Short Histories are authoritative and elegantly written introductory texts which offer fresh perspectives on the way history is taught and understood in the twenty-first century. Designed to have strong appeal to university students and their teachers, as well as to general readers and history enthusiasts, *Short Histories* comprise novel attempts to bring informed interpretation, as well as factual reportage, to historical debates. Addressing key subjects and topics in the fields of history, the history of ideas, religion, classical studies, politics, philosophy and Middle East studies, these texts move beyond the bland, neutral 'introductions' that so often serve as the primary undergraduate teaching tool. While always providing students and generalists with the core facts that they need to get to grips with, *Short Histories* go further. They offer new insights into how a topic has been understood in the past, and what different social and cultural factors might have been at work. They bring original perspectives to bear on current interpretations. They raise questions and—with extensive bibliographies—point the reader to further study, even as they suggest answers. Each text addresses a variety of subjects in a greater degree of depth than is often found in comparable series, yet at the same time in a concise and compact handbook form. *Short Histories* aim to be 'introductions with an edge'. In combining questioning and searching analysis with informed historical writing, they bring history up to date for an increasingly complex and globalized digital age.

For more information about titles and authors in the series, please visit: https://www.bloomsbury.com/series/short-histories/

A Short History of . . .

the American Civil War	Paul Anderson, Clemson University, USA
the American Revolutionary War	Stephen Conway, University College London, UK
Ancient Greece	P.J. Rhodes, Emeritus, Durham University, UK
the Anglo-Saxons	Henrietta Leyser, University of Oxford, UK
Babylon	Karen Radner, University of Munich, Germany
the Byzantine Empire: Revised Edition	Dionysios Stathakopoulos, University of Cyprus, Cyprus
Christian Spirituality	Edward Howells, University of Roehampton, UK
Communism	Kevin Morgan, University of Manchester, UK
the Crimean War	Trudi Tate, University of Cambridge, UK
English Renaissance Drama	Helen Hackett, University College London, UK
the English Revolution and the Civil Wars	David J. Appleby, Nottingham University, UK
the Etruscans	Corinna Riva, University of Erfurt, Germany
Florence and the Florentine Republic	Brian J. Maxson, East Tennessee State University, USA
the Hundred Years' War	Michael Prestwich, Emeritus, Durham University, UK
Judaism and the Jewish People	Steven Leonard Jacobs, The University of Alabama, USA
Medieval Christianity	G.R. Evans, Emeritus, University of Cambridge, UK
the Minoans	John Bennet, British School of Athens, Greece
the Mongols	George Lane, University of London, UK

the Mughal Empire — Michael H. Fisher, Emeritus, Oberlin College, USA

Muslim Spain — Amira K. Bennison, University of Cambridge, UK

the New Kingdom of Egypt — Robert Morkot, Independent Scholar

the New Testament — Halvor Moxnes, University of Oslo, Norway

the Normans — Leonie V. Hicks, Canterbury Christ Church University, UK

the Ottoman Empire — Baki Tezcan, University of California, Davis, USA

the Phoenicians: Revised Edition — Mark Woolmer, Independent Scholar

the Reformation — Helen L. Parish, University of Reading, UK

the Renaissance in Northern Europe — Malcolm Vale, Emeritus, University of Oxford, UK

Revolutionary Cuba — Antoni Kapcia, Emeritus, University of Nottingham, UK

the Russian Revolution: Revised Edition — Geoffrey Swain, Emeritus, University of Glasgow, UK

the Spanish Civil War: Revised Edition — Julián Casanova, Central European University, Hungary

the Spanish Empire — Felipe Fernández-Armesto, University of Notre Dame, France, and José Juan López-Portillo, University of Oxford, UK

Transatlantic Slavery — Kenneth Morgan, Brunel University, UK

the Tudors — Richard Rex, University of Cambridge, UK

Venice and the Venetian Empire — Maria Fusaro, University of Exeter, UK

the Wars of the Roses — David Grummitt, University of Kent, UK

the Weimar Republic — Colin Storer, University of Warwick, UK

A Short History of Judaism and the Jewish People

STEVEN LEONARD JACOBS

BLOOMSBURY ACADEMIC
LONDON • NEW YORK • OXFORD • NEW DELHI • SYDNEY

BLOOMSBURY ACADEMIC
Bloomsbury Publishing Plc
50 Bedford Square, London, WC1B 3DP, UK
1385 Broadway, New York, NY 10018, USA
29 Earlsfort Terrace, Dublin 2, Ireland

BLOOMSBURY, BLOOMSBURY ACADEMIC and the Diana logo
are trademarks of Bloomsbury Publishing Plc

First published in Great Britain 2024

A catalogue record for this book is available from the British Library.

A catalog record for this book is available from the Library of Congress.

ISBN: HB: 978-1-3502-3590-8
          PB: 978-1-3502-3646-2
          ePDF: 978-1-3502-3657-8
          eBook: 978-1-3502-3658-5

Series: Short Histories

Typeset by RefineCatch Limited, Bungay, Suffolk
Printed and bound in Great Britain

To find out more about our authors and books visit www.bloomsbury.com
and sign up for our newsletters.

Contents

Acknowledgments   ix

1 Introduction   1
2 Beginnings Until the Monarchy   19
3 Kingdoms of Judah and Israel   41
4 Social Structures and Institutions of Ancient Israel   57
5 Before the Destruction of the First Temple to
   Alexander the Great   83
6 The Second Temple Period and the Conflicts
   with "Hellenism" and "Romanism"   93
7 Aftermath of the Roman War to the Seventh Century   115
8 The Eighth to the Fifteenth Centuries: The Middle Ages   123
9 The Sixteenth and Seventeenth Centuries: The Middle
   Ages and Transitions   141
10 The Eighteenth and Nineteenth Centuries: Pre-Modernity
   to Modernity   153
11 The Twentieth and Twenty-First Centuries and Beyond:
   Modernity   173
12 The Twenty-First-Century Moment and Beyond and
   Conclusions   197

Bibliography   209
Index   229

Acknowledgments

To Fortress Press, Minneapolis, MN, USA, for its gracious permission to use chapter one, "The Cycles of History," from my book, *The Jewish Experience: An Introduction to Jewish History and Jewish Life* (2019), as the basic outline of this new book.

To my students in my REL 224 class "Introduction to Judaism," who continue to inspire me with their dedication to learning, their questions and inquisitive natures, and their all-around good cheer. They make me a better teacher and a better scholar.

To my colleagues in the Department of Religious Studies at The University of Alabama, Tuscaloosa, AL, USA—Russell T. McCutcheon, Chair; Keisha Harris; Oleg Kyselov; Daniel Levine; Nathan R.B. Loewen; Richard Newton; Steven Ramey; Merinda Simmons; Edith Szanto; Vaia Touna; Theodore Louis Trost; Jeri Wieringa—who continue to create a supportive learning and scholarly environment for all of us to put forth our best efforts, and whose ongoing interactions further create a sense of community second to none.

To my wife Louanne, a dedicated teacher and scholar in her own right, and our children, Hannah Beth Millman, Naomi Jacobs Pryor, and Shea Clayton Jacobs, their spouses, Adam Millman, Christopher Pryor and Suzanne Daniels, and our wonderful grandchildren—Elizabeth Greer Millman, Savannah Drew Millman, Liam Allen Millman, Laun Albert Pryor, Jacob Alan Pryor, Molly Daly and Dorothy Jacobs—whose own *joie de vivre* has made the writing of this book a particular joy in and of itself.

And to my parents—Ruth Jacobs-Arrill and Ralph Albert Jacobs—and my stepfather Daniel Arrill—to whom this book is dedicated. Your own love of learning and commitment to our Jewish people and our Judaism continue to bear fruit.

1

INTRODUCTION

Just as in the academic study of religion there is no one universally agreed-upon definition of what we mean when we use the world "religion," so, too, there is no one universally accepted understanding of what we mean by "Judaism," denominational differences at times affecting the definition, along with historical circumstances (e.g., Jews labeled as such, even those with non-Jewish mothers, by the Soviet Communist regime suffered because of it, and later emigrated to Israel). Complicating this picture even more, there is, equally, no agreed-upon understanding of who the totality of the Jewish people is, either historically or contemporarily. Biblically, the Israelites traced their status and lineage through their male parent, subdivided into the three divisions within their society (high priestly families biologically connected to Aaron, Moses' older brother; others within the tribe of Levi; and, lastly, the remaining members of the Israelite tribal community and communities). Post-biblically, rabbinically and talmudically, identity status was shifted to either one whose female parent was Jewish (a shift in collective identity from Israelite to Jew), or one who underwent the formal rite we know today as "conversion," though it did not even exist in the biblical period. Historically, one married into, or chose to live within and among Israelites, or was captured and later freed but chose to remain. Thus, for approximately the first four thousand years of Israelite/Jewish existence and history, identity was male-based; for approximately the next two thousand years, it was and is female-based. In 1983, however, the Reform or Liberal or Progressive religious denominational movement in the United States resolved, through its rabbis at their annual convention, that the Jewish identity of children could now be determined through *either* male or female parent, provided the commitment was to raise that child within the orbit of the Jewish community, the child itself undergoing *significant* Jewish rites of passage (*brit milah* [circumcision], naming, consecration, bar/bat mitzvah, and/or confirmation) without necessarily, however, undergoing any act formally recognized as conversion. Thus, their actual "Resolution on Patrilineal Descent," after a relatively brief excursus surveying the contemporary situation, concluded:

> The Central Conference of American Rabbis declares that the child of one Jewish parent is under the presumption of Jewish descent. This presumption of the Jewish status of the offspring of any mixed marriage is to be established through appropriate and timely public and formal acts of identification with the Jewish faith and people. The performance of these *mitzvot* [obligatory commandments] serves to commit those who participate in them, both parent and child, to Jewish life.
>
> Depending on circumstances, *mitzvot* leading toward a positive and exclusive Jewish identity will include entry into the covenant, acquisition of a Hebrew name, Torah study, Bar/Bat Mitzvah, and Kabbalat Torah (Confirmation). For those beyond childhood claiming Jewish identity, other public acts or declarations may be added or substituted after consultation with their rabbi.[1]

This decision is still marked even today by rancorous debate and unresolved tensions among the various denominational communities, with Reform and Reconstructionist liberal Judaisms lining up on one side, and narrower Orthodox (both Hasidic and non-Hasidic) and centrist Conservative Judaisms on the other.[2] Today, then, the waters tend to be somewhat muddy as to who is or is not a Jew, depending on parental status or denominational affiliation, including conversionary practice, which tend to differ somewhat in specifics[3]—all this despite Israel's first prime minister David ben Gurion's (1886–1973 CE) bold suggestion that "a Jew is anyone who considers himself such!"[4]

THE OPERATING DEFINITION OF JUDAISM

Thus, attempting to define either Judaism and/or the Jewish people is a tricky enterprise at best. It is, however, a place to begin as we explore a complex and complicated history, recognizing, even at this early outset, that we simply cannot divorce the *religion* of Judaism from the people who continue to be its living embodiment. Although scholar and

University of California historian David Biale (b. 1949) strongly argues that, early on, the biblical books of Job, Song of Songs and Esther, and later figures such as Dutch philosopher Baruch Spinoza (1632–77), Lithuanian philosopher Salomon Maimon (1753–1800), German poet Heinrich Heine (1797–1856), Austrian and psychoanalyst Sigmund Freud (1856–1939), German-American theoretical physicist Albert Einstein (1879–1955) and others bespeak a secularism that is, perhaps somewhat unequally, part of this story as well.[5] What follows, then, is this author's own working definition of Judaism, less so the Jewish people, which will serve as the initial frame of reference around which this book is organized:

> **Judaism** is the evolving cultural[6] and religious expressions of the people, Jews—
> originally known as Hebrews or Israelites—over the course of the generations,
> in response to their and others' changing perceptions of themselves,[7] their
> historical journeys, their stories and ideas, their celebrations, and their
> understandings of their relationship with their God.[8]

SOCIOLOGICALLY SPEAKING

Sociologically, any group, however defined, expresses its collective identity through its behaviors (in this case cultural and religious), bracketed by both its ideas and its stories or myths. Over time, those behaviors change, buffeted about by both internal and external threats to its survival, and adapting itself to changing historical circumstances, new, different, and challenging reinterpretations of its own existence and the like. Historical groups that have long survived—and the Jews certainly count themselves among them, following an historical trajectory close to six thousand years of continually identified existence—are those who continue to successfully negotiate and renegotiate both the internal and external understandings of what it means to be members of the group, both individually and collectively.

In addition, all manner of group behavior constitutes the group's culture, from so-called "high culture" and ennobling behaviors (e.g., religion, the arts, literature) to "low culture" and disgracing behaviors (e.g., violation of moral and ethical norms in defiance of group ideals). The Jews are no exception to the latter, to be sure, from those patriarchs of the Hebrew Bible who lied to protect themselves (e.g., Abraham informing King Abimelech of Gerar that Sarah was his sister rather than his wife) to those who deceived and manipulated those even within their same family (e.g., Jacob's deception of his father Isaac in his quest for the latter's blessing, or his manipulation of his older brother Esau, exchanging food for birthright), to those who maintained themselves within the criminal elements of society, particularly in the nineteenth and twentieth centuries (e.g., US gangster Meyer "Little Man" Lansky [1902–83 CE]). Thus, to tell the story of the Jews is to attempt to tell the whole story of the Jews and Judaism without blinders, to include both the best and the worst in this migratory trek of several thousand years, especially through Europe, North and South America, and the Middle East. Further complicating the telling of this overall Jewish story, however, has been both the neglect of the Sephardic/Spanish and beyond Jewish communities throughout history and the role, place, function, and influence of women on the evolution of Judaism and the Jewish people.

THE IMPORTANCE OF THE LITERARY TRADITION

Important in sustaining Jewish group survival have been both the stories that the Jews have told themselves about themselves and those told to others about themselves and their relationship to Jews. Such stories (and myths) are powerful psychological tools, not only in times of stress and threat but in times of celebration as well. Added to these stories are the ideas that the founders of Judaism have crafted, that the Jewish people have embraced, and that later generations have enlarged and reinterpreted in response to changing historical circumstances.

Significantly, at least for the last two thousand years, the Jews have valued literature and literacy, and the values reflected therein in the production not only of their sacred Torah/Hebrew Bible—what Christians refer to as the "Old Testament" but with a decidedly different focus and reordering of the post-initial first five texts by Roman Catholic, Orthodox, and Protestant religious communities—but of their ancillary rabbinic and other texts as well, Talmud, Midrash, Codes, Responsa. Prior to this, however, it is our scholarly understanding that the stories, laws, poems, hymns, psalms, and the like were, at a minimum, at least a thousand years if not older in their original Israelite formulations and tellings and retellings before becoming the Hebrew Bible/Torah.[9] Three thousand years at the very least from their original dreams to their contemporary manifestations, a long if somewhat uneven journey.

THE CENTRALITY OF THE GOD OF ISRAEL

The interwoven story of the Jews and Judaism cannot fully be told without reference to the God of Israel, as understood and already present in the first sentence of the Hebrew Bible Bereshith/Genesis 1:1 ("In the beginning of creating, God, with [the use of] the heavens and the earth . . ."),[10] and even more fully present at Sinai with not only those Israelites already there but the generations yet to be born, entering into a covenantal relationship for all time (Devarim/Deuteronomy 29:14–15). This singular incorporeal creator God, vitally concerned with the affairs of humanity and, most particularly and especially, Israelite humanity remains a distinctive contribution of the Jewish people to the civilizing and humanizing of our collective humanity along with such concepts as the perhaps mistranslated labelled "Ten Commandments" (Hebrew, *Aseret Ha-Dibrot*/"Ten Essential Statements") and the Sabbath itself.[11]

JUDAISM, JEWISH PEOPLE, AND GOD

Thus, when all is said and done, the history or story of "Judaism" cannot be disconnected from either the Jewish people or its God, however each element of this tripartite reality is understood both historically and contemporarily. Together they constitute a somewhat seamless garment, embroidered over countless generations by countless persons in countless locales. At the same time, this garment is always unfinished, as each generation of Jews continues to add its own distinctive features, changing that which was previously created to fit the moment, and knowing only too well that the next generation of Jews will repeat this threefold tradition of preserving that from the past deemed worthy of preservation, adapting from the past that deemed worthy of adaptation, and innovating where past historical experience is deemed insufficient (e.g., the rabbinic ordination of women, gays, and transgendered persons).

This journey of the Jews and Judaism, then, tells the story of the Israelites prior to the inauguration of the monarchy under Samuel (*c.* 1070–*c.* 1012 BCE) and Saul (*c.* 1037–*c.* 1010 BCE), from the migratory and settled periods of Judah and Israel to the destruction of the First and Second Temples (586 BCE and 70 CE) to their 2,000-year wandering primarily throughout the European continent and elsewhere and into the modern period, with the recreation of the Third Jewish Commonwealth on May 14, 1948, Medinat Yisra'el/the State of Israel, and now the twenty-first century. It is a journey filled with peaks and valleys, successes and failures, creations, and destructions, but framed by the seeming indestructibility not only of the Jewish people but of the Judaic religion as well. It is also of necessity an all-too-brief story told here, globally attempting to tell a broad story while elaborating somewhat on many, many topics worthy of elaboration, but not all of them.

Finally, the complexity of the Jewish story is not one easily written, and any number of scholars and others have attempted to weigh in with a theorized understanding of the whys and the hows of how this story has been, is, and should be told and written. Equally, the writings of such persons as, for example, Dean Bell of the Spertus Institute for Jewish Learning and Leadership, Chicago, Illinois, David Myers, University of California, Moshe Rosman of Bar-Ilan University, Israel, and the late Yosef Yerushalmi (1932–2009) of Columbia University, New York, and others is addressed here as well and helps to frame what follows in subsequent chapters.[12]

HISTORIOGRAPHY, THE JEWS, AND JUDAISM

There is no dearth of historical books about the people, places, and events of the past in the multiplicity of the world's languages. Less so about the theorizing about how we *do* history and history-writing—that field of exploration which scholars have termed historiography. In the American context, two books loom large in English: David Lowenthal's (1923–2018) *The Past Is a Foreign Country* (Cambridge: Cambridge University Press, 1985) and Hayden White's (1928–2018) *Metahistory: The Historical Imagination in Nineteenth Century Europe* (Baltimore, MD: Johns Hopkins University Press, 1973). A relatively recent brief survey of the field is that of the University of Kentucky historian Jeremy D. Popkin's (b. 1948) *From Herodotus to H-Net: The Story of Historiography* (New York, NY: Oxford University Press, 2016).[13]

Judaically- and Jewishly-speaking, as well as historically, there have been those concerned both with the meaning and the writing of Jewish history—the "Jewish story," if you will—for example: Polish-born American historian Salo Wittmayer Baron (1895–1989);[14] Russian-British social and political theorist, philosopher, and historian Isaiah Berlin (1909–97);[15] Jewish-Russian historian, writer, and activist Simon Markovich Dubnow (1860–1941);[16] late professor of modern history at the Hebrew University of Jerusalem Judah Leib Talmon (1916–80);[17]

and, contemporarily, president of the Shalom Hartman Institute of North America Yehuda Kurtzer (b. 1977).[18] Others who have also addressed Jewish historical writing and Jewish historians include: German-Jewish historian Michael Brenner (b. 1964);[19] educator and internationally known scholar of Jewish and medieval studies historian Amos Funkenstein (1937–95);[20] and Chancellor emeritus of the Jewish Theological Seminary, New York, and professor of Jewish history Ismar Schorsch (b. 1935).[21, 22]

On a somewhat discordant note, however, and of concern to both non-Jewish and Jewish scholars has been the abuse of historical work and writings to further political, religious-theological, and/or other ends, and which have been addressed beginning with German philosopher, cultural critic, and philologist Friedrich Nietzsche (1844–1900).[23] Others who have written of their similar concerns include English historian George Kitson Clark (1900–75);[24] former Brandeis University professor of history David Hackett Fischer (b. 1935), whose book *Historians' Fallacies: Toward a Logic of Historical Thought* (New York, NY: Harper Perennial, 1970) addressed such "errors" as question-framing, factual verification, factual significance, generalization, narration, causation, motivation, composition, false analogy, semantical distortion, and substantive distraction; Amy S. Kaufman and Paul V. Sturtevant;[25] University of Toronto historian Margaret MacMillan (b. 1943);[26] University of California historian David N. Myers (b. 1960);[27] the late Haitian scholar Michel-Rolph Trouillot (1949–2012).[28]

Rounding out these references, persons, and concerns, Judaically understood, is a topic of importance but one usually not discussed: that of how the censorship of such texts throughout history—by both Jewish and non-Jewish censors—has influenced both the writing and understanding of the past. The work of Moshe Carmilly-Weinberger (1908–2010), late rabbi and professor at Yeshiva University, New York, remains somewhat singularly unique.[29]

Lastly, and of special concern, is how the Holocaust/Shoah was and is understood and presented early on and presently. Thus, the writings of Michael André Bernstein (1947–2011) of the University of California,[30] New York University professor David Engel (b. 1951),[31] and University of California, Los Angeles, Professor Mark L. Smith[32] loom large.

NB [Latin, *nota bene*, "Note well"]: My purpose in citing all these persons and their writings is not to overwhelm you, the reader, at the outset. Rather, it is twofold: to provide you with additional opportunities to further your own interests in the work of creditable, noteworthy, and important historians and their work, and, in all honesty, to "complexify" rather than simplify the telling of the Jewish story.

HISTORY AND MEMORY

History remains the reasonably objective writing and presenting of the past based upon the amassing of the available collected evidence, subject always to revision as more evidence is uncovered, and, importantly, also to provide an interpretive understanding of what has been shared. Memory, however, tends to be a somewhat more subjective rendering of those same people, places and events as other aforementioned agendas—political, economic, religious-theological, etc.—surface. A good example, Jewishly, would be the biblical presentation of Passover, as recorded primarily in the Book of Exodus. Objective scholarly investigation finds itself at odds with the biblical account—a gradual emigration of the ancient Israelites and others (the so-called *asafsuf/*"riff-raff") during a disintegrating period of the Egyptian pharaonic monarchy rather than a singular event, which remains subjectively at the very heart of the evolution of the Jewish religious tradition, thought, ethics, and practice.[33] Judaically, no discussion of the distinction between history and memory can exclude—must include—the seminal work of Columbia University historian Yosef Hayim Yerushalmi (1932–2009), *Zakhor: Jewish History and Jewish Memory*, wherein he argues most strongly that their objective and subjective agendas are decidedly different.[34]

Of late, however, there has developed far more appreciation of the role, purpose, and function of memory in the writing and understanding of history itself.[35] Thus, "witness accounts"—both past and present—have come to occupy a more prominent place than has been previously accorded them; even checking the data of who, what, where, and why in those tellings has not diminished their importance. Significantly, the journal *History & Memory* (published by Indiana University Press) is now more than thirty years old and addresses the nexus between history and memory. A quick scan of issues between 1998 and 2021, volumes ten to thirty-three, reveals more than twenty contributions/articles specifically on Jews and Judaism with the overwhelming majority focusing on the Holocaust/Shoah[36] and only one, somewhat surprisingly, on the Israeli-Palestinian situation.[37]

Finally, and not to be given short shrift, our current and future pre- and post-occupation with new media and the various technologies they represent is of particular concern to historians. If not, should it be? How will the documentary evidence of the past—the actual *physical* specimens—be preserved for future generations of researchers? Is their digitization the best method to ensure that their ultimate preservation be guaranteed or insured? Who and under what criteria and circumstances will access and permission be granted to such information? Who will grant that access and what criteria are to be recognized in the granting of that access? Will that very electronic access shape the way in which the material itself is written, understood, analyzed, and presented? Questions such as these and others are reflected in the writings of both Stanford University intellectual and cultural historian Abby Smith Rumsey[38] and Rutgers University Professor of Judaic Studies Jeffrey Shandler.[39]

ISRAELITES, HEBREWS, HABIRU (HAPIRU, 'APIRU), SHASU, JUDEANS, AND JEWS—AND "JEWISH GENETICS"[40]

Over the course of their history, the people known today as "Jews"—as distinct from "Israelis," best understood as *citizens* of the State of Israel, who may or may not be Jews (e.g., Arabs, Muslims, Christians, Samaritans, etc.)—have been known by various names. What follows, then, are brief comments on these names, although the following chapters are intended to tell their story regardless of and including these designations or labels.

First off, the most common well-known ancient names for this people are "Israelites" or "Hebrews." The name "Israel" is almost universally understood today, following Bereshith/Genesis 32:28 ("Then the man said, 'Your name will no longer be Ya'akov/Jacob, but Yisra'El/Israel, because you have struggled with God and with humans and have been enabled'")[41] and 35:10 ("God said to him, 'Your name is Ya'akov/Jacob, but you will no longer be called Ya'akov/Jacob; your name will be Yisra'El/Israel.' So, he named him Israel."), as an initial reference to the patriarch Ya'akov/Jacob—Yisra'El—who "wrestled" and thus became the "father" of his descendants who took his new name as their own. Significantly, however, the name does also appear in the texts of Ebla (the so-called "Amarna Letters," fourteenth century BCE[42]) as well as the Egyptian Merneptah Stele (thirteenth century BCE) to designate a foreign, conquered people rather than a distinct nation- or city-state. If, however, its etymological root derives from *śarah* ("to rule, contend, have power, prevail over"), and El/God is its subject, then it designates God as the one who fights or struggles with and over this same people. Historically understood, and for our purposes as well, Israelites were a tribal confederation speaking a common language in the ancient Near East and residing primarily in Canaan during Iron Age I (1200–550 BCE). The term "Hebrews" is, however, somewhat more complicated. The Hebrew word *avar* means to pass or cross over, to pass or cross through, to pass by, or, possibly, to pass or cross on. Thus, the designation *Ivri* (pl. *Ivri'im*) may refer to those who "crossed over" the Jordan River, or the Great River, the Euphrates, and therefore a label to a group of wanderers, migrants, refugees, travelers, or even mercenaries. Attempts to link this translated name to the Habiru/Hapiru, while still regarding this same group as synonymous with the Israelites—or even the Egyptian term "Shasu" or Akkadian "Shutu"—remain problematic, as the late Moshe Greenberg (1928–2010) of the Hebrew University, Israel, has noted in his important study, *The Hab/piru*: "The proposed equation of 'Apiru with the Biblical Hebrews involves problems of a philological, ethnic-social, and historical nature."[43]

Following the destruction of the ten northern tribes by the Assyrians in 721 BCE, the remaining southern tribes of Judah and Benjamin—Judah, the larger, Benjamin, the smaller—began to refer to themselves collectively as "Judeans" from which we derive our contemporary label "Jews," though we remain somewhat in the dark about when this actual change occurred. (A good case, perhaps, could be made that this change from Judeans to Jews made sense after the destruction of the Second Temple by the Romans in the year 70 CE, as this again migratory and wandering people either self-designated or other-designated themselves and further distinguished themselves from the original Jewish Christians—itself a problematic term—who would evolve into essentially "gentile"[44] Christians.)[45]

Today, the world knows this lineally descended people as "Jews" (Hebrew, *Yehudim*, "followers of the One God," though not all Jews are themselves committed religious practitioners and/or believers). Thus, collectively, Jews are, perhaps, best understood as an interwoven mix of religiously committed people coupled with those who have clustered into somewhat ethnically diverse populations, and united both by their own self-understanding and others' understanding of them as well. Today as well, most Jews are those we label "Ashkenazim" from the Hebrew *Ashkenaz* ("Germany") and trace their roots to locales of origin in Western Europe, Poland, and Russia and places in between. The second group are the "Sephardim" from the Hebrew *Sepharad* ("Spain"), though more generally the Iberian Peninsula, including Greece. The third group are the "Mizrakhim" (or "Easterners"), from the Hebrew *Mizrakh* ("East"), used to refer to Jews from the Middle East, Western and/or Central Asia, and North Africa, whom some in the West have labeled inaccurately "Oriental Jews."

Lastly, and finally, the newly-emerging field of scientific genetic studies— not without controversy to be sure—has encouraged some Jews to enquire as to their historical places of origin, and connection. Two recent books, one by a journalist, Jon Entine, *Abraham's Children*,[46] the other by a scientist, David G. Goldstein, *Jacob's Legacy*,[47] may whet the appetite of you, the reader, to pursue your own curiosity vis-à-vis these matters.[48]

NOTES

1 www.jewishvirtuallibrary.org/reform-movement-s-resolution-on-patrilineal-descent-march-1983. See, also, Aaron Hughes, *Defining Judaism: A Reader* (London and Oakville, CT: Equinox, 2010), and *The Invention of Jewish Identity: Bible, Philosophy, and the Art of Translation* (Bloomington: Indiana University Press, 2010).

2 For ease of understanding, both Reform and Reconstructionist Judaism may be viewed as both liberal and progressive in our understanding of these terms; Orthodoxy, perhaps even better understood as "Orthopraxy," is a narrower and more historical-traditional and literalist read of religious Judaism; and Conservative Judaism, originally self-defined in the 1800s in Germany as "Positive-Historical Judaism," was and is an attempt to bridge the so-called "religious divide" between left and right religious expressions of Judaism.

3 For example, all the different denominations of religious Judaism require both educational and religious practice components, but neither Reform nor Reconstructionist Judaisms require ritual immersion (*mikveh*) and male either symbolic or full circumcision, whereas both Orthodox and Conservative Judaisms do.

4 On October 27, 1958, Ben-Gurion sent a letter to forty-five rabbis, scholars, and other academics posing the question:

If the mother is non-Jewish and has not been converted, but both she and the father agree that the child shall be Jewish, should it [*sic*] be registered as Jewish on the basis of the expression of the parents and their declaration in good faith that the child does not belong to another religion, or is any further ceremony of any kind required, in addition to the agreement and the declaration of both parents, for the child to be registered as a Jew? (14)

Steven Leonard Jacobs

All forty-five responded. Forty-three have been translated into English and published: Baruch Litvin, *Jewish Identity: Modern Responsa and Opinions on the Registration of Children of Mixed Marriages: David Ben Gurion's Query to Leaders of World Jewry: A Documentary Compilation*, ed. Sidney B. Hoenig (Jerusalem and New York, NY: Feldheim Publishers, 1970).

5   David Biale, *Not in the Heavens: The Tradition of Jewish Secular Thought* (Princeton, NJ, and Oxford: Princeton University Press, 2011).

6   "Culture" is herein understood as the customs, arts, social institutions, achievements, beliefs, and ways of life of a particular group of people and transmitted down through the generations.

7   See, for example, Klaus Hödl, "Major Trends in the Historiography of European Ashkenazic Jews from the 1970s to the Present," *Jewish History* 35, nos 1–2 (2021): 153–77, wherein he and others argue for a more carefully nuanced exchange and interactive relationship between Jews and Christians, and how each have significantly and importantly influenced each other.

8   Both Menahem Mansoor and Robert Seltzer follow this same orientation: Menahem Mansoor, *Jewish History and Thought: An Introduction* (Hoboken, NJ: KTAV Publishing House, 1991); Robert M. Seltzer, *Jewish People, Jewish Thought: The Jewish Experience in History* (Upper Saddle River, NJ: Prentice Hall, 1980). See, also: Moshe Rosman, *How Jewish Is Jewish History?* (Oxford and Portland, OR: The Littman Library of Jewish Civilization, 2007); S.N. Eisenstadt, *Jewish Civilization: The Jewish Historical Experience in a Comparative Perspective* (New York, NY: SUNY Press, 1992); and Samuel A. Oppenheim, *The Historical Evolution of Judaism: With Comparisons to Other Systems of Thought* (Jacksonville, FL: Mazo Publishers, 2012).

9   For easing of understanding, Talmud is that 500-year accumulated body of literary wisdom which remains the source not only of Rabbinic Judaism but Jewish theology and law (*halakhah*) as well. Midrash is the literary tradition of commentaries on the Hebrew Bible, including fanciful stories of its people, places, and events. Codes are then the various abstracted collections of Jewish civil and religious behaviors around which Jews have historically patterned their lives. Responsa is thus the answers given by authoritative rabbis in various geographic, historical, and contemporary locales to specific and practical questions of Jewish behaviors. Torah is that collection of texts regarded as the holy and sacred to Jews offering insights to the God of Israel and what that God expects of the Jewish people. It is also known as the Hebrew Bible or Holy Bible and consists of the so-named "Five Books of Moses" (Genesis, Exodus, Leviticus, Numbers, Deuteronomy), fifteen books of "Prophets" (e.g., Isaiah, Jeremiah, Ezekiel, and twelve lesser-known persons), and a third literary collection known as the "Writings" (e.g., Psalms, Proverbs, Ruth, Esther).

10 This translation is the author's own and more in accord with the actual Hebrew language rather than the popular: "In the beginning, God created the heavens and the earth." It also points us to the realization that God's creative genius made use of pre-existent matter to bring order out of chaos rather than, as the Latin would have it, *creatio ex nihilo*, "creation out of nothing."

11 Significantly, the rabbis of the Jewish religious tradition do not label them the *Aseret Ha-Mitzvot* (obligatory commandments) but *Dibrot*, and thus essential and foundational understandings without which no society can either survive or endure beyond its own initial creation.

12 See the Bibliography for a list of those writers examined but by no means exclusively so.

13 Others worth examining are: Joyce Appleby, Lynn Hunt, and Margaret Jacob, *Telling the Truth About History* (New York, NY, and London: W.W. Norton & Co., 1994); Reuven Brenner, *History: The Human Gamble* (Chicago, IL, and London: University of Chicago Press, 1983); Edward Hallett Carr, *What Is History?* (New York, NY: Vintage Books/Random House, 1961); Ernest Gellner, *Plough, Sword, and Book: The Structure of Human History* (Chicago, IL: University of Chicago Press, 1988); Anthony Grafton: *Bring Out Your Dead: The Past as Revelation* (Cambridge, MA, and London: Harvard University Press, 2001); George Walsh, *The Role of Religion in History* (New Brunswick, NJ, and London: Transaction Publishers, 1998); Gordon S. Wood, *The Purpose of the Past: Reflections on the Uses of History* (New York, NY: Penguin Books, 2008); and C. Vann Woodward, *The Future of the Past* (New York, NY, and Oxford: Oxford University Press, 1989). Undergirding all of these texts, to be sure, is that of R.G. Collingwood, *The Idea of History*, rev. ed. (Oxford and New York, NY: Oxford University Press, 1993). Interestingly enough, that of Jewish scholar Marc Bloch (1886–1944), murdered by the Nazis, *The Historian's Craft*, trans. Peter Putnam (Manchester: Manchester University Press, 1954), is a general series of essays rather than one with a specific Judaic focus.

14 Salo W. Baron, *History and Jewish Historians: Essays and Addresses* (Philadelphia, PA: Jewish Publication Society of America, 1964).

15 Isaiah Berlin, *Historical Inevitability* (Oxford and New York, NY: Oxford University Press, 1954).

16 Simon Markovich Dubnow, *Jewish History: An Essay in the Philosophy of History* (Philadelphia, PA: Jewish Publication Society of America, 1903).

17 J.L. Talmon, *The Nature of Jewish History: Its Universal Significance* (London: The Hillel Foundation, 1957).

18 Yehuda Kurtzer, *Shuva: The Future of the Jewish Past* (Waltham, MA: Brandeis University Press, 2012).

19 Michael Brenner, *Prophets of the Past: Interpreters of Jewish History*, trans. by Steven Rendall (Princeton, NJ, and Oxford: Princeton University Press, 2006).

20 Amos Funkenstein, *Perceptions of Jewish History* (Berkeley: University of California Press, 1993).

21 Ismar Schorsch, *From Text to Context: The Turn to History in Modern Judaism* (Hanover, NH: Brandeis University Press, 1994).

22 Equally important are three edited collections all attempting to assess those who work and who have worked in the field of Jewish history and their own *Weltanschauungen* (world perspectives) that have shaped and influenced their work: Dean Philip Bell (ed.), *The Routledge Companion to Jewish History and Historiography* (London and New York, NY: Routledge, 2019), 48 contributions; Jonathan Frankel (ed.), *Reshaping the Jewish Past: Jewish History and the Historians* (Oxford and New York, NY: Oxford University Press, 1994), 96 contributions; and David N. Myers and David B. Ruderman (eds.), *The Jewish Past Revisited: Reflections on Modern Jewish Historians* (New Haven, CT, and London: Yale University Press, 1998), 10 contributions.

23 Friedrich Nietzsche, *The Use and Abuse of History for Life*, trans. Adrian Collins (1874; Minneola: Dover Publications, 2019).

24 G. Kitson Clark, *The Critical Historian* (London: Heinemann, 1967).

25 Amy S. Kaufman and Paul B. Studevant, *The Devil's Historians: How Modern Extremists Abuse the Medieval Past* (Toronto: University of Toronto Press, 2020).

26 Margaret MacMillan, *Dangerous Games: The Uses and Abuses of History* (New York, NY: Modern Library, 2009).

27 David N. Myers, *The Stakes of History: On the Use and Abuse of Jewish History for Life* (New Haven, CT, and London: Yale University Press, 2018).

28 Michel-Rolph Trouillot, *Silencing the Past: Power and the Production of History* (Boston, MA: Beacon Press, 1995).

29 Moshe Carmilly-Weinberger, *Censorship and Freedom of Expression in Jewish History: Great Ideological and Literary Conflicts in Judaism from Antiquity to Modern Times* (New York, NY: Sepher-Hermon Press/Yeshiva University Press, 1977). See, also, Eric Berkowitz, *Dangerous Ideas: A Brief History of Censorship in the West, from the Ancients to Fake News* (Boston, MA: Beacon Press, 2021).

30 Michael André Bernstein, *Foregone Conclusions: Against Apocalyptic History* (Berkeley: University of California Press, 1994). His text, in many ways, is a more contemporary riff on Salo Baron's rejection of what he regarded as "the lachrymose view of Jewish history."

31 David Engel, *Historians of the Jews and the Holocaust* (Stanford, CA: Stanford University Press, 2010).

32 Mark L. Smith, *The Yiddish Historians and the Struggle for a Jewish History of the Holocaust* (Detroit, MI: Wayne State University Press, 2019).

33 See Pamela Barmash and W. David Nelson (eds.), *Exodus in the Jewish Experience: Echoes and Reverberations* (Lanham, MD: Lexington Books, 2015), which explores this very theme, as well as James K. Hoffmeier, *Israel in Egypt: The Evidence for the Authenticity of the Exodus Tradition* (New York, NY, and Oxford: Oxford University Press, 1996). See, also, James K. Hoffmeier, Alan R. Millard, and Gary A. Rendsburg (eds.), *"Did I Not Bring Israel Out of Egypt?" Biblical, Archaeological, and Egyptological Perspectives on the Exodus Narratives*, Bulletin for Biblical Research Supplement 13 (Winona Lake, IN: Eisenbrauns, 2016).

34 Yosef Hayim Yerushalmi, *Zakhor: Jewish History and Jewish Memory* (Seattle and London: University of Washington Press, 1996). Renewed and recent attention to this work has resulted in two books: Yosef Hayim Yerushalmi and Sylvie Anne Goldberg, *Transmitting Jewish History: In Conversation with Sylvie Anne Goldberg*, trans. Benjamin Ivry (Waltham, MA: Brandeis University Press, 2021); and David N. Myers and Alexander Kaye (eds.), *The Faith of Fallen Jews: Yosef Hayim Yerushalmi and the Writing of Jewish History* (Waltham, MA: Brandeis University Press, 2014). Earlier discussions include: Robert Chazan, "The Timebound and the Timeless: Medieval Jewish Narration of Events," *History & Memory* 6, no. 1 (1994): 5–34; Amos Funkenstein, "Collective Memory and Historical Consciousness," *History & Memory* 1, no. 1 (1989): 5–26; David N. Myers and Amos Funkenstein (1992), "Remembering 'Zakhor': A Super Commentary [with Response]," *History & Memory* 4, no. 2 (1992): 129–48.

35 See, for example: Geoffrey Cubitt, *History and Memory* (Manchester: Manchester University Press, 2007); Michael S. Roth and Charles G. Salas (eds.), *Disturbing Remains: Memory, History, and the Crisis in the Twentieth Century* (Los Angeles, CA: Getty Research Institute, 2001); and Joan Tumblety (ed.), *Memory and History: Understanding Memory as Source and Subject* (London and New York, NY: Routledge, 2017). Relevant to this text is Ronald Hendel, *Remembering Abraham: Culture, Memory and History in the Hebrew Bible* (Oxford and New York, NY: Oxford University Press, 2005).

36 Examples of which are: Mark A. Wolfgram, "From the Visual to the Textual: How Nazi Control of the Visual Record of Kristallnacht Shaped the Postwar Narrative," *History & Memory* 33, no. 2 (2021): 107–34; Janek Gryta, "Creating a Cosmopolitan Past: Local and Transnational Influences on Memory Work in Schindler's Factory, Kraków," *History & Memory* 32, no. 1 (2020): 34–68; Ewa Wolentarska-Ochman, "Collective Remembrance in Jedwabne: Unsettled Memory of World War II in Postcommunist Poland," *History & Memory* 18, no. 1 (2006): 152–78; Slawomir Kapralski,

"Battlefields of Memory: Landscape and Identity in Polish-Jewish Relations," *History & Memory* 13, no. 2 (2001): 35–58. Additionally, there are several Holocaust-related texts concerned with memory, memorializing, and presenting the Shoah as our physical distance from that past continues to encroach upon our memory of that event: Geoffrey H. Hartman, *Holocaust Remembrance: The Shapes of Memory* (Oxford: Blackwell, 1994); Janet Jacobs, *Memorializing the Holocaust: Gender, Genocide and Collective Memory* (London and New York, NY: I.B. Tauris, 2010); Ronit Lentin (ed.), *Re-Presenting the Holocaust for the 21st Century* (New York, NY, and Oxford: Berghahn Books, 2014); Daniel Levy and Natan Sznaider, *The Holocaust and Memory in the Global Age*, trans. Assenka Oksiloff (Philadelphia, PA: Temple University Press, 2006); Alan Mintz, *Popular Culture and the Shaping of Holocaust Memory in America* (Seattle and London: University of Washington Press, 2001); Oren Baruch Stier, *Committed to Memory: Cultural Meditations of the Holocaust* (Amherst: University of Massachusetts Press, 2003).

37 Elie Podeh, "History and Memory in the Israeli Educational System: The Portrayal of the Arab-Israel Conflict in History Textbooks (1948–2000)," *History & Memory* 12, no. 1 (2000): 65–100.

38 Abby Smith Rumsey, *When We Are No More: How Digital Memory is Shaping Our Future* (New York, NY, and London: Bloomsbury Press, 2019).

39 Jeffrey Shandler, *Holocaust Memory in the Digital Age: Survivors' Stories and New Media Practices* (Stanford, CA: Stanford University Press, 2019).

40 For ease of discussion and throughout this book, we group Jewish populations into three main "clusters": *Ashkenazim* (Jews in Germanic countries, including Russia, broadly defined); Sephardim (Jewish in Spanish-speaking and related countries); and *Mizrakhim* (Jews of the Middle East and African continent). See, also, Graham Harvey, *The True Israel: Uses of the Names Jew, Hebrew and Israel in Ancient Jewish and Early Christian Literature* (Boston, MA, and Leiden: Brill Academic, 1996), which further expands our understandings of these terms in the past.

41 Again, this translation is the author's own as the "wrestling match" between Ya'akov/Jacob and his unnamed opponent does not result in victory, but, rather, one which enables Ya'akov to go forth in search of the blessings that the God of Israel has reserved for him.

42 The designations BCE and CE are used by both scholars and Jews as "Before the Common Era" and "Common Era" to acknowledge the commonality of dating but not to reference BC and AD "Before Christ" and "Anno Domini" (Latin for "In the year of the Lord" [i.e., Jesus Christ]).

43 Moshe Greenberg, *The Hab/piru* (New Haven, CT: American Oriental Society, 1955), 91.

44 This term "gentile" was originally, biblically, a later translation of the Hebrew term *goi* which simply meant "nation"; Israel itself being termed a *goi kadosh* (holy nation). Over time, within Jewish circles, it became a term simply for non-Jews and, later, within those same communities, one of opprobrium.

45 See Daniel R. Schwartz, *Judeans and Jews: Four Faces of Dichotomy in Ancient Jewish History* (Toronto: University of Toronto Press, 2014), as well as the e-book edited by Timothy Michael Law and Charles Halton (2014), *Jew and Judean* (Marginalia Ioudaios Forum).

46 Jon Entine, *Abraham's Children: Race, Identity, and the DNA of the Chosen People* (New York, NY: Grand Central Publishing, 2007).

47 David B. Goldstein, *Jacob's Legacy: A Genetic View of Jewish History* (New Haven, CT, and London: Yale University Press, 2008). Also, worth noting in this context is the work of Harry Ostrer, MD, *Legacy: A Genetic History of the Jewish People* (Oxford and New York, NY: Oxford University Press, 2012). The author of this text decided, more out of curiosity than anything else, to submit his own DNA to one of the genetic testing services available online. The result "89.1 percent Jewish; 8.4 percent Italian (?); 2.5 percent Spanish (?)," the latter two not part of any family story or lore with which I am or was at all familiar. What one does with such information, other than an already-known affirmation, remains a questionable and, perhaps for some, problematic concern or issue. For a somewhat different slant on such questions, see Avner Falk, *A Psychoanalytic History of the Jews* (Madison, NJ: Fairleigh Dickinson University Press, 1996).

48 A good initial survey of relevant articles on "Jewish genetics" is found in Steven Weitzman, *The Origin of the Jews: The Quest for Roots in a Rootless Age* (Princeton, NJ, and Oxford: Princeton University Press, 2017), 370–80.

2

BEGINNINGS UNTIL THE MONARCHY

WHAT ARE WE TO DO WITH THE TORAH/HEBREW BIBLE/OLD TESTAMENT?

To the extent to which we are willing—and able—to consider ourselves historians of ancient Israel's past, and whether or not we are able to read the texts of the Torah/Hebrew Bible/Old Testament in the original languages of Hebrew and Aramaic or any other ancient Middle Eastern language (e.g., Akkadian, Babylonian, Egyptian, Sumerian), the question should naturally arise:

> To what degree are the texts before us accurate (and objective?) depictions of the actual persons, places, and events they describe and present to us? And, second, have these texts gone through any kind of editing process, either at the time of their writing or subsequently, and thus reflect the tendenz/orientation of their authors and/or editors?

For much of the last 2,000 years, Jews, Christians, and, to a lesser extent, so-called "secularists" have by and large accepted the historicity of that depicted therein as accurate, e.g., there *was* an Abraham, Isaac, Jacob, Moses, Joseph, Joshua, David, Solomon, etc., and, while some of their "stories" may possibly require questioning, in the main, they were and are as their authors/editors intended to share them with their audiences—and with us.[1]

It is only in the post-Enlightenment modern era that serious-minded scholars and students of this literature—Jews and non-Jews alike—coupled with the rise of archaeology, began to question these depictions as seeing in their telling two interwoven threads, or, as Duke University Bible scholar Marc Zvi Brettler would have it, "while it is true that '*historical* Israel' must be distinguished from '*biblical* Israel', the biblical text will remain fundamental in reconstructing ancient Israelite history."[2] In line with Brettler, noted American archaeologist at the University of Arizona until his retirement in 2002, William G. Dever reminds us as well that: "The basic traditions about ancient Israel now enshrined in the books of Exodus [to] Numbers and Joshua through Kings cannot be read uncritically as a satisfactory history, but neither can they be discarded as lacking any credible historic information."[3]

In an earlier text as well, Dever also reminds his readers—us—that there are, in fact, many different kinds of histories:

> We may distinguish: (1) political history, the history of great public figures and institutions; (2) intellectual history, the history of formative ideas; (3) socio-economic history, the history of social and economic structures; (4) technological history, the history of things and their use; (5) art history, the history of aesthetics; (6) ideological history, the history of how certain concepts, specifically ethnic[4] and religious, have shaped culture; (7) natural history, the history of the environment and natural world; and (8) perhaps a culture history, or total history.[5]

Three "larger than life" people who helped to set the stage for this rethinking of ancient Israel's past were the Frenchman Jean Astruc, the Dutchman Baruch Spinoza, and the German Julius Wellhausen. Each cast a critical eye on the text of the Hebrew Bible and, in doing so, further complicated our understanding of that Bible which we inherited and which remains so central to both the Jewish and Christian faiths and central as well to their/our educational curricula and liturgical practices.

For Jean Astruc (1684–1766), medical doctor and professor, the two names for God found in the Book of Genesis, "Yahweh" and "Elohim," reflected two different authors, though he still claimed Mosaic authorship for much of the text. Given the tenor of the times, his *Conjectures on Genesis* (1753) was published anonymously. For philosopher Baruch Spinoza (1632–77), whose iconoclasm would ultimately lead to his excommunication, the Hebrew Bible/Old Testament was the work of many writers over many generations but most assuredly not the work of Moses or any other single author and certainly not God. For German biblical scholar and orientalist Julius Wellhausen (1844–1918), the Pentateuch (the "Five Books"—Genesis to Deuteronomy) was a multi-layered text: the "J" or Jahwist author(s) or school; the "E" or Elohist author(s) or school; the "P" or priestly editor(s) or school; and "D" or Deuteronomist editor(s) or school. While this last assessment fell out of favor for much of the twentieth century, it has experienced something of a renewal of interest, with modifications to be sure, in the twenty-first. These seminal thinkers and others have all contributed to the overall and ongoing debate about the use or not of the Hebrew Bible as the *primary* source with which to write a solid history of ancient Israel before the period of the monarchy, the monarchy itself, and the history of the Southern Kingdom (Judah and the tribes of Judah and Benjamin) versus the Northern Kingdom (Israel and the nine other tribes, Levites resident in both locales) after their split and the destruction and assimilation of the north by the Assyrians (which some have labeled "Neo-Assyrians") in 721 BCE.

Today, though the terms "minimalists" and "maximalists" are rarely used in current scholarship, they continue to represent a serious division and ongoing debate (at times rancorous) regarding Israel's ancient historic past: those for whom the Hebrew Bible is nothing more than a post-period, constructed and largely fictionalized, set of texts refashioned by later largely unknown authors for social, political, economic, and religious reasons—elites one and all—versus those for whom the texts represent a reasonable historical assessment of that same past and who are comfortable with the notion that the ancient writers had their own understanding of their past, even if their subjective retelling differs at times markedly from our present desire to be as objective in our retellings as humanly possible based on the available evidence. Representative of the former, sometimes referred to as the "Copenhagen School" because of the academic home of some of the authors, include Philip R. Davies,[6] Israel Finkelstein,[7] Niels Peter Lemche,[8] Thomas L. Thompson,[9] and Keith Whitlam.[10] Representative of the latter includes William Dever, James K. Hoffmeier,[11] and K.A. Kitchen.[12] Forty years ago, American biblical scholar Millar Burrows (1889–1980) suggested that:

> The basic, distinctive presumption of all ancient Hebrew ideas about history is the conviction that in human history the one, eternal living God is working out his [*sic*] own sovereign purpose for the good of his creatures, first for his chosen people, and through them the rest of humankind ... the divine purpose of creating a holy people, a kingdom of priests, through whom all the families of the earth may be blessed, is painfully and patiently wrought out. ... At the heart of the Hebrew idea of history is the assurance that Israel is God's chosen people, but this involves not merely privilege but obligation.[13]

With regard to those who "do" ancient Israel's history today, J. Maxwell Miller, Emeritus Professor at Emory University, Atlanta, GA, is largely correct when he writes:

Most biblical scholars, therefore, fall somewhere between the two extremes [minimalist vs. maximalist]. . . . On the one hand, they proceed with confidence that the Bible preserves authentic historical memory. On the other hand, they recognize that the Bible is not a monolithic document, that its different voices reflect different perceptions of ancient Israel's history, that these perceptions usually are heavily influenced by theological and nationalistic interests, and that some of the biblical materials were not intended to be read as literal history in the first place. The historian's task, therefore, is to separate the authentic historical memory from its highly theological and often legendary context.[14]

Summarily, then, Lester L. Grabbe, Emeritus Professor of Hebrew Bible and Early Judaism at the University of Hull, UK, outlines where we go from here:

1. Writing the history of ancient Israel and Judah is no different from writing any other history.
2. The minimalist argument that the biblical text cannot be used except where there is external confirmation has often been supported in our investigation; however, as a working principle, it is inadequate.
3. Particular sorts of information are more likely to be trustworthy than others: wherever an Israelite or Judahite ruler is mentioned in an external source, the biblical text is shown to have the genuine name, the correct sequence of rule, and the approximate time of the person's rule in every case where there are sufficient external comparative sources to make a determination.
4. The most fruitful method is the multiple-source approach.
5. The social sciences can sometimes provide important models for and approaches to understanding the data.[15]

Finally, a word about archaeology, the uncovering and recovery of "things and stuff" from our past, which continues to play an important role in furthering our understanding of Israel's past as well. Again, William Dever provides us with a good summary, arguing "archaeological data can be a 'primary' source for history-writing—indeed, sometimes superior to biblical and other ancient Near Eastern texts" because:

1. Archaeological data in the broadest sense are by definition 'external' to the texts and therefore constitute an *independent* witness.
2. Archaeological data, unlike texts, have not been deliberately edited and altered in meaning over time by continuous commentary, so they allow us to leap across the centuries and encounter a past reality directly.
3. Archaeological artifacts constitute *realia*, as much as do texts.

4. While surviving ancient texts will always be relatively scant, and largely the result of accidental finds, archaeological evidence is potentially almost unlimited.
5. The analysis of ancient texts will and should proceed, although I think with diminishing results.[16]

BEGINNINGS UNTIL THE MONARCHY

If one fancies oneself a devotee of the so-called great man (person) theory of history—largely attributed to the nineteenth-century Scottish essayist Thomas Carlyle (1795–1881)—Israel's beginnings, at least according to the Torah or Hebrew Bible itself, can well be told in terms of its patriarchs, Abraham, Isaac, Jacob, Joseph, and Moses (and, perhaps, Joshua). Collectively larger-than-life figures, their stories dominate the first two books of the Hebrew Bible or Torah, Bereshith/Genesis, and Shemot/ Exodus, and the last two books Bamidbar/Numbers and Devarim/ Deuteronomy.

In doing so, however, one tells only a partial story, a series of "biohistories"—if we may invent such a term—and misses a far larger picture. For the story of the Israelites or Hebrews or Jews is not only a story of individuals writ large, however large they were and are, but instead is the story of an ancient people, a collectivity as it were, whose present-day descendants perceive themselves as *lineal* inheritors of that which has preceded them (more on this in chapter four).

THE "FOUNDERS"

As already noted, the Torah/Hebrew Bible/Old Testament tells the foundation story of the people of ancient Israel in terms of its larger-than-life personages Abraham, Isaac, Jacob, Joseph, Moses, and Joshua, presented to us in the biblical books Bereshith/Genesis, Shemot/Exodus, Bamidbar/Numbers, Devarim/Deuteronomy, and Yehoshua/Joshua. So, who then were the important figures? What do we know and who do we not know? (The book of Vayikra/Leviticus "interrupts" the historical story to inform us, its hearers and readers, how the sacrificial religion of ancient Israel was to be practiced by its high priests and attendants— *cohanim* (high priests) and *Levi'im* (others of the tribe of Levi trained in the rituals as well). It also provides the foundational underpinnings of Israel's moral-ethical standards: chapters eighteen to twenty-two, the so-called "Holiness Code").

Abraham

Born a Chaldean from the city of Ur, already an old and wealthy man, Abraham (born Avram) responds to a voice he fully and truly believes to be that of a Singular Deity, commanding him to leave home and journey forth southeastward, and, in the process, becoming a great and blessed nation through his progeny ("as numerous as the stars in the sky and as the sand on the seashore," Bereshith/Genesis 22:17). After many adventures—including the near-sacrifice of the son of his old age Yitzhak/Isaac—what Jews refer to as the *Akedat* Yitzhak ("Binding" of Isaac) and Christians as the "Sacrifice" of Isaac (understanding it as prefiguration of the Christ-event)—he, along with his primary wife, Sarah (born Sarai), and others, arrives "home" to live out his days. When Sarah dies, he purchases the Cave of Machpelah in or near Hebron from Ephron the Hittite, rather than accepting it as a gift, where, according to Jewish, Christian, and Islamic traditions, Sarah and he, Isaac, Jacob, Leah, and Rachel are all buried. (Known today as the Cave/Tomb of the Patriarchs, venerated by religious Jews, Christians, and Muslims, it is also the site of the Islamic holy place *al-Haram al-Ibrahimi*/Sanctuary of Abraham, where, tragically, in 1994, American ex-pat Baruch Goldstein, MD [1956–94], murdered 29 Palestinians and wounded 125 others while at prayer before himself being killed.)[17]

Though accorded the honorific by Jews as Avraham *Avinu* ("Abraham our Father" or "Abraham our Patriarch," who scholar Jon Levenson of Harvard University calls "the biological progenitor of the Jews and the father of Judaism, the first Jew"[18]), neither his story nor time period can be confirmed either textually or archaeologically. Scholarly consensus today tends to date the texts/stories as presented in Bereshith/Genesis to the so-called "Persian Period" of the late sixth century BCE—the post-Babylonian exilic period—and understands them as resolving the tensions between those who left and returned and those who stayed. Likewise, Abraham is further accorded the rabbinic respect along with Yitzhak/Isaac and Ya'akov/Jacob in the formulaic beginning to many Jewish prayers: "Praised are You, Adonai our God, God of our patriarchs, God of Abraham, God of Isaac, God of Jacob . . ."[19]

24

Isaac

Beloved son of Abraham's and Sarah's old age, his name Yitzhak may, perhaps, be best translated as "Laughing Boy" as both Abraham and Sarah laughed at news of her intended pregnancy, though she would later recant when questioned directly. He was, however, not the first-born: that would fall to Ishmael (Arabic, Isma'il, and mentioned seventeen times in the Qur'an), son of Sarah's maid, Hagar, and both banished from the family due to Sarah's discomfort at the conception, though it was she herself who encouraged her husband because of her own barrenness.[20] As was the case previously, no textual or archaeological evidence has thus far been found to support either him directly or his story. He would go on in later rabbinic and Jewish tradition, however, to become the symbol of unwavering commitment to the God of Israel, up to and including one's own death, especially during the tribulations of the Middle Dark Ages (i.e., martyrdom).[21]

Contrary to popular opinion, however, of the notion of Isaac blindly following his father up Mount Moriah *à la* chapters twenty-two and twenty-three of Bereshith/Genesis, rabbinic understanding of him was that of a mature 37-year-old man, to wit, Sarah was ninety at his birth and dies at 127 in the chapter following. (Some *midrashim*/legendary add-on stories attribute it to a heart attack, the result of having been told what was transpiring and being informed by none other than ha-satan, the prosecuting angel of the heavenly hosts who would, again, surface in Sefer Iyov/the Book of Job.)

Jacob

Ya'akov, the son of Isaac and grandson of Abraham, is a far more enigmatic character who both manipulates his older brother Esau—food for change in status—and deceives his father—first-born blessing. His name may, perhaps, best be understood as "Heel Grabber"—from the Hebrew word *ekev*/heel—who came out of his mother's womb clutching the heel of his twin older brother. (Evidently, as will be the case with others throughout the Hebrew Bible, God uses flawed human beings to accomplish divine tasks.)

Of far more import, however, is the wrestling match with the *ish* (another man? God? angel? Christ?) which will result in his significant name change from Ya'akov to Yisra'El ("God Wrestler"; Bereshith/Genesis 32:22–32) and, thus, the name by which his followers and descendants will identify themselves to themselves and to others as well: *Yisraelim*/Israelites. Equally, significantly, he will become the father of twelve sons (the twelve tribes) though his four wives: Leah, Rachel, Bilhah, and Zilpah. As was the case with his predecessors, no textual, historical, or archaeological evidence has thus far surfaced to substantiate his existence.

Joseph

Son of Jacob and Rachel, grandson of Isaac, and great-grandson of Abraham, he is first presented to us in the biblical text as an obnoxious teenager who sees his lot in life as lording it over his older brothers, beloved of his father who makes for him a *k'tonet passim* (coat of many colors? symbolic of worldly authority?), and with the ability to correctly interpret dreams. Spirited out of his father's house when the brothers can no longer tolerate his unsufferable antics, he is sold into slavery, winds up in Egypt where he rises to the post of prime minister (?)/secretary of agriculture (?), saves the nation from famine, manipulates his brothers, who have come to Egypt to seek food/grain for their own starving flocks and herds, and reunites with his family. Prior to his death, he declares to his family his heartfelt desire to be buried in the land of his birth, which they honor, and thus, in so doing, established the tradition of the most religiously devout Jews to do the same today. Rabbinically, he is also said to the be ancestor of the Messiah son of Joseph who, along with the Messiah son of David, will wage war against the enemies of both the God and people of Israel and who himself with die in battle.[22]

Modern scholarship regards the Joseph stories as a Wisdom literary novella folded into the Book of Genesis, perhaps the work of a single author, and perhaps written in the early fifth century BCE. In the Islamic tradition, Joseph is the only prophet to whom a whole chapter (Sura XII) in the Qur'an is devoted. Nevertheless, while containing "bits of history" (e.g., both Egypt and ancient Israel did go through periods of famine and drought), he, too, comes up short as a character who can be historically confirmed.

Moses

No more important figure in the whole of the Jewish religious and historical tradition is that of Moses (Hebrew, Moshe, "one drawn from the waters" in accord with his birth story and thus saved from the murderous edict of the pharaoh for the slaughter of the newborn sons of the Israelites to prevent them from overpopulating the country and rebelling against the native Egyptians) who has long merited the rabbinic title Moshe *Rabbeinu*/Moses our rabbi, Moses our teacher. (While the Hebrew language itself has no capital letters as such, the title may be better understood as Moses *The* Rabbi, Moses *The* Teacher.) Raised as an Egyptian court prince by the unnamed pharaoh's daughter, he would flee Egypt after murdering a slave master for beating an Israelite, encounter the God of Israel at the Burning Bush, marry a Midianite (Ethiopian?), Zipporah, daughter of a Midianite priest Jethro, have two sons Gershom ("I was a stranger there") and Eliezer ("God is my help"), and return to Egypt to lead his people out of their bondage together with his older brother Aaron and older sister Miriam. Wandering the desert for four decades at the helm of a continuously disgruntled people, he would, ultimately, be denied his dream to lead them home to the land of their origins; that blessing would fall to his non-biological successor Joshua.[23]

Of the figure/person of Moses, scholarly consensus is somewhat divided between those who reject any notion of an historical personage and those who argue that there probably was someone in all likelihood—a pre-Mosaic figure perhaps—upon whom the stories were based though obviously embellished as well. Whatever one's own conclusions, he remains, however, after God, the dominating figure of the Torah/Hebrew Bible/Old Testament, and, according to Devarim/Deuteronomy 34, he dies at age 120 in full possession of his physical and (sexual) faculties, giving rise to the Jewish birthday wish as one ages, "May you, too, like Moses of old, live to be 120!" (In the Qur'an as well, other than Muhammed, he is mentioned more often than any other prophet, more than 500 times.)

Joshua

Joshua, unlike like his predecessor, was an excellent military tactician, but, like his predecessor, possessed of reasonability good administrative skills, and a religious heart to match. He was one of the twelve spies sent to scout out the land and assess its possibilities for the Israelites' return, but one of only two—along with Caleb, son of Jephunneh, who would go on to be given the priesthood in perpetuity as a reward—to announce to Moses and those assembled that they would overtake and overpower their enemies already resident there with the God of Israel on their side.

Tapped to succeed Moses, his significant ascension is marked by his *non-biological* relationship with Moses, Aaron, Miriam and family, and thus marks also an important and different way forward for the Israelites from their neighbors. (His name Yehoshua in Hebrew—"God is salvation"—becomes in Greek, Latin, and, later, English, Jesus.) After his successful military campaigns, according to the biblical account, it will be Joshua's responsibility to apportion the land to the various tribal groups. As with the problematic scholarly divisions noted above vis-à-vis Moses' own historicity, Joshua, too, like the previous "founders," cannot be confirmed textually, historically, or archaeologically.

* * *

Summarily, then, regarding these founding patriarchs of the early Israelite people and their religious community—who they were and how they come to be who they were—they metaphorically and perhaps even symbolically would go on to present their followers with a story writ large and one which has continued to engender commitment over the course of the generations. The very lessons of their lives, even if they cannot historically be verified by the tools of modern scholarship, have inspired and continue to inspire Jews, Christians, and Muslims to commit themselves to a God who seemingly communicated to a rather small and somewhat insignificant group of Semites in a faraway place and who continues to elicit those same commitments today.

AND GOD AS WELL

Far more complicated than the cases of the founders enumerated above is the case of the God of Israel, not only as presented in the Torah/Hebrew Bible/Old and New Testaments, and Qur'an, but also in scholarly thinking: how did a somewhat parochial deity (Shasu? Midianite? Canaanite?) come to supplant all other deities in all other ancient religious nation-states and assume the singular distinction of being the *only* true divine reality? Important at the outset is to recognize that, for ancient Israel, their initial acceptance of *monolatry* (other nations have other gods but Israel's God is ours alone) to *monotheism* (only Israel's God is the only God; all others are false) was and remains correct and beyond debate and discussion.

The Hebrew tetragrammaton of Yod-heh-vav-heh ("Yahweh"? "Yahweh?" and morphed into English as Jehovah) was, at least initially, understood and perceived by its ancient, committed Israelite adherents to be both a storm and warrior deity who would make fertile people, land, herds, and flocks and lead the Israelites successfully and militarily into battle against their enemies. By the time of the Babylonian captivity (586 BCE) and the building of the Second Temple under King Solomon (see chapter three), the actual pronunciation of God's name was both forbidden and unremembered. Even though these same Israelites accorded their fellow Canaanites respect for their own/other deities (see below), that respect quickly turned into both rejection and disrespect.

Worship of the God of Israel would come to be best expressed in the land of Israel upon their return from that same Babylonian captivity through the *hagim*/the three pilgrimage festivals: *Sukkot*/Booths in the fall and a reminder of both the harvest and planting season and the desert wandering after Egypt; *Pesach*/Passover, the celebration of the liberation itself; and *Shavuot*/Weeks, the celebration of the harvest and Moses' return with the Tablets of the Laws of God. (The evolution of these and other holy day celebrations from their biblical beginnings up to and including the present day and including denominational differences is a book in and of itself!)

In those same Tablets, Israel's God was announced as *incorporeal* (without bodily form) and *aniconic* (never to be depicted as statue or other image), in contradistinction to all of the Israelites' neighbors and experience. Why this remains so has long vexed scholars who have thus far proffered no meaningful explanation.

The scholarly literature about the earliest and later understandings of the God of Israel remains vast and growing. Among the more fascinating works are those of Jean Bottero,[24] Jonathan Goldstein,[25] Jonathan Kirsch,[26] Theodore J. Lewis,[27] Thomas Römer,[28] Peter Schäfer,[29] Mark S. Smith,[30] Francesca Stavrakopoulou,[31] and Robert Wright.[32]

MIGRATORY TRIBES

Scholarly consensus today regarding ancient Israel's beginnings suggests that the group's origins lay among the western Semitic migratory tribes of the region who traveled its highways and byways during the second millennium BCE—approximately 3,500 to 4,000 years ago at the outset. As the late Anson Rainey (1930–2011) of Tel Aviv University noted:

. . . the Israelites were originally Canaanites fleeing from the city-states of the coastal plain west of the hill country. . . . In the period archaeologists call Iron Age I, from 1200 to 1000 BCE, approximately 300 new settlements sprang up in the central hill country of Canaan that runs through the land like a spine from north to south . . . these were the early Israelites settling down.

There is no reason to doubt the principal assumption of the Biblical tradition that the ancient Israelites migrated as pastoralists from east of the Jordan.[33]

Thus, organized along patriarchal and tribal lines, they were primarily shepherds, pastoralists, whose own flocks, herds, and cattle dictated their journeys in their constant need and search for food. Some among them, however many we cannot say, hired themselves out as mercenaries, traveling not only with their portable wealth but with their families, servants, and tribes as well. At a time when the Egyptian empire dominated that part of the world, their journeys took them into and out of Egypt and into and out of their own lands as well.

Important to note in this context as well, these ancient Israelites, tribal clusters of varying size and leadership cadres, were not *Habiru* or *Hapiru* but, perhaps related to the *Shasu*. Again, Anson Rainey:

Habiru is not an ethnic designation. The *Habiru* are a social element . . . they are not from a single linguistic group. There seems to have been several different kinds of *Habiru*—but always of inferior status. The term itself has a negative connotation . . . *there is absolutely no linguistic relationship between Habiru and Hebrew ('ivri)*. But another term may indeed have something to do with the early Israelites, not linguistically but socially: namely the *Shasu* who are often found in Egyptian texts and inscriptions of the Late Bronze Age . . . the *Shasu* were pastoralists (nomads) who lived in symbiosis with sedentary populations but were prone to violence in times of distress. The term first appears in the 15th century BCE in Egypt. These *Shasu* were the main source of early hill-country settlements in Canaan that represent the Israelites' settling down. . . . *Israel was simply one group among many Shasu who were moving out of the steppe lands to find their livelihood in areas that would provide them with food in times of drought and famine.*[34]

If Anson Rainey and others are indeed correct, and the scholarly consensus would appear to be so, we have encountered a true conflict between the biblical telling of ancient Israel's origins attributed to the founding patriarchs and the work of objective scholarship. All nations and all people—indeed all groups sociologically—massage their own origin stories to shore up the psychological mindsets of their members and retain their numbers and active involvements. In this, the ancient

Israelites and contemporary Jewish people are no different from their neighbors, near and far, past and present. To thus confirm a different origin story from that of the Bible is *not* to dismiss outright the generations of later Jews, however, who understand themselves and their commitments as Jews as the lineal descendants of a somewhat shrouded past and a religious and covenantal commitment to the God of Israel and their people as causes for both celebration in the good times and healing and reconciliation in the bad times.

Thus, whatever else they were, the ancient Israelites who would evolve into today's Jews were in fact a Canaanite people, similar in some respects to their neighbors but different from them as well and/but who would survive them all.

EGYPTIAN MONARCHY

With the gradual integration of the Asiatic tribes or Western Semitic peoples known to us as Hyksos (an Egyptian term possibly meaning "foreigners" or "rulers of foreign lands," but one conceivably of their own self-designation), their takeover of the Egyptian monarchy between 1655 BCE and 1570 BCE—the so-called "Fifteenth Dynasty"—life by and large continued as it had under previous Egyptian rulers, at least initially. (The story of Joseph, who attained eminence at the highest levels of Egyptian government may very well date from this period.) It is also important to note as well that the Hyksos may have been preceded in their takeover by Canaanites who had already settled in the rich and fertile Nile Valley during the earlier thirteenth (approximately 1803–1649 BCE) and twelfth (approximately 1938–1750 BCE) Egyptian dynasties.[35] However, with the end of their period of hegemony and expulsion[36] and its reclamation by so-called native Egyptians, the tide turned against these migrants, ultimately resulting in their enslavement under pharaonic leadership. According to Shemot/Exodus 1:11, it was the slaves, not only Israelites, who built the store-cities of Pithom and Ramses for the pharaoh (now identified as Ramses II [1290–1224 BCE]). It was during his reign, a period of corruption and disintegration, that the Judaic archetypal redemptive experience known as *Y'tziat Mitzrayim*, the "going forth from Egypt"—the Exodus—took place, an event of such magnitude that it will forever be enshrined as one of the two central themes of Judaic religious life (the other being the *theophany* at Sinai, the "giving of the Torah").

Though nowhere recorded by Egyptians or other non-Israelite chroniclers (or at least not yet unearthed by archaeologists), within two centuries, these same Israelites conquered much of their former home and resettled in the land of Canaan. In so doing, they turned from their previous, pre-slavery, nomadic ways of life of quasi-independent tribal clusters to becoming agriculturalists, farmers, craftspeople, and settled religionists constantly on guard against invaders.

CONFEDERATION OF TRIBES

After the solitary leadership of the Egyptian court prince Moses, his designated non-dynastic successor, Joshua, and Moses' priestly older brother Aaron, leaders known as "judges" (Hebrew *shofetim*) stepped forth to govern what, for all intents and purposes, was a confederation of tribes, none acquiring supreme sovereignty over either the people or the land itself. It will then be at the end of this period of a series of transitional leaders, by the beginning of the eleventh century BCE that the Israelites will usher in their monarchy.

These aforementioned "tribal clusters" were named for the sons of the patriarch Jacob (Hebrew Ya'akov/"Heel Grabber," acknowledging his birth grasping the heel of his older brother Esav/Esau)/later renamed Israel (Hebrew, Yisra'El/"God Wrestler," based on his mysterious nighttime wrestling match with an *ish* [Hebrew, "man"—himself? another? rather than God, an angel, or later, in Christian tradition, the Christ, Jesus] across the Jordan River when he was all alone): Reuben, Simeon, Judah, Issachar, Zebulun, Benjamin, Dan, Naphtali, Gad, Asher, Ephraim, and Manasseh (Devarim/Deuteronomy 27:12-13); and each of whom would conquer and govern territorial space upon their return to Canaan. While there is no consensus when they united in something of a loose confederation, scholarly consensus is that they definitely did so at some point, in all likelihood for military and defensive, economic, and religious reasons, quite possibly already laying the groundwork for such during their wandering period and prior to their return and reflected in the Book of Judges. Important to this story as well, the tribes of Judah (larger) and Benjamin (smaller) governed in the south and the remaining nine tribes in the north as laid out in the Book of Joshua 13–19.

This "tribal history," biblically told and retold and accepted by both Jews and Christians, has had its critics in the modern period (e.g., German historian and sociologist Max Weber [1864–1920], American historian Ronald M. Glassman [b. 1937], English biblical scholar Arthur Peake [1865–1929], American economist Paul Davidson [b. 1930], and others), all of whom have argued either for the non-existence of the story as presented or modified somewhat. Historian Norman K. Gottwald, however, wrote his text *The Tribes of Yahweh* as an affirmation of the biblical account but told at a later date and after Israel's return.[37] Like so much else in the story of Israel's ancient past, biblical accounts have found themselves subject to rejection, harsh criticism, dismissal, and affirmation, either in whole or in part.

THE SPLIT BETWEEN JUDAH IN THE SOUTH AND ISRAEL IN THE NORTH: AFTER THE MONARCHY

While we shall address the United Monarchy under the reigns of Israel's kings, Saul, David, and Solomon, in the next chapter, relevant to this chapter is what occurred to the tribes after the death of Solomon: the divided kingdom—the result of his failure to name a successor and one able to maintain unity; the loss of the northern tribes after their takeover and absorption by the Assyrians in 721 BCE; and the mythic history of the "Ten Lost Tribes."

The southern tribes of Judah and Benjamin—the kingdom of Judah—were not subjected to the experience of their northern extended family and would flourish and remain a somewhat independent nation- (or city-?) state until first the Babylonian debacle in 586 BCE; they would return and rebuild until the Roman debacle in 70 CE, and twice the destruction of its capital Jerusalem (originally a hilltop fortress city called Jebus, inhabited by a Canaanite tribe, the Jebusites). After the Roman assault which would further prevent the Jews from even entering their holy city upon pain of death, this subjugated people would remain somewhat autonomous, though obviously politically, militarily, and economically diminished. Two events, however, would loom large in the telling of the Jewish story: first, the historically-questionable founding of a rabbinical academy under surviving rabbi Yohanan ben Zakkai post-70 CE and the historically-problematic "canonization" of the Torah/Hebrew Bible in 90 CE; and, second, the "publishing" of the Mishnah (the "Second Torah") under the acknowledged communal leadership of rabbi Yehudah the "Prince" (a political not regal term) in 220 CE. (More on this later on as well.) Importantly, however, post-70 CE, the wandering Jews would again leave their land of origin and migrate primarily westward to the European continent and beyond. Today's Jews see and understand themselves as primarily the lineal descendants of the Southern Kingdom.

As noted above, the "Jews" of ancient Israel experienced their first event of traumatic origins in their defeat at the hands of the Babylonian Empire in the year 586 BCE, and the taking into captivity of their religious, political, military, and economic leaderships, and, evidently, a significantly large portion of their overall population. Sociologically and politically, that defeat should have ended ancient Israel's story as the normative "way of the world" was for the defeated to surrender their own unique identity, embrace that of the victors, and with it embrace their religions and gods as well. "Wonder of wonders, miracle of miracles"—to quote one of the musical lines from the 1971 American hit play "Fiddler on the Roof"—the beneficent Babylonians allowed the defeated to cluster in their own neighborhoods, practice their own religious and unique ways, maintain some semblance of communal leadership—provided they paid their taxes and did not engage in any militarily insurrectionist activities. The captured Israelites evidently did as required and thus preserved their own integrity and way of life even in a foreign land, and thus set the stage for all future locales of Jewish residence and existence.

In 538 BCE, under the equally beneficent ruler Cyrus of Persia, also known as "Cyrus the Great" (600–530 BCE), who defeated the Babylonians, the door was opened for return. A sizeable remnant began returning home, according to the biblical text, under the later administrative leadership of Nehemiah (b. c. 473 BCE) and the religious leadership of Ezra (c. 480–440 BCE) though at different times. The remaining resident community in Babylonia would, however, continue to flourish and would go on to establish important rabbinical academies (e.g., the two most well-known in the cities of Sura and Pumbedita) and later produce the Babylonian Talmud (BT), which would become the foundational document for surviving Jewish life. Based on its extensive commentaries on the Mishnah of Palestine, produced in 200 CE but far less complete, the BT continues to nourish Jewish life throughout the world. Thus, the "religion of the rabbis," addressing all aspects of Jewish communal life, looms large in enabling Jewish survival for more than 2,000 years.

With regard to the Northern Kingdom of Israel, the seeming result of King Solomon's failure to designate a successor and thus a splitting of the tribal configuration from a now-controversial questionably united kingdom (at least according to the biblical texts – more on this later), the dates of its existence would appear to be between 930 BCE and 720 BCE when it was successfully invaded and conquered by its neighbors the Assyrians. As was normative in the ancient world, the resident population, including those removed into captivity, surrendered their god who had "failed" them and embraced the god-system of the victors and, ultimately, their own distinctive customs and ways of life to become part of this larger collectivity—with one exception: the Samaritans, who continued in the region of Samaria and who claimed partial Israelite identification, but who, today, exist wholly as a separate entity even while living in the modern State of Israel.[38] The Mesha Stele (also known as the Moabite Stone), dated 840 BCE, details the defeat of the kingdom of Israel by King Mesha of Moab, and reasonably confirms that account found in 2 Kings 3:4-28.[39]

Of continuing interest to some within both the larger Jewish and Christian communities but thoroughly discounted by the scholarly community (defeat equaled both absorption and disappearance) has been the ultimate fate of the so-called "Ten Lost Tribes", going so far as to claim the Eskimos, Native Americans, Vikings, the Pashtuns of Afghanistan/Pakistan, and even the Chinese, or others (e.g., the Jews of Kashmir, Cochin in India, Beta Israel in Ethiopia, Igbo in Nigeria) as their descendants. Among even a smaller minority of Christians, there have been those who have suggested that, when the Christ returns, so, too, will the lost tribes of Israel reappear. Something of a modern-day Indiana Jones (a reference to the 1981 movie character in *Raiders of the Lost Ark*, Dir. Steven Spielberg, US: Paramount Pictures), British scholar and adventurer Tudor Parfitt has written a fascinating account of the myths beyond history, *The Lost Tribes: The History of a Myth* (London: Weidenfeld & Nicholson, 2003).[40]

* * *

We turn now in the next chapter to the question of the United Monarchy under the reins of ancient Israel's first three kings: Saul, the brilliant military tactician but a somewhat unstable leader and personality; David, the youthful and popular leader with a "religious heart" but a wayward body; and Solomon, whose wisdom obscured his own unpopularity but would be overlooked by later generations of Jews and Christians. As has been noted previously as well, this part of the story remains somewhat controversial.

NOTES

1   In the March/April 2014 issue of the *Biblical Archaeology Review*, Lawrence Mykytiuk of Purdue University, IN, published "Archaeology Confirms 50 Real

Steven Leonard Jacobs

People in the Bible," 40, no. 2: 42–5, 48–50, and in the May/June 2017 issue of the *Biblical Archaeology Review* 43, no. 3, "Archaeology Confirms 3 More Bible People," 48–52. See: www.biblicalarchaeology.org/biblepeople for the initial listing.

2 Marc Zvi Brettler, *The Creation of History in Ancient Israel* (London and New York, NY: Routledge, 1995), 140. See, also, Reinhard G. Kratz, *Historical & Biblical Israel: The History, Tradition, and Archives of Israel and Judah*, trans. Paul Michael Kurtz (Oxford and New York, NY: Oxford University Press, 2015), and Giovanni Garbini, *History & Ideology in Ancient Israel*, trans. John Bowden (New York, NY: Crossroad, 1988).

3 William G. Dever, *Who Were the Early Israelites and Where Did They Come From?* (Grand Rapids, MI, and Cambridge: William B. Eerdmans, 2003), 226.

4 See the discussion of "ethnogenesis" with which chapter four, "Social Structures and Institutions of Ancient Israel," begins.

5 William G. Dever, *What Did the Biblical Writers Know & When Did They Know It? What Archaeology Can Tell Us about the Reality of Ancient Israel* (Grand Rapids, MI, and Cambridge: William B. Eerdmans, 2001), 5.

6 Philip R. Davies, *In Search of 'Ancient Israel'* (Sheffield: Sheffield Academic Press: 1992), and *On the Origins of Judaism* (London: Routledge, 2011).

7 Israel Finkelstein and Neil Asher Silberman, *The Bible Unearthed: Archaeology's New Vision of Ancient Israel and the Origin of Its Sacred Texts* (New York, NY: Free Press, 2001).

8 Niels Peter Lemche, *The Israelites in History and Tradition* (London: SPCK; and Louisville, KY: Westminster John Knox Press, 1998).

9 Thomas L. Thompson, *The Mythic Past: Biblical Archaeology and the Myth of Israel* (New York, NY: Basic Books, 1999).

10 Keith W. Whitlam, *The Invention of Ancient Israel: The Silencing of Palestinian History* (London: Routledge, 1996). Edited collections include: Diana Vikander Edelmann (ed.), *The Triumph of Elohim: From Yahwisms to Judaisms* (Grand Rapids, MI: William B. Eerdmanns, 1996); Lester L. Grabbe (ed.), *Can a 'History of Israel' Be Written?* (Sheffield: Sheffield Academic Press, 1997); and Brian B. Schmidt (ed.), *The Quest for the Historical Israel: Debating Archaeology and the History of Early Israel* (Atlanta, GA: Society of Biblical Literature, 2007).

11 James K. Hoffmeier, *Israel in Egypt: The Evidence for the Authenticity of the Exodus Tradition* (Oxford and New York, NY: Oxford University Press, 1996).

12 K.A. Kitchen, *On the Reliability of the Old Testament* (Grand Rapids, MI, and Cambridge: William B. Eerdsmans, 2003).

13 Millar Burrows, "Ancient Israel," in *The Idea of History in the Ancient Near East*, ed. Robert C. Dentan, American Oriental Series Monograph 38 (New Haven, CT: American Oriental Society, 1955), 128–9.

14 J. Maxwell Miller, "Reading the Bible Historically: The Historian's Approach,"
in *To Each Its Own Meaning: Biblical Criticisms and Their Application*, ed.
Steven L. McKenzie and Stephen R. Haynes, rev. and expanded (Louisville, KY:
Westminster John Knox Press, 1999), 22.

15 Lester L. Grabbe, *Ancient Israel: What Do We Know and How Do We Know
It?* (London and New York, NY: T&T Clark, 2007; rev. ed.: 2017), 222–3.

16 Dever, *What Did the Biblical Writers Know & When Did They Know It?*,
89–90.

17 Ibrahim/Abraham is mentioned in 35 Suras (chapters of Qur'an), second only
to Musa/Moses.

18 Jon D. Levenson, *Inheriting Abraham: The Legacy of the Patriarch in Judaism,
Christianity, and Islam* (Princeton, NJ: Princeton University Press, 2012), 3.

19 The latest iteration of the American Reform/Liberal/Progressive Siddur/
Prayerbook, *Mishkan T'filah: A Reform Siddur* (New York, NY: Central
Conference of American Rabbis, 2007), reads (in translation): "Blessed are
You, Adonai or God, God of our fathers and mothers, God of Abraham, God
of Isaac, God of Jacob, God of Sarah, God of Rebecca, God of Rachel, and
God of Leah."

20 Thus, one possible "reading" of the Palestinian Arab/Israeli Conflict is that it is
a "family feud": same father, different mothers.

21 See, for example: Søren Kierkegaard, *Fear and Trembling*, trans. Alastair
Hannay (New York, NY: Penguin, 1986); Jon D. Levenson, *The Death and
Resurrection of the Beloved Son: The Transformation of Child Sacrifice in
Judaism and Christianity* (New Haven, CT, and London: Yale University Press,
1995); and Shalom Spiegel, *The Last Trial: On the Legends and Lore of the
Command to Abraham to Offer Isaac as a Sacrifice*, trans. Judah Goldin
(Woodstock, VT: Jewish Lights, 1993).

22 According to the first of the two prophets, Zechariah, as reflected in the text
(1–8 and 9–14), both of whom apparently wrote during the fifth century BCE,
in chapter 1:18–21 (Tanakh, Zechariah 2:1–4) we find the following: "Then I
looked up, and there before me were four horns. I asked the angel who was
speaking to me, 'What are these?' He answered me, 'These are the horns that
scattered Judah, Israel and Jerusalem.' Then the Lord showed me four
craftsmen. I asked, 'What are these coming to do?' He answered, 'These are the
horns that scattered Judah so that no one could raise their head, but the
craftsmen have come to terrify them and throw down these horns of the
nations who lifted up their horns against the land of Judah to scatter its
people.'" (NIV) Jewish interpretive tradition regards these "four craftsmen" as
four messianic figures: Messiah ben Joseph, who will die in war against the
enemies of God and Israel; Messiah ben David, the "ultimate" and "true"
messiah (and the one understood by later Jewish Christians and gentile

Christians as Jesus); Elijah who will herald the end of the world (the eschaton); and the Righteous Priest," though not a focus of Jewish messianic speculation (BT Sukkah 52b). Interestingly and significantly, Cyrus the Great of Persia was also seen as a messiah of sorts having prodded and encourage those Israelites wanting to do so to return to their Holy Land from their Babylonian exile.

Though modern scholarship is largely undecided when these messianic speculations made their initial appearance, there is a whole host of rich and fascinating contemporary literature. See, for example: Daniel Boyarin, *The Jewish Gospels: The Story of the Jewish Christ* (New York, NY: The New Press, 2012); Susannah Heschel, *Abraham Geiger and the Jewish Jesus* (Chicago, IL: University of Chicago Press, 1998); Israel Knohl, *The Messiah before Jesus: The Suffering Servant of the Dead Sea Scrolls*, trans. David Maisel (Berkeley: University of California Press, 2000); Israel Knohl, *The Messiah Confrontation: Pharisees versus Sadducees and the Death of Jesus*, trans. David Maisel (Philadelphia, PA: Jewish Publication Society, 2022); Peter Schäfer, *The Jewish Jesus: How Judaism and Christianity Shaped Each Other* (Princeton, NJ: Princeton University Press, 2012); Peter Schäfer, *Jesus in the Talmud* (Princeton, NJ: Princeton University Press, 2007); Geza Vermes, *Jesus in His Jewish Context* (Minneapolis, MN: Fortress Press, 2003); Geza Vermes, *Jesus the Jew: A Historian's Reading of the Gospels* (Philadelphia, PA: Fortress Press, 1973); and Michael O. Wise, *The First Messiah: Investigating the Savior Before Christ* (San Francisco, CA: Harper, 1999).

For those contemporary Orthodox Jews who await his appearance, they stand fast with Maimonides, who affirmed in his "Thirteen Principles of Faith," "I believe with perfect faith in the coming of the Messiah, and even though he tarries, yet will I wait for him." Conservative Jews remain somewhat divided on the issue; Reform and Reconstructionist Jews reject altogether such a belief, opting instead for a belief in a forthcoming "messianic age" to be brought about by the concerted efforts of all good people of faith.

23 A beautiful meditative reflection of Moses' thinking as he sat upon Mount Nebo watching from afar as the Israelites entered the Promised Land is that of Samuel Sandmel, *Alone atop the Mountain* (Garden City, NY: Doubleday, 1973).

24 Jean Bottéro, *The Birth of God: The Bible and the Historian*, trans. Kees W. Bolle (University Park: Pennsylvania State University Press, 2000).

25 Jonathan Goldstein, *Peoples of an Almighty God: Competing Religions in the Ancient World* (New York, NY: Doubleday, 2002).

26 Jonathan Kirsch, *God Against the Gods: The History of the War Between Monotheism and Polytheism* (New York, NY: Viking Compass, 2004).

27 Theodore J. Lewis, *The Origin and Character of God: Ancient Israelite Religion Through the Lens of Divinity* (New York, NY: Oxford University Press, 2020).

28 Thomas Römer, *The Invention of God*, trans. Raymond Guess (Cambridge, MA, and London: Harvard University Press, 2015).

29 Peter Schäfer, *Two Gods in Heaven: Jewish Concepts of God in Antiquity*, trans. Allison Brown (Princeton, NJ: Princeton University Press, 2020).

30 Mark S. Smith, *The Early History of God: Yahweh and the Other Deities in Ancient Israel* (Grand Rapids, MI, and Cambridge: William B. Eerdmans, 2002), and *God in Translation: Deities in Cross-Cultural Discourse in the Biblical World*, 2nd ed. (Grand Rapids, MI, and Cambridge: William B. Eerdmans, 2010).

31 Francesca Stavrakopoulou, *God: An Anatomy* (New York, NY: Alfred A. Knopf, 2022).

32 Robert Wright, *The Evolution of God* (New York, NY: Back Bay Books, 2009).

33 Anson Rainey, "Inside, Outside: Where Did the Early Israelites Come From?" *Biblical Archaeological Review* 34, no. 6 (2008): 45, 50.

34 Anson Rainey, "Shasu or Habiru: Who Were the Early Israelites?" *Biblical Archaeological Review* 34, no. 6 (2008): 52–3; 54–5 (emphases added).

35 The Hyksos reign paralleled somewhat that of the Egyptians themselves during the seventeenth (1580–1550 BCE) and sixteenth (1649–1582 BCE) dynasties based in their capital Thebes, but, often, their relationship was marked by hostility and conflict (i.e., war).

36 Their own expulsion may, in fact, be the "inspiration" for the biblical story of the Exodus itself. To quote the unknown and unnamed author of "Hyksos" in *Wikipedia*: "The current consensus among archaeologists is that, if an Israelite exodus from Egypt occurred, it must have happened instead in the Nineteenth Dynasty [1292–1189 BCE], given the first appearance of a distinctive Israelite culture in the archaeological record. *The potential connection of the Hyksos to the exodus is no longer a central focus of scholarly study of the Hyksos.* Nevertheless, many recent scholars continue to posit that the Exodus narrative may have developed from collective memories of Hyksos expulsions from Egypt, and possibly elaborated on to encourage resistance to the 7th century domination of Judah by Egypt": https://en.wikipedia.org/wiki/Hyksos (emphasis added).

37 Norman K. Gottwald, *The Tribes of Yahweh: A Sociology of the Religion of Liberated Israel, 1250–1050 B.C.E.* (Maryknoll, NY: Orbis Books, 1979).

38 With regard to the Samaritans (from the Hebrew *Shomronim*/Keepers or Guardians [of the Torah]), today's Jews know very little of this small group originating among the ancient Israelites, their Torah, liturgical, ritual, and legal practices, other than their annual lamb slaughter on Mount Gerizim in Israel, and/or the "Parable of the Good Samaritan" in the New Testament with its negative cast on levitical priestly leadership (Gospel of Luke, 10:25–37). The

scholarly and popular literature is, however, vast and fascinating. See, for example: Robert T. Anderson and Terry Giles, *The Keepers: An Introduction to the History and Culture of the Samaritans* (Peabody, MA: Hendrickson Publishers, 2002); Gary S. Knoppers, *Jews and Samaritans: The Origins and History of Their Early Relations* (Oxford and New York, NY: Oxford University Press, 2013); and Reinhard Pummer, *The Samaritans: A Profile* (Grand Rapids, MI, and Cambridge: William B. Eerdmans, 2016).

39 Somewhat earlier, 1208 BCE, the now-famous Merneptah Stele of Egypt details the victory of Pharaoh Merneptah (d. 1203 BCE) over his enemies and includes the tantalizing line (27), "Israel is laid waste and his seed is not." The reference is not to a nation- or city-state but, rather, to Israel as people-group. Two other ancient references to Israel as a people are the Tel Dan Stele (870–750 BCE), which tells of the killing of Jehoram, son of Ahab, king of Israel, and the two Assyrian Kurkh Monoliths (879–852 BCE), which record the defeat of King Ahab of Israel.

40 An equally well written account is that of Zvi Ben-Dror Benite, *The Ten Lost Tribes: A World History* (New York, NY: Oxford University Press, 2009).

3

KINGDOMS OF JUDAH AND ISRAEL

BEFORE THE MONARCHY: THE TIME OF THE JUDGES

Joshua's failure to name a designated successor, one equally capable of both unifying and administrating the tribal confederation, led to something of a leadership void into which stepped a group of leaders to whom we have given the name "judges" (Hebrew, *shofetim*, from the root *shin-pe-tet*, i.e., those who make *mishpatim*/judgments). Unlike our Western notion of those who sit on high benches and pronounce their rulings, these men *and women* were civil, religious, and even military leaders, respected by all, and evidently capable of leading their collective people until the time of the monarchy. Their stories are found within the Book of Shofetim/Judges with the exception of Shmu'el/Samuel and Eli, whose own stories are told within the two books which bear the former's name. Thus, we may easily chart them as follows, and date their leadership prior to the eleventh century BCE, and divide them into so-called "major judges" and "minor judges":[1]

Othniel	3:7–11	(Fought the Arameans)	Major
Ehud	3:12–30	(Fought the Midianites and Moabites)	Minor
Shamgar	3:31	(Fought the Philistines)	Minor
Deborah	4–5	(Fought the Canaanites)	Major
Gideon	6–8	(Fought the Midianites and Amalekites)	Major
Abilmelech	9	(Status questionable, result of treachery)	?
Tola	10:1–2	(Served twenty-three years)	Minor
Yair	10:3–5	(Served twenty-two years)	Minor
Jepthah	11:1–12:7	(Fought the Ammonites)	Major

Ibzan	12:8–10	(Served seven years)	Minor
Elon	12:11–12	(Served ten years)	Minor
Abdon	12:13–15	(Served eight years)	Minor
Samson	13–16	(Fought the Philistines)	Major
Eli	1 Samuel 1:9		Major
Samuel	1–2 Samuel[2]		Major

Most well-known by later generations of Jews, Christians, and Muslims are Deborah (the only woman among them), Gideon, Samson (the author's Hebrew namesake!), and Samuel who would later play a key role in the anointing of the military leader Sha'ul/Saul as Israel's first monarch. Uncomfortably, however, their stories and lives, like too many others, cannot be fully confirmed by history and archaeology only textually, though the consensus of modern scholarships is that these persons and their stories are part of what we may call "Deuteronomistic history," and, perhaps, the work of a single author or limited group of authors. Their stories are, equally, somewhat repetitive: after committing themselves to the God of Israel covenantally, the Israelites backslide somewhat, are threatened by a variety of enemies, and thus required leaders—judges—to do battle with those same enemies and thus ensure Israelite survival.

THE UNITED MONARCHY: ~ 1047–930 BCE

These dates, and those which follow, are, of course, our best "guesses" based on all available evidence, including that which appears in collateral texts of other ancient nation-states. This designation "United Monarchy" thus becomes a catchall term to include the reigns of Israel's first three kings—Saul, David, and Solomon—and all the nine northern tribes—Israel—and the two southern tribes of Judah and Benjamin—Judah, with the Levites dispersed among both. After Solomon's death the kingdoms would split and lead ultimately to Israel's destruction and incorporation into the Assyrian kingdom (721 BCE) and, later, the Babylonian captivity (586 BCE). Between the two tragedies, we encounter the "Age of the Prophets," described below. (It goes without saying, of course, that modern scholars remain divided as to this historicity between those who support it with modifications and those who deny it and/or see it as an over-exaggeration of the time period and/or literary construct.)

REIGN OF SAUL: ~ 1047–1010 BCE

According to the books of the Hebrew Bible, specifically 1 and 2 Samuel, we learn that the eleventh-century prophet Shmu'el/Samuel (whose own story is one of the most fascinating in the whole of the Hebrew Bible) is tasked with the communal responsibility to find a king for his nation. He first communes with the God of Israel, whom he regards as Israel's only legitimate ruler. To his surprise, according to the text, the God of Israel accedes to this request; and the necessity for a strong military leader who can unite the tribes and protect them as well finds him anointing Saul, the son of Kish, a member of the tribe of Benjamin, as Israel's first king (1 Samuel 9–11). Though strong in the ways of the military and nearly successful in routing the Philistines, and fully aware of the need for tribal unity in a confederation-style government, his failures at the helm will, ultimately, result in his break with Samuel. A later battle with the Philistines at Gilboa and looming defeat force Saul to take the dramatic action of his own suicide by falling on his sword in order to avoid the humiliation and ignominy that would come with capture, according to 1 Samuel.[3] Yet, in 2 Samuel, an Amalekite is responsible for Saul's death, and it is David who puts the Amalekite to death. Even more sorrowful, 1 Samuel 31 and 2 Samuel 1 and 1 Chronicles 10 portrays the Amalekites recovering his body as well as his three sons, beheading them, and displaying their bodies. (Perhaps the truth of his ultimate fate lies somewhere between these three stories.)

A close reading of Saul's life and story in the Hebrew Bible present us with a personality suffering, perhaps, from quasi-legitimate paranoia. After all, as Israel's first king, he is, potentially, the target of assassination, the norm in his world, with which he certainly was familiar. To assuage his own fears, his son-in-law, popular in his own right as a poet, singer, and lesser military hero, David, is brought in to work his therapeutic musical magic but to no avail. Saul perceives David's growing popularity itself as reason for concern, and it is David himself who must flee the royal court as Saul becomes more and more convinced that his own death is part of David's agenda. With his apparent suicide, however, the people do anoint David as Israel's second king, leaving us to wonder, perhaps, whether or not David himself did in fact have his own "royal agenda."

REIGN OF DAVID: ~ 1008–970 BCE

Reigning for almost forty years, David is successful in further uniting the northern and southern tribes, and, most significantly, establishing Jerusalem, the former hilltop fortress city of the Canaanite Jebusites, Jebus, as his capital, and, with it, bringing the Ark of the Covenant, symbol of Israel's religious authority and divine favor, to rest there.[4] All this during the military and political decline of the powerful nations of Egypt and Mesopotamia. Said to be the author of many of the psalms contained within Sefer Tehillim/Book of Psalms (evidence of his poetic genius as well as his love for the God of Israel), David is also successful in engaging in peace treaties with his neighbors, for example, Hamath and Tyre. Thus, even today, many religious Jews regard the period of David's monarchy as Israel's historic "golden age," made even more positive for those who affirm belief in a personal messiah who will trace his own lineage back to the royal Davidic household (as the unknown author of the Gospel of Matthew does with regard to Jesus's lineage in the opening verses of his text as well). Historical debates among scholars as to the accuracy of David's life and stories, however accurate or inaccurate, have not apparently impacted these religious communities.

However, whatever plans David had for a dynastic chain of successors initially went awry with the death of his son Amnon (responsible for the rape of his sister Tamar) by his third-born son, Absalom, and Absalom's own death at the hands of David's general, Joab, during a rebellious military campaign (2 Samuel 13–18). Adonijah, David's first-born son and the legitimate claimant to the throne is passed over in favor of Solomon, David's sixteenth son and son of Bathsheba, assuming the throne. He, in turn, will rule the kingdom for more than thirty years.

Here, too, a close reading of the text certainly addresses David's initially adulterous relationship with Bathsheba, but, on reflection, may also suggest not that she was seduced and ensnared by a powerful king, but, rather, that she was a woman whose own agenda was, ultimately, to see one of her sons on the throne of Israel. And, given the vagaries of history being what they were and are, she saw her dream realized.

REIGN OF SOLOMON: ~ 970–931 BCE

Be that as it may, Sh'lomo/Solomon becomes Israel's third king in a time of relative peace and is recognized far and wide, then and now, for his wisdom, as evidenced by the parable of the two harlots both claiming motherhood of the same child (1 Kings 3:16–28). His genius, however, lay in his seeming ability to enter into alliances with his neighbors as well as his success in realizing his father's dream of building in Jerusalem a temple to the glory of the God of Israel. Both successes, however, come at a price, and cause us to realize a more nuanced portrait of him than the overwhelmingly positive one in the popular imagination.[5] His life and story are found within the biblical books of 2 Samuel, 1 Kings, and 2 Chronicles. His Hebrew name Sh'lomo is derived from the Hebrew root *shin-lamed-mem*, and, thus, is, perhaps, best translated as "Peaceful One" or "Peaceful Ruler." Jewish tradition also attributed to him authorship of the Song of Songs in his youth; Proverbs in his mature years, and Ecclesiastes in his old age (none of which can be independently verified). He is also said to be the author of the apocryphal books known as the Wisdom of Solomon, Odes of Solomon, and Psalms of Solomon, but, again, this cannot be independently verified. Archaeologists themselves, to date, have not been able to verify either his Temple building or his supposedly sumptuous and lavishly furnished palace. However, the copper mines at Timna, said to be under his authority, have been found.

As is par for the course in any nation-state relationship, Solomon's alliances resulted in ambassadorial entourages journeying to Jerusalem, together with their own idol-worshipping representatives, to take up residence, which the populace, in turn, viewed as acts of desecration of a holy city. (His own foreign non-Israelite wives and concubines, however, were permitted their non-Israelite worship of their deities.) Furthermore, the building of the First Temple would require vast *corvées* (unpaid labor) drawn from the Israelite population as well as vast sums of capital to purchase the required goods (e.g., cedar wood from the trees of Lebanon), purchases that could only have been made by extraordinarily heavy taxation, again a significant source of discontent. Moreover, while the Babylonian Talmud indicates that the Temple was, in fact one of the wonders of the ancient world, it would take a long passage of time for it to be viewed as such in the minds of the ordinary citizenry and later Jews in subsequent memory.

One of the most fascinating and intriguing stories is that of his supposed relationship with the Queen of Sheba (Ethiopia). The account, said to have been written in the fourteenth century, tells that she journeyed to Jerusalem, bore a son from their relationship who would go on to become King Menelik I of Axum and found a 2,900-year dynasty, initially

Jewish and later Christian up to and including Haile Selassie (1892–1975), emperor of Ethiopia from 1930 until his overthrow in 1974. As the story goes, Menelik was given a replica of the Ark of the Covenant, which was then switched, and he returned home with the original where it supposedly remains to this day under the guardianship of priests in a church site closed to the prying eyes of others.

Lastly, the Masonic Order, its lodges, temples, rituals, and fraternity trace their origins to Solomon and his building of the First Temple; much of its work was secretive and closed to outsiders.

SACRIFICIAL WORSHIP IN ANCIENT ISRAEL

Now, with the centralization of worship in Jerusalem at the First Temple, and the institution of an authoritative priesthood, attention must also be paid to the actual form of sacrificial worship as demonstrated in Sefer Vayikra/Book of Leviticus. Prior to the building of the Temple, levitical priests conducted their sacrificial rituals throughout the land of Israel but they ceased to do so once the Temple of Solomon was erected in Jerusalem.

Sacrifices of animals—and humans, to a lesser extent—to the gods of the ancient Near East was common to the religions enshrined therein. That said, however, one possibly correct understanding of the *Akedat Yitzhak*/"Binding" of Isaac in Bereshith/Genesis 22 and his near sacrifice at the hands of his father Avraham/Abraham and the substitutionary offering of the ram caught by its horns in the bushes was the rejection of human sacrifice on the part of the ancient Israelites. Nonetheless, the animal sacrificial system as it developed may best be termed cultic and non-democratic/non-participatory. That is to say, the Israelites brought their animals to the priests (*cohanim*) to be prepped by the priests' "assistants" (*Levi'im*), then, the Israelites, along with the appropriate meal and libation (drink) offerings, watched what took place, and returned to their homes feeling certain that the God of Israel had accepted their sacrificial gifts, and all would be well. (Only later, with the rise of the Pharisees [Hebrew, *Perushim*/"Separatists"] during the Roman period would Israelite worship provide a contested alternative form of commitment to God based on knowledge and male inclusivity.) It should also be noted that, with the destruction of the Second Temple by the Romans in 70 CE, the sacrificial system ceased to be and would only return with the rebuilding of the Third Temple, a contemporary preoccupation on the part of some devout Jews and some devout

Christians (who regard it as a necessary requirement for the Christ's eventual return). Obvious as well, during the period of the Babylonian captivity (see below), the sacrificial system was suspended and thus necessitated and redirected Israelite worship toward study of the sacred Torah, prayers said by all (priests no longer serving as intermediaries between Israelite humanity and the God of Israel), and the development of personal observance and heightened ethical practice—all hallmarks of an evolving diasporic Judaism to this day.

In the Torah/Hebrew Bible/Old Testament, the Hebrew word *korban* ("to bring forward," i.e., to God; pl. *korbanot*) is used to designate these animal sacrifices and designed to win God's favor (fertility of land, animals, and people; success in war), homage (thanksgiving for success; spared harm), and pardon (from sins; personal and collective violations). Our English word "sacrifice" is derived from the Latin word *sacrificare*, "to make sacred" from the human realm to the divine realm. Thus, the sacrifices of the ancient Israelites, however regulated, were meant and understood to be "gifts" to God, willingly offered without hesitation as the proper way to maintain this primary relationship between God, individuals, families, tribes, and the whole people.

As found early on in Sefer Vayikra/Book of Leviticus, they are:

Olah	Burnt offering	1:6–8:13
Minhah	Grain offering	2; 6:14–23[6]
Zevach Shelamim	Well-being offering	3; 7:11–
Hatta't	Sin/Purification offering	4:1–5:13; 6:24–30
Asham	Guilt Offering	5:14–6:7; 7:1–10

The animals themselves, depending on the wealth of the individual Israelites, ranged from bulls, goats, and sheep to doves and pigeons.

Mention must also be made in this context of the "scapegoat"— *Azazel* ("one removed" or "one sent out")—as presented in Leviticus 16:21–22, and upon which is symbolically placed the sins and impurities of the entire Israelite people as it is led outside the community to wander in the desert wilderness and ultimately to die:

> [21] He [Aaron] is to lay both hands on the head of the live goat and confess over it all the wickedness and rebellion of the Israelites—all their sins—and put them on the goat's head. He shall send the goat away into the wilderness in the care of someone appointed for the task. [22] The goat will carry on itself all their sins to a remote place; and the man shall release it in the wilderness. [NIV]

It is a continuing tragic irony of Jewish history that the Jewish people have become the world's scapegoats upon whom all or seemingly all of the problems, crises, and various political, economic, social, religious, and military conundrums and manifestations have been placed and all-too-often resulting in the violent deaths of the Jews themselves.[7]

DOWNFALL OF THE TWO KINGDOMS

Unfortunately for the people of Israel, with Solomon's death, there was no designated successor, no great unifier able to maintain such, and the nation split into the Northern Kingdom of Israel under Jeroboam, with its capital at Shechem, and the Southern Kingdom of Judah under Rehoboam, with its capital at Jerusalem. For the next three-plus centuries, the thrones of both the north and the south would experience all the court intrigues associated with royalty, including murders and assassinations, some occupying the seat of royalty longer than others. The Northern Kingdom would survive only until 721 BCE, when it would be conquered by the Assyrians; the south only until 586 BCE, when it would be conquered by the Babylonians. Between the two downfalls, however, the ancient Israelites would experience the "Age of the Prophets," whose religious-literary gifts to succeeding generations of Jews, Christians, Muslims, and others remain the finest religious-ethical literature in all of Western civilization.

THE ASSYRIAN CAPTIVITY: ~ 721 BCE

The Northern Kingdom of Israel was conquered by the armies of the Assyrian rulers Tiglath-Pileser III (795–727 BCE) and Shalmaneser V (d. 722 BCE) after an extended military conflict which may very well have ranged close to two decades. (Some scholars have suggested that it began in 740 BCE, while others have opted for a beginning date of 733 BCE.) The "final nail in the coffin," so to speak, would be at the hands of Sargon II (d. 705 BCE). As would be the case with the later Babylonian captivity, the religious, political, military, and economic leaderships were all taken into exile as well as a sizeable portion of the resident population. Unlike their southern confreres, however, they were not allowed to reassemble in their own neighborhoods, not allowed to practice their religious ways, and not allowed to maintain any semblance of national or ethnic cohesion. Thus, the nine northern tribes, plus their levitical priestly cohorts, found themselves adapting to Assyrian ways for survivalist purposes, individually, familially, and collectively, embracing the religious, social, and political systems of their victorious overlords, and, ultimately, assimilating themselves out of existence. (The myth of the so-called "Ten Lost Tribes" has been previously addressed.)

THE AGE OF THE PROPHETS

Now bereft of a much larger, even if somewhat divided, constituency, the Southern Kingdom of Judah (the tribes of the larger Judah and the smaller Benjamin, and their own levitical cohort) made haste to remain united, even if subject to repeated corruption from its own religious, political, and economic leaderships. It is into this "void" that the residents of Judah found themselves confronted by the fifteen remarkable men (no women!) whose sermonic *cris de coeur* spared no one in their largely unsuccessful attempts to bring the people back to their announced and proper relationship with the God of Israel. These men, whose plaintive discourses comprise the second section of the Torah/Hebrew Bible/Old Testament, were the *nevi'im* ("prophets", from the Hebrew word *navi*, "one who brings [the Word of God] to the people *and* who brings the people's words to God"; an uneven dialogue of sorts). To be sure, there were others "tapped" by God and bringers of divine injunctions (e.g., Samuel, Gad, Nathan, Elijah, Elisha), as well as guilds of so-called ecstatics who were trained/schooled to whip themselves into some sort of religious frenzy and thus speak (in tongues?) holy words to their people. However, it remains these fifteen who, having been enshrined in the sacred text itself, have remained our enduring legacy, divided, similar to the aforementioned judges into "majors" (3) and "minors" (12).[8] They are:

> Isaiah (~ eighth–seventh century BCE; actual dates unknown), perhaps the most messianic of all the prophets due to chapters 52 and 53 of his text (which some Christians affirm accurately predict the coming of the Christ).[9] Today's scholars continue to assert that the Book of Isaiah is not one text of one prophet, but rather three, or possibly four, texts and persons merged into one (Deutero-Isaiah chapters 40–66, Trito-Isaiah chapters 56–66, and, maybe, Quatro-Isaiah, chapters 60–66). The repetitive themes throughout are the holiness of God, Jerusalem as God's holy city, messianism, a surviving remnant, and a heightened sense of morality and moral responsibility.

Jeremiah (~ 650– ~ 570 BCE). Relatively unpopular because of his harsh pronouncements, he would spend time in prison, but accompany the exiles into their Babylonian captivity. He is the only prophet whose secretarial assistant is named, one Baruch ben [son of] Neriah, but his example suggests that other prophets had such assistants as well. For Jeremiah, the key to Jewish survival was making peace with their new reality—settling into the land of Babylon, and working for the welfare of the community. By extension, throughout Jewish history, this means resolving the ongoing tension between where one lives and where one can best and more fully be a follower of Judaism's religious ways: only back in the land of Israel (the "Zionist position"); in *galut* (in exile, the historical temporary reality but necessitating *aliyah*/emigration); or in the *t'futzah* (the diaspora, the continuing positive Jewish story outside the land).

Ezekiel (~ 622– ~ 570 BCE) "preached" both the destruction of Judah, having witnessed it first-hand, and prophesied the ultimate redemption and return of the Judahites to their homeland, where a future Temple would be constructed, specifically chapter 37 (the resurrection of the dry bones and their return). He, too, accompanied his people into their Babylonian exile and was a member of the priestly class. His fantastic visions, especially in the first chapter of his text, gave rise to that theological enterprise known as *Ma'aseh Merkavah* or *Chariot Mysticism*, and would later evolve into that understanding of Jewish theological thinking and biblical commentary known as *Kabbalah* ("received tradition," attesting, according to its own adherents, to its own ancient authenticity).

* * *

Hosea (eighth century BCE, and, if so, one whose very prophetic mission may have taken place in the Northern rather than the Southern Kingdom). Mixing doom with restoration, it was his life's story as he tells it in the text of God's commanding him to marry the *zonah*/prostitute Gomer whose unfaithfulness mirrors that of the people of Israel, but who, like God, remains willing to accept her/their return but only in faithful repentance.

Joel (ninth century BCE? or fifth or fourth century BCE?). Problematic in that his all-too-brief text (four chapters), which tells of a devastating plague of locusts—common in the Near East—is both ahistorical (it cannot be dated) and metaphorical, reminding the Israelites that their enemies are locust-like in their destructive capabilities, but non-specific as well. Further, no autobiographical information is included which would further our knowledge of him.

Amos (d. 745 BCE)—perhaps the most literarily sophisticated in its writing by one who claimed to be merely a simple orchard tender. Amos repeatedly inveighed against Israel's misdeeds and equally comforted those distressed by his criticisms. He is also the first to use the Hebrew word *galah* (to go into exile) as punishment for Israel's sins.

Obadiah (?)—one whose name is best translated as either "servant of God" or "slave of God" (*eved Yah*). He rails against the sins of Edon—arrogance, hubris, violence, bystanderness, gloating, looting, and betrayal—all of which are understood metaphorically to categorize the Israelite people's own iniquities.

Jonah (ninth century BCE? –eighth century BCE), the one prophet whose "prophecy" is only found in 3:4 ("Forty more days and Nineveh will be overturned"). His story of reluctance and finally submission to the will and command of God not only reminds the people of their own reluctance, at times, but ultimate acceptance of their covenantal responsibility, but also of God's forgiving nature toward all humanity. Nineveh, a real place which was ultimately destroyed (612 BCE), may equally have served in the minds of the prophet's audience as to their ultimate fate vis-à-vis their rejection of God. Some scholars have even suggested that it is, in fact, more novel than historical text (the person of Jonah cannot be historically verified) and simply ends rather than concludes, giving rise to the tantalizing theory that, perhaps, a bit of text remains undiscovered.

Micah (?)—said to have been a contemporary of Isaiah, Amos, and Hosea, he preached both the destruction of Jerusalem because of Israel's dishonesty and idolatry and, at the same time, that the nation-state would be restored under God's sovereignty, Israel's enemies would be destroyed, and Israel would make peace with her neighbors.

Habakkuk (seventh century BCE)—again, a prophet about whom no biographical information is found within his text. Yet his importance is reflected in two passages: 1:12–17 where he asks why God allows the wicked to devour the righteous, and 2:1–5 where he answers that the wicked will fall but the righteous will live by their faith, a Q and A which have haunted religious thinkers of all traditions for generations.

Nahum (?)—one whose name may best be translated as "Comforter" (i.e., one who gives succor to a hurting people/community). He may equally be described as "the prophet of outraged humanity" in his condemnation of the fall of Nineveh and the destruction of all who oppress Israel and oppose the God of justice.

Zephaniah (?)—a prophet whose name has two possible and different meanings, "one whom God has hidden/concealed" or "God's northerner," and who, like both his predecessors and successors, prophesied against the wickedness of the various nation-states, Judah included, but whose ultimate fate would be the survival of a "saving" if somewhat diminished remnant, which has, most assuredly, been the Jewish story up to and including the present day.

Haggai (sixth century BCE)—said to be something of a post-exilic prophet, his name is best translated as "My [God's] Festival Prophet." His concern was

51

the rebuilding of the Temple and the great events which Judah would experience in the future as the result of it.

Zechariah (?)—another post-exilic prophet whose name has two possibilities, either "God's Rememberer" or "God's Man/Male," and whose text, unevenly divided, scholars suggest bespeaks not one but two different authors: "first" Zechariah 1–8 concerned with Israel's return from Babylonia; and "second" Zechariah 9–14 concerned with the doom of Israel's enemies, the restoration of Israel and the rebuilding of the Sanctuary. Like Ezekiel before him, first Zechariah is a man possessed of visions (eight all told in chapters 1–6) but nowhere near as powerful or graphic as those of his predecessor.

Malachi (fifth century BCE), one whose name means "My [God's] Messenger." Malachi prophesied against what he regarded as Israel's degenerate priesthood, the failure of the people to pay their tithes, and a reduction in the people's religious commitment as the result of their marriage to and influence of their foreign wives. (Upon the exiles' return, Ezra would later call for their divorce.)

In carefully reading and reflecting upon the words of Israel's fifteen *nevi'im*—the only time this designation is applied in the Jewish religious tradition—one cannot but be inspired by their linguistic exaltations even in translation, their ethical hyper-awareness to people and events surrounding them, and the applicability to those concerns today, which is why rabbis, priests, and ministers continue to draw upon them to share with their own congregations and communities in their sermonic endeavors.

THE BABYLONIAN CAPTIVITY: ~ 586 BCE

When all is said and done, we may perhaps somewhat gently characterize Israel's prophets as "holy failures" for, despite all of their remonstrations, they were unable to get their people back on the proper and true religious track and re-imbue and re-energize them to take to heart their unique relationship with the God of Israel as one of covenantal responsibility which would manifest itself in divine protection. Thus, both the earlier Assyrian captivity and now this later Babylonian captivity were for all those seriously concerned with the *meaning* of these two mega-events not the failure of God to protect God's people, but the people's failure to live up to their own commitments to the God of Israel.

Textually, the Babylonians begin their destruction of Judah possibly as early as 597 BCE only to conclude their work by 581 BCE, for which there is solid archaeological evidence. (Those who remained in Judah, perhaps the majority, now found themselves in a client-state called

Yehud.) For the next fifty years, the exiles in Babylonia would find themselves striving mightily and apparently successfully to keep their community together in this foreign land until a momentous sea change took place with the defeat of the Babylonian Empire by the Persian Empire under Cyrus the Great at the Battle of Opis in 539 BCE. Once firmly in power and prior to his death, Cyrus decreed that Judahites who wished to return to their homeland could do so—not all but many did leave, led in different moments by the civil administer Nehemiah and the religious leader Ezra, but led, according to the Book of Ezra by Prince Zerubbabel (b. 566 BCE) and Joshua the Priest. It would take nearly half a century to organize those willing to do so, but once initiated, it would eventually result in success: strengthening the fortifications surrounding Jerusalem and preparing for the rebuilding of the Second Temple (built 521–516 BCE) (but which would meet its own destruction under the Roman oppressors in 70 CE).

The Babylonian captivity and the return of the exiles would remain throughout subsequent Jewish history the foundational event of later Jewish survival (after the return from Egypt, of course, despite its own historical difficulties). In its aftermath, the Torah/Hebrew Bible would later be canonized as the Jewish people's authoritative text (until its supplementation by the Talmud of Babylonia, and, to a lesser extent, the Talmud of Palestine or Jerusalem [the *Talmud Yerushalmi*—YT], both expansions of the Mishnah of Judah the Exilarch in the second century CE); the Hebrew alphabet (Greek, *alpha-beta*; Hebrew equivalent, *aleph-bet*) adopted as we have it today; the appearance of a new class of religious leaders, scribes, and sages and an increase in literary production; and, ultimately, the realization and recognition that the people of Israel could survive communally and religiously as a collectivity in the diaspora, as it has continued to do so up until the present moment.[10]

* * *

Before continuing with the history of Judaism and the Jewish people, let us take a slight detour and examine the social structure of ancient Israel now back in the Holy Land of Israel, the subject of the next chapter.

NOTES

1 For a re-thinking of their status as "minors," see Alan J. Hauser, "The 'Minor Judges': A Re-Evaluation," *Journal of Biblical Literature* 94, no. 2 (1975): 190–200.

2   Others who may also be said to have been judges were Joel and Abiah (1 and 2 Samuel), Keniah and his sons (1 Chronicles), and Amariah and Zebadiah (2 Chronicles).

3   Rabbinic reinterpretation of Saul's seemingly noble act became for them one of discomfiture and a later violation of religious norms, as well as a story from which no lessons should be learned. Suicide remains a violation of the sacred and a desecration of a "holy vessel" (the human body) made in the likeness/ image of God, following Bereshith/Genesis 1:27 ("So God created man in His own image, in the image of God created He him; male and female created He them"). Such acknowledged people (in the presence of two male witnesses) cannot be buried in the sacred soil of a Jewish cemetery, though doubtful cases can—along the edges or borders.

4   Contemporarily, both the late Yasir Arafat (1929–2004), chairman of the Palestinian Liberation Organization (1969–2004) and president of the Palestinian National Authority (1994–2004), and Faisal Husseini (1940–2001), a Palestinian politician who held a variety of important posts, falsely claimed, without substantive evidence and thoroughly discredited, that today's Palestinians are the descendants of the ancient Jebusites.

5   See, for example, Isaac Kalimi, *Writing and Rewriting the Story of Solomon in Ancient Israel* (Cambridge: Cambridge University Press, 2019), for a thorough and insightful overview of this changing understanding.

6   Said to be mixed with the finest of olive oils and the finest of flours.

7   The literature regarding scapegoats and scapegoating—Jews and others—is vast and intriguing. See, for example: Charlie Campbell, *Scapegoat: A History of Blaming Other People* (London and New York, NY: Duckworth Overlook, 2011); Tom Douglas, *Scapegoats: Transferring Blame* (London and New York, NY: Routledge, 1995); Andrea Dworkin, Scapegoat: *The Jews, Israel, and Women's Liberation* (New York, NY: The Free Press, 2000); René Girard, *The Scapegoat*, trans. Yvonne Freccero (Baltimore, MD: Johns Hopkins University Press, 1986); Kenneth M. Gould, *They Got the Blame: The Story of Scapegoats in History* (New York, NY: Association Press, 1944); Marek Halter, *Why the Jews? The Need to Scapegoat*, trans. Grace McQuillan (New York, NY: Arcade Publishing, 2020); Henri Hubert and Marcel Mauss, *Sacrifice: Its Nature and Functions*, trans. W.D. Halls (Chicago, IL: University of Chicago Press, 1964); Sylvia Brinton Perera, *The Scapegoat Complex: Toward a Mythology of Shadow and Guilt* (Toronto: Inner City Books, 1986); Raymund Schwager, *Must There Be Scapegoats? Violence and Redemption in the Bible*, trans. Maria L. Assad (San Francisco, CA: Harper & Row, 1987); and John B. Vickery and J'nan M. Sellery, eds., *The Scapegoat in Ritual and Literature* (Boston, MA: Houghton Mifflin, 1972).

8   Prior to the fifteen prophets, also included in the second section of the Torah/
    Hebrew Bible/Old Testament are the Books of Joshua, Judges, 1 and 2 Samuel,
    and 1 and 2 Kings, which are, technically speaking, not prophetic texts at all,
    but are intended to advance Israel's historical story.
9   Isaiah's reference to the "Suffering Servant" in these chapters is and has been
    understood by Jews throughout history as the Jewish collectivity, while, again,
    Christians understand the reference as directly referring to the Christ.
10 See, for example: Peter R. Ackroyd, *Exile and Restoration: A Study of Hebrew
    Thought of the Sixth Century B.C.* (Philadelphia, PA: The Westminster Press,
    1968); Rainer Albertz, *Israel in Exile: The History and Literature of the Sixth
    Century B.C.E.*, trans. David Green (Atlanta, GA: Society of Biblical
    Literature, 2003); and Daniel E. Fleming, *The Legacy of Israel in Judah's Bible:
    History, Politics, and the Reinscribing of Tradition* (Cambridge: Cambridge
    University Press, 2012).

4

SOCIAL STRUCTURES AND INSTITUTIONS OF ANCIENT ISRAEL

BY WAY OF AN INTRODUCTION: ETHNOGENESIS

Contrary to the Torah's/Hebrew Bible's telling of the origins of ancient Israel—from God's command to the Chaldean Avram/Abraham to flee Ur and journey to the land southward; to his son Yitzhak/Isaac, more a transitional figure; to Ya'akov/Jacob who would become Yisra'El/Israel, and thus the name of the collectivity as well; and aided by the Israelite/Egyptian court prince Moshe/Moses after Egypt's earlier foreign/Israelite leader Yosef/Joseph—modern scholarly consensus remains that the ancient Israelites were, in all likelihood, a sub-sect of Canaanites, more resident in the highlands, but, quite possibly, with additional members from the lowlands as well as Yahwistic followers who themselves may have fled Egypt for reasons of safety, security, and freedom from servitude.[1]

Charting the development of early Israelite social structures and institutions, however, is no easy task, complicated even more so by the paucity of materials found directly in the Hebrew Bible/Old Testament itself. Thus, much of our theoretical understandings are derived from comparisons to other cultures with whom the ancient Hebrews most likely came into contact.[2]

Before doing so, however, it is well to begin at the beginning and explore the idea of *ethnogenesis*—the formation and development of an ethnic group—by applying this concept of ethnicity to ancient Israel and whether or not it was, in fact, a decidedly observable ethnic community, one distinguished by a set of unique characteristics from its neighbors. (Collaterally relevant terms to keep in mind are: *ethnoarchaeology*—the ethnographic study of peoples for archaeological reasons in terms of their material remains [How was it made? For what purpose?]; *ethnocentrism*—applying one's own community's culture as the standard by which to evaluate others' cultures, practices, behaviors, beliefs, and the peoples themselves, more often inferiorly rather than equally; *ethnonationalism*—defining one's own or others' nation in terms of ethnicity; and *ethnoreligion*—understanding a group of people unified by their own ethnic and religious background and present.)

Because both James C. Miller[3] and Pekka Pitkänen[4] cite John Hutchinson's and Anthony D. Smith's 1996 book *Ethnicity*, it is also important to enumerate what they believed to be the main or primary features of ethnicity:

1. A common *proper name*, to identify the "essence" of the community
2. A myth of *common ancestry* rather than a fact, a myth that includes the idea of a common origin in time and place, and that gives an *ethnie* a sense of fictive kinship
3. Shared *historical memories*, or better, shared memories of a common past or pasts, including heroes, events and their commemorations
4. One or more *elements of common culture* which need not be specified but normally include religion, custom, or language
5. A link with a *homeland*, not necessarily its physical occupation by the *ethnie*, only its symbolic attachment to the ancestral land, as with diaspora peoples
6. A *sense of solidarity* on the part of at least some sections of the *ethnie's* population.[5]

Both Miller and Pitkänen appear to conclude, therefore, that ancient Israel more than meets the criteria to be labeled an ethnic community, based on the biblical texts themselves and such archaeological discoveries as distinctive pottery bowls, residence/house structures, male circumcision, and the now somewhat disputed absence of pig bones.[6]

Two caveats, however. Israeli archaeologist Avraham Faust, author of *Israel's Ethnogenesis: Settlement, Interaction, Expansion and Resistance*, has written summarily:

Today, however, it is widely acknowledged that ethnic identity is flexible, and that it is subjective rather than objective.

Ethnic identity must be defined in relation to other groups. What are important are not the unifying elements of the group, but the differences one group maintains from another group or groups.

It is clear that people in the past, just as people today, directly and indirectly, used material items to transmit messages about their identity.[7]

Any effort to understand Israel's ethnogenesis must therefore examine Israelite ethic identity as part of a larger study of Israelite society . . . .

It is also important to distinguish between two different questions: (1) When did a people named Israel first appear? And (2) where did those people come from?

Patterns of behavior and material items that seem meaningful during Iron Age II [1000–800 BCE] include the avoidance of pork, a tradition of not decorating pottery, male circumcision and use of the four-room house. The common denominator of many of these traits (and others, e.g., burial in simple inhumations during most of this period, the limited use of royal inscriptions) is an ethos of simplicity and perhaps even a form of equalitarian ideology. This ethos may very well have been used by the Israelites to define their boundaries in relation to other, more hierarchical groups. In short, this ethos helped to differentiate them from others.[8]

In his book *Israel's Ethnogenesis*, Faust notes additionally—as do most other scholars—"Merneptah's [Egyptian victory] stele of the late thirteenth century BCE informs us of the existence of a new ethnic group by the name of Israel, and by doing so suggests it to be a group of importance at the time."[9]

Having now established, not without controversy to be sure, that, at least by the thirteenth century BCE, there was a distinctive ethnic group known both to itself and to others as Israel, let us look, therefore, more closely at its social structures and institutions. Each of the topics addressed—(1) tribes; (2) urbanization; (3) family and life cycle (women, children, birth, marriage, death, inheritance, education, literacy, writing); (4) civic life (kings, kingdom/monarchy, slaves, scribes, law); (5) economic life and trade; (6) military and wars; (7) religion (cult, Temple, priests, calendar, others); and (8) culture (art, music, dance, literature)—is worthy of far more lengthy addesseses than these relatively brief summaries herein provided. (Collectively, the literature, resources, and archaeological evidence for each are vast.)

TRIBES AND PATRIARCHAL STRUCTURES

This much, however, does make sense to us: the overarching structure was that of the tribe, based on a patriarchal model. (Matriarchal modeling will come to the fore in the post-biblical or rabbinic period and continues to dominate Jewish identity up to and including the present day.) Originally, the tribes themselves were at least initially nomadic or semi-nomadic, their wanderings governed by the need for food for their herds, primarily goats, sheep and cattle. Prior to the monarchy, probably for reasons of safety, security, and survival, the tribes were loosely governed by a council or councils of elders, elected from within their own tribes, whose own elevation was, likely, based on age, experience, and socio-cultural and possibly economic status. Within their tribe, families were likewise patriarchal (alpha-male dominant by virtue of age and fatherhood); clusters of tribes—here we may use the term *clans*—coming together and constituting the various tribes identified within the Hebrew Bible/Old Testament. According to Bereshith/Genesis 48–50, the patriarch Ya'akov/Jacob (later Yisra'El/Israel) fathered twelve sons, each of whom would then occupy his own territory within the land of Israel, except for the tribe of Levi, who would, ultimately, serve as priests of the Holy Temple—first, the Aaronide priesthood with direct biological links to Aaron, Moses' older brother, and, then, the remaining members of the Tribe of Levi. In order of their birth, they were Reuben, Simeon, Levi, Judah, Dan, Naphtali, Gad, Asher, Issachar, Zebulun, Joseph, and Benjamin. (After the destruction of the Northern Kingdom by the Assyrians in 721 BCE, nine of the tribes and their Levites would be lost, and the Southern Kingdom would be inhabited by Judah and Benjamin only and their Levites.)

RISE OF URBANIZATION

The drive toward settlement brought with it more and more cultivation of the land itself, fruit trees and harvestable grains, and new classes of craftspeople and artisans. Urbanization coupled with conquest saw the status of the ruling elders increase and, concomitantly, increased the importance of both households and the smaller clan units. Out of such an evolving settled society came the monarchy, held in power by increasingly larger and larger landowning households, clans, and tribes, and, within it, the increasing social stratification known to us today: peasants and slaves (captives, residents, Israelites) to work the land; small landowners working the land themselves, possibly with the assistance of hired laborers; various governmental functionaries required for the success of the monarchy (e.g., administrators, scribes, accountants, military leaders and subordinates, and the like); levitical religious leaders as worship comes to occupy more and more a central place in Israelite life; and artisans, merchants, and businesspeople.

It should also be noted here that one of the threads that runs throughout the Torah/Hebrew Bible/Old Testament is the ambivalence of the Israelites toward urban, as opposed to pastoral, life. Ironically, however, later Jewish society survived, and religious and cultural productivity would all be contingent on urban life, and it is only with the rise of the modern State of Israel in the twentieth century that we see a truly positive return and renewed celebration and valuation of pastoral life in the development of both the *kibbutzim* and the *moshavim*, Israel's collective farming settlements.

FAMILY AND LIFE CYCLE

We begin, or course, with what is perhaps the most oft-quoted biblical expression of the positive role of the wife and mother in ancient Israel, recognizing at the same time that its application only makes sense when its description is that of a woman of some economic wherewithal or substance, that of Proverbs 31:10–31:

> [10] A wife of noble character who can find?
> She is worth far more than rubies.
> [11] Her husband has full confidence in her
> and lacks nothing of value.
> [12] She brings him good, not harm,
> all the days of her life.
> [13] She selects wool and flax
> and works with eager hands.
> [14] She is like the merchant ships,
> bringing her food from afar.
> [15] She gets up while it is still night;
> she provides food for her family
> and portions for her female servants.
> [16] She considers a field and buys it;
> out of her earnings she plants a vineyard.
> [17] She sets about her work vigorously;
> her arms are strong for her tasks.
> [18] She sees that her trading is profitable,
> and her lamp does not go out at night.
> [19] In her hand she holds the distaff

and grasps the spindle with her fingers.
[20] She opens her arms to the poor
and extends her hands to the needy.
[21] When it snows, she has no fear for her household;
for all of them are clothed in scarlet.
[22] She makes coverings for her bed;
she is clothed in fine linen and purple.
[23] Her husband is respected at the city gate,
where he takes his seat among the elders of the land.
[24] She makes linen garments and sells them,
and supplies the merchants with sashes.
[25] She is clothed with strength and dignity;
she can laugh at the days to come.
[26] She speaks with wisdom,
and faithful instruction is on her tongue.
[27] She watches over the affairs of her household
and does not eat the bread of idleness.
[28] Her children arise and call her blessed;
her husband also, and he praises her:
[29] "Many women do noble things,
but you surpass them all."
[30] Charm is deceptive, and beauty is fleeting;
but a woman who fears the LORD is to be praised.
[31] Honor her for all that her hands have done,
and let her works bring her praise at the city gate.

That having been said/written—however poetically beautiful its expression—we must keep in mind that (1) the society itself, like the tribes and clans, was patriarchal, and (2) women, at all levels, occupied a lesser status. A woman's role was "confined" to that of household manager, including meal preparation,[10] recipient of sex, and the bearer and rearer of children, males favored over females; and motherhood was seen as the supreme familial and communal honor and value. (Evidence, however, that the Hebrew Bible's/Old Testament's authors wrestled with these rather limiting understandings and the inclusion of love as a value is found both in the story of Ya'akov/Jacob and his favored wife, Rachel, and the entire text of *Shir Ha-Shirim*/Song of Songs.)

Girls were, in all likelihood, engaged to be married relatively soon after they experienced puberty (age twelve or thirteen), such "arrangements" being the result of the father's contractual agreement with the father of the groom-to-be (able to sustain such a marriage economically and thus likely to be older by several years). A *mohar*—mistranslated as "bride price" and leading to the unfortunate misunderstanding as *purchasing* a wife—was in reality a gift given in good faith and, ultimately, "sealing the deal." Though a length of time was the norm between engagement and marriage, upon the completion of the marriage ceremony itself (about which we know nothing), marital festivities, possibly lasting as long as week (eating, drinking and toasting, and dancing) took place. Men were permitted to marry more than one wife (polygyny rather than polygamy) only when they were able to support them economically; women were restricted to being the wives of only one husband.

Significantly, adultery (a married woman having intercourse with someone other than her husband or later discovery of early premarital sexual activity) and/or barrenness (inability to produce sons) were grounds for divorce. The husband was required, according to ancient Hebraic law, to write or have someone else write for him a *sefer kritut* (a scroll/book/document of divorce, literally a "document of cutting," thus rendering the marriage terminated). Archaeologically, no such document has ever been found and the Torah/Hebrew Bible/Old Testament itself provides us with no text whatsoever. (The later rabbinic instrument of the *get*—Hebrew for twelve lines [*gimmel* = three; *tet* = nine]—is an interpretive evolution of that understanding and document.)

In those situations where a husband died without heirs and a widow was left bereft and vulnerable, ancient Israel instituted the system of *yibbum* or Levirate marriage, whereby the brother of the deceased was *obligated* to marry the widow, and the child (son) of that new marriage was understood as the son of the deceased and his property/estate/inheritance was preserved. (Refusal to do so would result in a humiliating public ceremony known as *halitzah*—a sandal was removed from his foot while seated, and he was thus known as someone who dishonored his late brother's memory.[11])

Positively, the birth of children—again, more so sons than daughters—was and remains in Jewish religious tradition the supreme value in the context of marriage. (The first commandment, according to the rabbinic reading of the Hebrew Bible/Old Testament was "Be fruitful and multiply and fill the earth," Bereshith/Genesis 1:28. Rabbinic reading of the text meant, at the least, one son and one daughter.) Historically, wives were assisted in childbirth by midwives, as we know from the famous story of Moses and the midwives, Shifrah and Puah, who aided his mother, Jocheved, but refused the Pharaoh's demand that the male babies of the Israelites be murdered.

Boys were circumcised (removal of the *glans penis* at the head of the penis) at eight days after birth, following God's injunction to Abraham than he and all the males of his household enter into a covernantal relationship. In its ritual evolution, boys, after the surgical procedure, are presented to the public and given their Hebrew names. For example, this author's name is Shimshon Liezer ben Yosef David HaLevi, in accord with that tradition (Steven Leonard son of Ralph Albert, the Levite).[12] No such ceremonies—physical or other—celebrated the birth of daughters until the late Middle Ages, when fathers were called to the Torah to offer blessings before and after the reading of the Scriptures, and the later twentieth century onward when liberal rabbis began writing creative liturgies to celebrate their birth (e.g., eighth-day prayer ceremonies, and, somewhat uniquely, the piercing of the ears and the placing of small gold studs into those ears).

Also addressed concerning children is the Torah's/Hebrew Bible's/Old Testament's concern with sibling rivalries—Isaac and Ishmael, Jacob and Esau, Joseph and his brothers. In these instances, it is the younger who succeeds and supplants the older, perhaps ancient Israel's own somewhat unique way of affirming the "newness" of its own religious-ethnic-moral traditions in contradistinction to those of its neighbors—Egypt, Mesopotamia, Philistia, Assyria.

As regards education, literacy, and writing in ancient Israel, we are somewhat in the dark in that the Torah/Hebrew Bible/Old Testament tells us very little. As the majority of ancient Israel's population were agriculturalists—farmers—the odds were that formal education in terms of textual learning, literacy, writing, and archived documents were rare. Most likely, fathers and mothers taught their children the moral and ethical (and religious) imperatives that were necessary to sustain the family and community: "Train up a child (son?) in the way that he should go, and when he is old, he will not depart from it" (Proverbs 22:6). While schools (and teachers) were in evidence in other ancient kingdoms and civilizations (Egypt, Mesopotamia, Sumer, Ugarit), we have no evidence of such in ancient Israel. More than likely, as scholarly consensus would have it, writing and literacy arose in ancient Israel as it did elsewhere out of necessity, as societies which engaged in trade required other business and accounting activities and kings needed royal and military records kept, giving rise to a scholarly class we label "scribes" (i.e., those who can write), though here too, we have no evidence of the training required for such professional responsibilities. As to literate kings and prophets in ancient Israel, the results are mixed: some of both could read and write;

others could not.[13] Recent archaeological finds, however, have now suggested that literacy throughout the Southern Kingdom of Judah may, in fact, have been more widespread by the seventh century BCE than previously thought.

While hieroglyphics and cuneiforms were not part of ancient Israel's story but common elsewhere in the Middle East (e.g., Egypt, Babylonia), Philistia's move from pictograms to an early alphabetic system resulted in the origins of a proto-Hebraic/Semitic written alphabet which, ultimately, resulted in the Hebrew characters we have today. Common scholarly consensus remains that the texts of the Torah/Hebrew Bible/Old Testament were, in all likelihood, already set down in writing during the so-called "Persian Period," after Judah's return from the Babylonian captivity—roughly 538–400 BCE—suggesting that the writing, reading, and sharing of those texts would have occurred somewhat earlier. Perhaps, during the period of the captivity, such intellectual pursuits were part of the survivalist agenda, and, upon their return, became the agenda of the reconstituted nation-state.

Finally, given the reality of life, the ever-present fear of invasion and the necessity of military defense of a somewhat vulnerable population, and the hot climate of the ancient Near East, death necessitated relatively quick burial directly in the ground or in caves without coffins—as illustrated by the story of Abraham purchasing the cave at Machpelah for his beloved wife, Sarah, which would become the resting place for him as well as the later patriarchs. Embalming, unlike in ancient Egypt, was not the norm in ancient Israel, nor was cremation. Klaas Spronk draws an important distinction between "good death" and "bad death" in ancient Israel:

> In the view of the ancient Israelites, as expressed in the Hebrew Bible, death is good or at least acceptable: (1) after a long life ["The days of our years are three score years and ten (70); and if by reason of strength they be fourscore years (80)," Psalm 90:10]; (2) when a person dies in peace; (3) when there is continuity with the relation with the ancestors and heirs; and (4) when one will be buried in one's own land [e.g., Joseph informing his family of his desire to be buried in the land of his kin at the end of the Sefer Bereshith/Book of Genesis, necessitating both transport and embalming]. Death is experienced as bad when: (1) it is premature; (2) violent, especially when it is shameful [e.g., when a man is killed by a woman: Canaanite commander Sisera killed by Jael in Sefer Shofetim/Book of Judges]; (3) when a person does not have an heir; and (4) when one does not have a proper burial.[14]

Lastly, the Torah/Hebrew Bible/Old Testament addressed the question of inheritance, which, initially, became Mosaic law. Primogeniture—the designation of the first-born son's entitlement to a double portion of the estate, the remainder to be divided among the remaining male siblings— was the norm (Deuteronomy 21:17). Interestingly and significantly, the practice was challenged by the five daughters of Zelophehad in Sefer Bamidbar/Book of Numbers:

> 27 [1] The daughters of Zelophehad son of Hepher, the son of Gilead, the son of Makir, the son of Manasseh, belonged to the clan of Manasseh son of Joseph. The names of the daughters were Mahlah, Noah, Hoglah, Milkah and Tirzah. They came forward [2] and stood before Moses, Eleazar the priest, the leaders and the whole assembly at the entrance to the tent of meeting and said, [3] "Our father died in the wilderness. He was not among Korah's followers, who banded together against the LORD, but he died for his own sin and left no sons. [4] Why should our father's name disappear from his clan because he had no son? Give us property among our father's relatives." [5] So Moses brought their case before the LORD, [6] and the LORD said to him, [7] "What Zelophehad's daughters are saying is right. You must certainly give them property as an inheritance among their father's relatives and give their father's inheritance to them. [8] Say to the Israelites, 'If a man dies and leaves no son, give his inheritance to his daughter. [9] If he has no daughter, give his inheritance to his brothers. [10] If he has no brothers, give his inheritance to his father's brothers. [11] If his father had no brothers, give his inheritance to the nearest relative in his clan, that he may possess it. This is to have the force of law for the Israelites, as the LORD commanded Moses.'"[15]

CIVIC LIFE: GOVERNMENT AND MILITARY

From individual families within tribal clans, to governing patriarchal tribal clans, to something of a loose confederation of tribes for reasons to safety, security and survival,[16] to preliminary unification under King Saul, to strengthening and settlement under King David, to a settled nation-state under King Solomon, to its dissolution into two "kingdoms" (Israel and Judah), from his failure to name a unifying successor, to the Assyrian destruction of Israel to the north (721 BCE) and the Babylonian destruction of Judah to the south (586 BCE), to the return and re-establishment of the nation-state, to its second destruction at the hands of the Roman oppressors (70 CE), it would appear that, like its surrounding neighbors, the Jewish people were intent on exploring various forms of political governance which would enable it to survive and flourish and maintain its own unique religious identity. Short on specifics, the Torah/Hebrew Bible/Old Testament does not provide us with concrete details in the main as to how exactly the Jewish people were governed: e.g., how decisions were made and implemented; how decrees became common knowledge and were thus executed; what roles scribes and other administrators, including tax collecors, played in the hierarchy and how they were trained to do so; and the like.

Norman Gottwald successfully argues in his book *The Politics of Ancient Israel*[17] that the Hebrew Bible/Old Testament describes ancient Israel's political leaders as both governmental and religious leaders and thus makes its difficult to separate one understanding of their roles from that of the other, and, similarly, in the case of the institutions themselves: "Not only is the politics obscured by religion [seventh century BCE] but the reformist religion used to assess politics [thirteenth century BCE and following] was unknown to the political leaders on whom it is unfairly foisted."[18] He then goes on to cite the following conclusions:

1. Ancient Israel passed through three major zones of political organization in its long history from the 13th–12th centuries to the end of the biblical period . . . the **tribal era** (*ca.* 1225–1000 BCE), the **monarchic era** (*ca.* 1000–586 BCE), and the **colonial era** (*ca.* 586 BCE–135 CE).
2. The determinative literary voices of the Hebrew Bible speak from a colonial context in which traditions from tribal and monarchic times are assembled, often revised or glossed, and included either within or alongside fresh traditions.
3. An examination of the rich trove of archaeological finds and abundant information about ancient Near Eastern states demonstrates that the Israelite monarchic experience recounted in the Hebrew Bible is a familiar instance of the many small to mid-size tributary monarchies in Syro-Palestine, many of whom interacted commercially, diplomatically, and militarily with Israelite states.
4. Taking into account advances in knowledge of the multiple, often competitive forms of preexilic Israelite religion, it is reasonable to conclude that the cult of Yahweh, while a creative force in the tribal era and the official state religion under the monarchy, was neither dominant enough nor sufficiently unified in its diverse manifestations to shape the politics of the Israelite states in a decisive manner, even though various versions of Yahwism were enlisted in political causes and conflicts.
5. The frequent claim that somehow the covenant-based religion of Yahwism, stemming from Moses and associated with reforming kings such as Joash,

Hezekiah, and Josiah, was controlling or even influential in monarchic politics appears mistaken.

6. Less biblical and extrabiblical information is available concerning tribal and colonial politics.

7. The cultural and religious vibrancy of Israel's tribal era, surviving as a substratum under the monarchy, eventually fructified the energies and commitments of colonial Israelites to fashion a fundamentally "a-political" mode of communal life.

8. The politics recounted or implied in the Hebrew Bible, however, is not sufficient to grasp the full course of biblical politics vis-à-vis its religion.[19]

Thus, as noted, we remain somewhat in the dark regarding the implementation in concrete details of exactly how the ancient Israelite community, once it moved to a settled nation-state, did the actual work of governing, who did what, and how they did what they did.

Militarily speaking, however, we are on reasonably safe grounds to realize that, for ancient Israel, both tribally and settled, the world was, at times, a frightening place, one where wars were already being fought, were soon to be fought, and/or their potential was right around the corner. The Torah/Hebrew Bible/Old Testament cannot be read without the stories of its wars and the roles played by Moses in the conflict with the Egyptian pharaonic monarchy, kings Saul and David and their enemies, Solomon and his diplomatic alliances to stave off that potential, and Joshua's necessary battle to reclaim and retake the land itself. Then, too, ancient Israel's warlike "adventures" cannot be fully divorced from the Israelites' own understanding that it was the God of Israel who would enter into battle with them to ensure their success and legitimate their rationale for doing so. (Failures in battle were, however, the results of Israel's own human deficiencies and never attributed to divine error.) Obvious as well, the Assyrian destruction of the Northern Kingdom of Israel in 721 BCE and the Babylonian destruction of the Southern Kingdom of Judah in 586 BCE were the result of military failures in both locales. Other notable conflicts must include: (1) the Battle of Qarqar (853 BCE); (2) the siege of Lachish (701 BCE); (3) the Battle of Megiddo (609 BCE); (4) the first siege of Jerusalem (605 BCE); and the (5) second siege of Jerusalem (587 BCE).[20] Post-biblically, the Maccabean revolt of 164 BCE, which would give rise to the Hasmonean kingdom, and the insurrection against the Roman invaders/overlords between 66 and 70 CE,[21] which would precipitate 2,000 years of wandering until the birth of the Third Jewish Commonwealth on May 14, 1948, as well as the modern State of Israel's subsequent wars (1956, 1967, 1973, 1981 and 2006) round out the picture. Archaelogy as well has further increased our knowledge of ancient Israel's wars by the discovery of various weapons (e.g., short spears, long spears, knives, hurling stones, etc.) at these sites. Thus, as the text of Sefer Kohelet/Book of Ecclesiastes reminds us, "for everything there is a season ... a time for war and a time for peace" (3:1–8).[22]

ECONOMICS AND SLAVERY

Ancient Israel was first and predominantly an agricultural community, initially demanding, perhaps, a nomadic and semi-nomadic existence dictated by the necessity of movement, moving on as fresh grazing lands were required for flocks and herds and after naturally growing staples were harvested. Trading with others for necessities not grown or made likewise demanded interaction with other communities with whom they came into contact. Plunder and booty, the result of periodic and/or successful military confrontrations, would similarly enable ancient Israelites to further increase and perhaps store and preserve various kinds of foodstuffs. Once settled, initially in the hill country but then expanding further into the lowlands, thereby increasing their territory, the Israelites—increasingly agriculturally aware—instituted two rather remarkable ideas: (1) the sabbatical year at the end of every seven-year cycle, by which the land was allowed to lie fallow to be replenished by natural processes; and (2) the jubilee year at the end of every 49-year cycle (seven times seven) by which the land and the people, both slave and free, were reenergized. (We do not know how regularly these lofty ideals were put into practice.)

We do know, however, that, with increasing settlement and stability, something of a class society began to take shape: individual households and smaller village communities responsible for their own agricultural productivity, and larger "estates" needing workforces including Israelite "slaves" (better, indentured servants who had the possibility of release) and non-Israelite slaves who remained so for life. The priestly class as well needed to be supported—primarily, the high priestly class of *cohanim* (those who could trace their lineage back to Aaron, Moses' older brother), but the remainder of the levitical clan was certainly similarly advantaged; and both would benefit from a sacrificial system by which some some animal parts were reserved/saved for human consumption.

We understand that some form of taxation was instituted, as evidenced by the reign of King Solomon, who taxed his subjects to the point that they protested, but which enabled him to purchase those things he deemed important (e.g., cedar wood from Lebanon) to build the Temple to the glory of God. First fruits—of both animals and harvested products—were themselves a form of taxation which went through the priestly system as "gifts to God" but were as well defrayed (?) to futher support the religious functionaries.[23]

As noted above, the enslavement of men and women, both Israelite (primarily because of indebtedness) and non-Israelite (through either purchase or capture), was very much an aspect of ancient Israel's economic structure, as it was throughout the ancient Near East. It should, however, be noted as well that, while the laws pertaining to both were harsh—as regards Israelite slaves less so—the slaveholders/slaveowners were instructed to treat their slaves with a reasonable modicum of dignity and to see to their needs. Physical abuse of a slave in either category would have been regarded as a violation of the legal and moral codes of the people themselves.[24]

LAW

Just as religion (below) was central to ancient Israel's sense and awareness of self, so, too, was the legal structure by which the people developed, the two most obvious examples being the *B'rith*/Covenant between Israel and God and the *Aseret Ha-Dibrot*, the latter usually (mis)translated as the "Ten Commandments" but, more accurately, the "Ten Essential Statements," without which their society could not endure.

As regards the former, the Covenant with God entered into in the theophanic moment at Mount Sinai was a relatively simple contract with profound consequences throughout Jewish history. In "contractualese," God, as the Party of the first part, had two obligations: (1) to insure the safety and security of this people; and (2) to insure the fecundity of land, animals, and people. The Israelites, as the party of the second part, had two obligations as well: (1) to honor God through the observance and celebration of Israel's holidays, holy days, festivals, and fast days (discussion of which will come later in this text); and (2) to honor God by the observance of a moral/ethical standard to the highest possible degree. Violations of either on the part of Israel would/could result in military failure, slavery, banishment from the land, and the land itself left to ruination.

As regards the latter, the words of the statutes appear in the Hebrew Bible/Old Testament twice with slight variation: Shemot/Exodus 20:2–17 and Devarim/Deuteronomy 5:6–21. Honoring an incorporeal deity (without bodily form); not abusing God's name; the sanctity of the Sabbath (an act of *imitatio Dei* derived from the Genesis story of creation); honoring parents; not murdering, committing adultery, stealing or coveting others' possessions form the core of their societal values. Later post-biblical/rabbinic scholars would literally mine the Hebrew Bible/Old Testament and derive 613 *mitzvot*/laws/commandments to be observed and further develop a religious Judaism characterized by a *halakhic*/legal way of life, biblically-based but further elaborated upon through both the Babylonian Talmud, primarily, and the Palestinian/ Jerusalem Talmud, secondarily. This orientation to and of Judaism as a legally-constituted set of behaviors covering and governing all aspects of life remains true today for Orthodox Jews, somewhat less so for Conservative Jews, and even less so for Reform, Reconstructionist, and Humanist Jews.

Furthering their rabbinic commitment to the God of Israel as the only God in existence, the rabbis also included what have come to be called the "Seven Noahide Laws" applicable to all humankind and derived from Bereshith/Genesis 2 and 9: (1) not to worship idols; (2) not to blaspheme the name of God; (3) to establish courts of justice; (4) not to murder; (5) not to commit adultery; (6) not to rob; and (7) not to eat flesh that has been cut from a living animal.[25]

CULTURE

Summarily, William Brown, in his important article "Ancient Israelite Art," reminds us that art in ancient Israel was very much a reality almost from Israel's very earliest beginnings:

> Ancient Israel, and therefore its art, existed from about the 10th century BCE until the late 8th century BCE and used both local and imported materials, as demonstrated by local limestone used for stamp seals and carved ivories that were possibly imported from Phoenicia. Common motifs in ancient Israelite art include plants flanked by animals, astral symbols (such as sun-disks and stars), adapted forms of Egyptian symbols (such as winged sphinxes, uraei [serpents], and falcons), various animals (such as lions, ostriches, and bulls), and monsters (such as Cherubs-creatures akin to the Lamassu [hybrid beings, human and

animal]) . . . it is not clear who created the art . . . it is not exactly clear how or where objects were manufactured.

Israelite materials and objects tell stories about society 2,700 years ago. Art reveals many aspects of the Kingdom of Israel: ongoing trade of luxury items among the upper class; perspectives on cult rituals, deities, and sacred objects; international networks; cultural concerns; and the role of cults and deities in ancient Israel.

Ancient Israelite art is not particularly unique, though, and observations regarding materials and techniques also apply to art in the broader Levant during the Iron Age.[26]

He, therefore, concludes:

The Kingdom of Israel created and received art as part of social activity. Though their art forms and motifs were not particularly unique in and of themselves, what was unique is how the art was used to bolster ancient Israel's legitimacy in relation to other powers. Israel displayed art to demonstrate its power (Samaria ivories), participate in regional politics (stamp seals), express religious ideas, and create sacred spaces for cultic rituals. Simply put, the Kingdom of Israel used art in order to communicate ideas, among themselves and to others.[27]

That having been said, two examples of art—one positive and one negative—come readily to the fore when thinking about the Hebrew Bible/Old Testament.

Positively, in Shemot/Exodus 31:1–6 and chapters 36 to 39, one Bezalel (whose name would later be used for modern Israel's own Academy of Art and Design, established in 1906) was appointed by Moses—at God's instigation and with the support of the people—to both oversee and participate in the building of the Ark of the Covenant, the sacred furniture, the holy oils and incense, and the priestly garments initially worn by Aaron and his sons, along with his assistant Oholiab the Danite and himself said to be somewhat of an architect and embroiderer. Textually, Oholiab is said to be the ultimate craftsperson, working with metals, stone, and wood.

Negatively, in that same biblical book, we have the infamous story of the "Golden Calf" (Hebrew, *eggel ha-zahav*), constructed under Aaron's guidance, during Moses' absence atop Mount Sinai during which time he would engrave the *Aseret Ha-Dibrot* (Ten Commandments), literally, at God's bidding. Perhaps a stand-in for God's very presence, it may have been a re-thought depiction of the Egyptian bull-god Apis. In order to fashion it, the Israelites contributed gold earrings, ornaments and whatever other jewelry they had taken with them when they fled Egypt.[28] Whatever else we might say with regard to that incident—in which Moses, assisted by the Levites who did not participate in such a "sin," orchestrated the deaths of those violators—the sculpture itself (we, of course, have no depictions whatsoever) must have been visually aesthetically pleasing.

Both stories, however, are, at the very least, biblical examples of artistic expression from early on in ancient Israel's history.

Architectually, while we have no depictions of Solomon's First Temple nor the rebuilt/restored Second Temple until its Roman destruction, this much we do know based primarily on archaeological evidence: as the overwhelming majority of the ancient Israelites were agriculturalists— small, subsistence farmers, larger collective farms, and even larger estate farms—the basic living structure was the now-labeled "four-room house": a place of shelter, safety, and work, and where such tasks as food preparation, pottery and basket making, implement fashioning, and provision storage would take place. Scholars have also suggested that religious, social/cultural, and political gatherings took place there as well. The construction of these dwellings was, in all likelihood, an extended familial and communal responsibility and heavily labor-intensive.[29]

Returning to Sefer Shemot/the Book of Exodus, 15:20–21, after Israel's successful flight from Egypt and the drowning of the enemy's military, we read:

> [20] Then Miriam the prophet, Aaron's sister, took a timbrel in her hand, and all the women followed her, with timbrels and *dancing*. [21] Miriam sang to them: "Sing to the LORD, for he is highly exalted. Both horse and driver he has hurled into the sea."

After David's victory over the Philistines, we read, Judges 11:34:

> [34] When Jephthah returned to his home in Mizpah, who should come out to meet him but his daughter, *dancing* to the sound of timbrels! She was an only child. Except for her he had neither son nor daughter.

A third example is that of David's slaying of Goliath, 1 Samuel 18:6:

> [6] When the men were returning home after David had killed the Philistine, the women came out from all the towns of Israel to meet King Saul with singing and *dancing*, with joyful songs and with timbrels and lyres.

In all these examples, dancing was associated with military victories. (We shall address singing and musical instrumentation below.)

Steven Leonard Jacobs

Religiously, dancing was also associated with religious observance as well, as we learn from Psalm 149:3: "Let them praise his name with *dancing* and make music to him with timbrel and harp"; and 150:4: "Praise him with timbrel and *dancing*, praise him with the strings and pipe." We are certainly on reasonably solid ground to suggest that celebratory dancing was associated with both circumcision rituals and wedding feasting.

While we have already addressed the idea of literacy and writing in the section regarding education, both family responsibility and communal scenarios necessitating literate "elites," consisting of scribes, governmental administrators, accountants, diplomats, and military functionaries, and some (but certainly not all) kings—we need to keep in mind the following: (1) literary record-keeping for religious and civic/military purposes was the norm throughout the ancient Near East, whether hieroglyphic, cuneiformic, pictographic, or rudimentary alphabetic systems;[30] (2) the scrolls of the Hebrew Bible/Old Testament were written down at some point so that the people could be taught by trained expositors both to understand and embrace the words and demands of the God of Israel and their authoritative priestly and royal classes; (3) at some point in the evolving history of ancient Israel, the people themselves became a literate community, a commitment that continues today and values education and knowledge as primary values. (One is reminded of the post-biblical talmudic statements that the community can tear down a synagogue to build a school but not the reverse, and that the Jerusalemites were mandated to build a school for the education of their young.)

As noted above with regard to the examples of dancing (and there were other occasions), both singing and musical instrumentation appear also to have been the norm in ancient Israel. There was and is no finer expression of these two cultural art forms than the 150 psalms found in Sefer Tehillim/Book of Psalms (literally, "*Books* of Praises"),[31] perhaps ancient Israel's very first songbook or hymnbook.[32] Then, too, contained within, as elsewere in the Torah/Hebrew Bible/Old Testament (e.g., 1 Samuel 16:14–23; 2 Samuel 6:5; 1 Chronicles 13:8) are mentions of harps or lyres—*kinorot*[33] or *neginot*, drums, cymbals, and rattles). There are also references to popular melodies of the day (Psalm 22, "Hind of the morning," Psalms 45 and 60, "Lilies," Psalms 9 and 46, "Softly"), various musical instruments (*sheminith*, an eight-stringed instrument, a *gat* or *gittith*, made in the town/village of Gath), and psalms to be presented by the *minatezakh* (translation, either "choirmaster" or "concertmaster"). Moreover, if the ultimate locale for the presentation of

74

this music was, in fact, the First Temple, then its choirs were in all likelihood trained musical Levites, both men and boys.

Though there are references to "trumpets" in the Torah/Hebrew Bible/ Old Testament, we are on shaky ground regarding their actual physical appearance. Firmer footing, however, is that with regard to *shofarot*— ram's horns—used for military clarion calls, communal gatherings, and religious convocations, and said to be of two types, straight and curved, and each capable of emiting piercing sounds as they are today for the inauguration and conclusion of the Jewish Holy Days of *Rosh Ha-Shana* (New Year) and *Yom Kippur* (Day of Atonement).

Both Jewish and Christian religious traditions regard King David as the author and/or inspiration for many of the psalms based on the designation in the superscription *l'David*, which can be understood as "to David" (written by another), "for David" (similarly), or "of David" (reflecting authorship). Contextually, it is impossible, however, to know which understanding is the correct one vis-à-vis any given psalm.

Ultimately, these 150 psalms, some more than others, have proven sources of inspiration for praying Jews and Christians for the last 2,000 years, are and have been continually expressed in many musical formats. Liturgically, for Jews, more than 250 psalmic verses have been found throughout the Jewish prayerbooks, both the *Siddur* (Sabbath and Festival) and *Machzor* (High Holy Day).[34]

Finally, culturally, pottery making and sculpting had both pragmatic and religious purposes. Jars, bowls, and cups of varying sizes and shapes served as storage containers, eating and drinking vessels, light-containing holders, and pots for cooking. Some, perhaps later as the potters and sculptors refined their art, may have been embellished with decorative motifs as well as the name of the artist or owner impressed into the handles. Additionally, both the *menorah* (Hebrew, "light containing holder") and *Ner Tamid* (ever-lit flame symbolizing God's enduring presence) in both the portable Tabernacle and later First (and Second) Temple would have benefited equally from the artists who made them.

What has not been addressed, however, is the question of painting, primarily representational art, which would directly contravene the divine commandment not to make any graven image of either God or humanity, following Exodus 20:4, and certainly not in the context of religious worship and cultic practice, unlike ancient Israel's neighbors who were not bound by such restrictions. In day-to-day realities, however, drawings and sketches of both people and animals were permitted, as well as toy dolls and other figurines (e.g., Rachel hiding her father

Laban's household idols, Genesis 31:34). Defying somewhat these aforementioned restrictions, however, was the third-century Dura-Europos synagogue in Syria (⊠ 244–256 CE, uncovered in 1932) and which included such scenes as the "Binding" of Isaac, the Israelites fleeing Egypt, the visions of the prophet Ezekiel, consecration of the Tabernacle, the Golden Calf, Samuel anointing David, and Mordecai and Esther from the Book of Esther, and Moses receiving the Tablets of the Law.

RELIGION[35]

Beyond question, the heart of ancient Israel's life was its commitment to the God of Israel without whom nothing made sense and with whom everything was possible. Yet, a realistic depiction of that commitment demands the recognition that Israel's own understanding was an evolving one (i.e., *monolatry* to *monotheism*), at first accepting (embracing? incorporating?) the diversity of gods present in the ancient Near East (Exodus 15:11: "Who among the gods is like you, ADONAI? Who is like you— majestic in holiness, awesome in glory, working wonders?"), but, ultimately, coming to the conclusion/recognition that Yahweh–God was and is the only true God of all humankind.[36] As Willam Brown notes vis-à-vis Israel's *henotheism* (the recognition and worship of many deities; however, the primary worship revolved around a single deity):

> Between the 10th century BCE and 7th century BCE, ancient Israelite and Judean religion was polytheistic . . . .
>
> As ancient Israelite and Judean religion moved closer and closer to monotheism between the 10th and 6th centuries BCE, the notion of family religion became incorporated into ancient Judah.
>
> Among the spectrums of how people in ancient Israel and Judah practiced religion, Asherah and Yahweh were both honored in cults. Priority, though, tended to be given to Yahweh.
>
> Worship of deities other than Yahweh seems to have been a regular part of life for people . . . henotheism was likely the norm for ancient Israelites and Judeans . . . .
>
> Although ofttimes considered to be taboo, divination was an important part of ancient Israelite and Judean worship (e.g., 1 Samuel 28, King Saul's visit to the ghostly "witch" of En-Dor).[37]

Taking this scholarly comprehension of how the ancient Israelites and later Jews came to understand themselves, and others to understand them as well, as followers of the singular deity of all humankind and to endure repeated trials and tribulations as the result of that commitment (isolation, dispossession, ghettoization, exile, annihilation) in no way, manner, shape or form lessens or minimizes that commitment. Nor has it ever done so in past centuries up to and including the present moment. Thus, the Jewish people—*Am Yisra'el* (the people of Israel), *Klal Yisra'el* (the world-wide Jewish collectivity), *Mishpakhat Yisra'el* (the Jewish family)—in their very existence continue to affirm, both despite everything that has transpired and because of everything that has transpired, the *B'rith*/Covenant between themselves and God as they understand it and to whom they committed themselves at Mount Sinai so very, very long ago.

* * *

After having surveyed these social and institutional realities somewhat, we now return to Israel's historical story in the next chapter.

NOTES

1 For an excellent overview of these understandings, see Jonathan Golden, *Ancient Canaan & Israel: An Introduction* (Oxford and New York: Oxford University Press, 2009).

2 See, for example: Nahman Avigad, Philip J. King, and Lawrence E. Stager (eds.), *Life in the Ancient World: Crafts, Society and Daily Practice* (Washington, DC: Biblical Archaeology Society, 2013) (E-book); S. Bendor, *The Social Structure of Ancient Israel: The Institution of the Family (Beit'Ab) from the Settlement to the End of Monarchy* (Jerusalem: Simor Ltd, 1996); Oded Borowski, *Daily Life in Biblical Israel* (Atlanta, GA: Society of Biblical Literature, 2003); William G. Dever, *The Lives of Ordinary People in Ancient Israel: Where Archaeology and the Bible Intersect* (Grand Rapids, MI: William B. Eerdmans, 2012); Richard J. Hess and M. Daniel Carroll (eds.), *Family in the Bible: Exploring Customs, Culture, and Context* (Grand Rapids, MI: Baker Academic, 2003); Philip J. King and Lawrence E. Stager, *Life in Biblical Israel* (Louisville, KY: Westminster John Knox Press, 2001); Leo G. Perdue, Joseph Blenkinsopp, John J. Collins, Carol Meyers, *Families in Ancient Israel* (Louisville, KY: Westminster John Knox Press, 1997); Roland de Vaux, *Ancient Israel: Its Life and Institutions*, trans. John McHugh (Grand Rapids, MI: William B. Eerdmans, 1960).

3 James C. Miller, "Ethnicity and the Hebrew Bible: Problems and Prospects," *Currents in Biblical Research* 6, no. 2 (2008): 174–5.

4   Pekka Pitkänen, "Ethnicity, Assimilation and the Israelite Settlement," *Tyndale Bulletin* 55, no. 2 (2004): 166–7.

5   John Hutchinson and Anthony D. Smith (eds.), *Ethnicity* (Oxford: Oxford University Press, 1996), v. Addressing that supposed "imagined" or "invented" past is the classic academic work by Benedict Anderson, *Imagined Communities: Reflections on the Origin and Spread of Nationalism*, rev. ed. (London and New York, NY: Verso, 2016).

6   See Max D. Price, *Evolution of a Taboo: Pigs and People in the Ancient Near East* (Oxford: Oxford University Press, 2021).

7   Further elaborating on these points, Aaron J. Brody and Roy J. King have written:

>   Our reconstruction of ancient ethnicities through archaeology gives no legitimacy to modern political assertions of historic claims over land in the Middle East . . . ethnicity is viewed by the authors as a social construct of group identity. Ethnic identity is not essential or primordial; as a component of social identity it is flexible, situational, and may change and develop over time. Ethnicity is not genetic, although groups may identify by kinship ties that are both real and fictitious. Elements of ethnicity, that is, the variety of identifiers that help to define individuals as in-group or out-group, and how these aspects are defined by the group itself and by outside groups, varies between social groups and may differ between different geographic regions and over different historic periods. Ethnicity may be more pronounced in the boundaries between groups, where self-awareness of ethnic identities may become emphasized.

>   Aaron Brody and Roy J. King, "Genetics and the Archaeology of Ancient Israel," *Human Biology Open Access Pre-Prints*, Paper 44 (2013) http:// digitalcommons.wayne.edu/humbiol_preprints/44.

8   Avraham Faust, "How Did Israel Become a People? The Genesis of Israelite Identity," *Biblical Archaeoology Review*, 35, no. 6 (2009): 66ff.

9   Avraham Faust, *Israel's Ethnogenesis: Settlement, Interaction, Expansion and Resistance* (London: Equinox, 2006), 228. See, also: Mark G. Brett, *Ethnicity and the Bible* (Boston, MA, and Leiden: Brill Academic Publishers, 2002); Erich S. Gruen, *Ethnicity in the Ancient World—Did It Matter?* (Berlin: Walter de Gruyter, 2020); Ann E. Killebrew, *Biblical Peoples and Ethnicity: An Archaeological Study of Egyptians, Canaanites, Philistines, and Early Israel, 1300–1100 B.C.E.* (Atlanta, GA: Society of Biblical Literature, 2005); and Kenton L. Sparks, *Ethnicity and Identity in Ancient Israel: Prolegomena to the Study of Ethnic Sentiments and Their Expression in the Hebrew Bible* (Winona Lake, IN: Eisenbrauns, 1998). Challenging many of the assumptions and understandings of these and other authors, however, is E. Theodore

Mullen, Jr., *Ethnic Myths and Pentateuchal Foundations: A New Approach to the Formation of the Pentateuch* (Atlanta, GA: Scholars Press, 1997).

10 The term for "house" in ancient Israel, biblically, was that of *beit Av* (i.e., of the father/patriarch), that of husband was *ba'al* (lord or master), and that of family was *mishpacha*, which may have also included multi-generations (i.e., grandparents) and extended familial relationships (i.e., uncles, aunts, cousins, nephews and nieces).

11 While most Jewish and Christian people believe that this institution was unique to ancient Israel, this was not and is not the case. Similar though somewhat different examples can be found in Islam, Scythia, Central Asia, India, Indonesia, Japan, Kurdistan, Kirghizstan, Korea, Manchuria, Somalia, Cameroon, Kenya, Nigeria, South Sudan, and Zimbabwe.

12 Among numerous terms found throughout the Hebrew Bible/Old Testament for children are *ben* (son); *bat* (daughter); *ach* (brother); *achot* (sister); *na'ar* (boy, youth), *almah* (young woman), *katan* (little one), *yeled* (child), and others as well. Because the Hebrew language is a gendered language as well, all male terms have female equivalents.

13 The prophet Jeremiah, for example, refers to his secretarial scribe, Baruch, the son of Neriah, the only one so named, which gives rise to the tantalizing theory that others had such assistants, though unnamed, as well.

14 Klaas Spronk, "Good Death and Bad Death in Ancient Israel According to Biblical Lore," *Social Science & Medicine* 58, no. 5 (2004): 987.

15 According to Joseph Jacobs and Julius H. Greenstone in the 1906 *Jewish Encyclopedia* (available online at www.jewishencyclopedia.com):

> The Rabbis elaborated the incomplete provisions of the Bible and established the following order of legal heirs: (1) sons and their descendants; (2) daughters and their descendants; (3) the father; (4) brothers and their descendants; (5) sisters and their descendants; (6) the father's father; (7) the father's brothers and their descendants; (8) the father's sisters and their descendants; (9) the father's father's father; and so on. (Maimonides, "Yad", Nahalot, 1–2; Shulhan 'Aruk, Hoshen Mishpat, 27, 276, 1.)

16 In the past, scholars and others have seemingly accepted the idea of an *amphictyony*, a well-organized confederation of tribes, paralleling somewhat the later Greek idea of such and given prominence by German historian Martin Noth (1902–68) in his 1930 book *Das System der zwölf Stämme Israels* ("The System of the Twelve Tribes of Israel"), itself based on the lists found in Genesis 49, Numbers 26, Judges 5, and Joshua 24. Refuting that understanding, however, is A.D.H. Mayes, "The Question of the Israelite Amphictyony," *Hermathena* 116 (1973): 53–63, who argues instead that the

Steven Leonard Jacobs

Israelites' pre-settlement unity was the result of a collective commitment to
embracing both the story of the Exodus as their historical validation and the
theophany at Sinai as their religious foundation.
17 Norman K. Gottwald, *The Politics of Ancient Israel* (Louisville, KY:
Westminster John Knox Press, 2001).
18 Norman Gottwald, "The Politics of Ancient Israel," *The Bible and
Interpretation: News and Interpretations on the Bible and Ancient Near East
History* (2001), available at: https://bibleinterp.arizona.edu/articles/2001/
politics (accessed 13 May 2023).
19 Ibid. See also his text, pages 246–7, for his restatement of these same
conclusions.
20 See, for example: Richard A. Gabriel, *The Military History of Ancient Israel*
(Westport, CT: Praeger, 2003); Chaim Herzog and Mordechai Gichon, *Battles
of the Bible* (London: Greenhill Books, 1978); Susan Niditch, *War in the
Hebrew Bible: A Study in the Ethics of Violence* (Oxford and New York, NY:
Oxford University Press, 1995); and Gerhard von Rad, *Holy War in Ancient
Israel*, trans. John H. Yoder and Marva J. Dawn (Grand Rapids, MI: William
B. Eerdmans, 1996).
21 See, for example: Lindsay Powell, *Bar Kokhba: The Jew Who Defied Hadrian
and Challenged the Might of Rome* (Barnsley: Pen & Sword, 2021); and Guy
Maclean Rogers, *For the Freedom of Zion: The Great Revolt of Jews against
Romans, 66–74 CE* (New Haven, CT, and London: Yale University Press,
2021).
22 Later rabbinic tradition would have much to say about war but also notes the
important distinction between what it regarded as a *milchemet mitzvah* (an
obligatory/defensive war) and a *milchemet reshut* (permissible war, i.e.,
territory or resources, but somewhat questionable). See Steven Leonard Jacobs,
"Holy Wars, Judaism, Violence, and Genocide: An Unholy Quadrinity?" in
Sara E. Brown and Stephen D. Smith (eds.), *The Routledge Handbook of
Religion, Mass Atrocity, and Genocide* (London and New York, NY:
Routledge, 2022), 37–43.
23 A fascinating study of ancient Israel's economy from a Marxist perspective is
that of Roland Boer, *The Sacred Economy of Ancient Israel* (Louisville, KY:
Westminster John Knox Press, 2015).
24 An interesting sidenote: during the American Civil War (1861–65), preachers
from both North and South addressed the fundamental issue of slavery, with
the Northerners fully condemning it outright, and the Southerners supporting
it. Both used biblical Old Testament texts in their arguments. The Southerners
were more accurate in their assessments, however, arguing that the Bible does
not condemn slavery as such, rather the abuse of slaves, not the institution of
slavery.

25 With regard to the prevalence of law and laws throughout the ancient Near East, see: Vadim Jigoulov, Jaco Gericke, and Steven Leonard Jacobs, *The Scriptures of Ancient Judaism: A Secular Introduction* (San Diego, CA: Cognella Press, 2020), "Legal Texts," 227–41; and Victor H. Matthews and Don C. Benjamin, *Old Testament Parallels: Laws and Stories from the Ancient Near East*, newly rev. and expanded 2nd ed. (New York, NY: Paulist Press, 1997).

26 William Brown, "Ancient Israelite Art," *World History Encyclopedia* (2020), available at: https://www.worldhistory.org/Israelite_Art (accessed 1 June 2022).

27 Ibid.

28 On a humorous note, in 2003, a dean of one of Egypt's law schools attempted to sue Israel for these "stolen" items. Israel, in turn, countersued Egypt for lost slave wages. Both suits went nowhere.

29 See, for example, Douglas R. Clark, "Bricks, Sweat, and Tears: The Human Investment in Constructing a 'Four-Room' House," *Near Eastern Archaeology* 66, no. 1/2, House and Home in the Southern Levant (2003): 34–43.

30 See, for example, John H. Walton, *Ancient Israelite Literature in Its Cultural Context* (Grand Rapids, MI: Zondervan Publishing House, 1989).

31 Etymologically, when the Hebrew word *mizmor* was translated into Greek in the Septuagint (LXX), the translator(s) selected the world *psalmos*, meaning a song or song text specifically sung to the accompaniment of a stringed instrument. This became the Latin *psalmus* and our English word psalm. It is also worthwhile to note that the books of Tehillim were five in number and their authors/editors/compilers may have thus seen in them a parallel to the Five Books of Moses, Bereshith/Genesis to Devarim/Deuteronomy.

32 While there may be a variety of ways to categorize these psalms, one such would be to regard them as psalms of praise, psalms of thanksgiving, elegiac psalms, pilgrimage psalms, meditative psalms, divine celebratory psalms, and moral-ethical psalms.

33 It is assumed that David himself used such an instrument when called to soothe King Saul's disturbed and disturbing frame of mind, but ultimately to no avail as Saul's paranoia would lead to David's flight.

34 For an excellent overview of music in ancient Israel, see Joachim Braun, *Music in Ancient Israel/Palestine: Archaeological, Written, and Comparative Sources*, trans. Douglas W. Stott (Grand Rapids, MI: William B. Eerdmans, 2002).

35 Among the many books addressing the religion of ancient Israel, the following may prove helpful: George A. Barton, *The Religion of Ancient Israel* (New York, NY: A.S. Barnes & Co., 1928); Susan Niditch, *Ancient Israelite Religion* (New York, NY: Oxford University Press, 1997); Patrick D. Miller, *The Religion of Ancient Israel* (Louisville, KY: Westminster John Knox Press; London: SPCK, 2000); Helmer Ringgren, *Religions of the Ancient Near East*,

trans. John Sturdy (Philadelphia, PA: Westminster Press, 1973); and H.H. Rowley, *Worship in Ancient Israel: Its Forms and Meaning* (London: SPCK, 1967).

36 See: Bottéro, *The Birth of God*; Lewis, *The Origin and Character of God*; Römer, *The Invention of God*; Smith, *The Early History of God*; Smith, *God in Translation*; Mark S. Smith, *The Origins of Biblical Monotheism: Israel's Polytheistic Background and the Ugaritic Texts* (Oxford and New York, NY: Oxford University Press, 2003); and Francesca Stavrakopoulou, *God: An Anatomy* (New York, NY: Alfred A. Knopf, 2022).

37 William Brown, "Ancient Israelite & Judean Religion," *World History Encyclopedia* (2017), available at: https://worldhistory.org/article/1097/ancient-israelite-judean-religion (accessed 1 June 2022). Along these same lines, see Francesca Stavrakopoulou and John Barton (eds.), *Religious Diversity in Ancient Israel and Judah* (London and New York, NY: T&T Clark, 2010); and Goldstein, *Peoples of an Almighty God*. Complicating this picture even further and arguing that "Yahwistic dualism" existed far longer than originally understood is the work of Daniel Boyarin, *The Jewish Gospels: The Story of the Jewish Christ* (New York, NY: New Press, 2012); and Peter Schäfer, *Two Gods in Heaven: Jewish Concepts of God in Antiquity*, trans. Allison Brown (Princeton, NJ: Princeton University Press, 2020).

5

BEFORE THE DESTRUCTION OF THE FIRST TEMPLE TO ALEXANDER THE GREAT

INTRODUCTION

In the year 721 BCE, invaders from the north, known as Assyrians, journeyed southward and destroyed the loose confederation of the nine Israelite tribes plus their Levites in the area. Though the Temple of Solomon was in the Southern Kingdom, in Jerusalem, the devastation caused by this destruction, both on those who were spared and those who experienced it should not be minimized or underestimated. A formerly unified people, even if contentiously so, saw its majority severed from its body, and, with it, the rise of a religious myth that has endured even today: that of the so-called "Ten Lost Tribes." Some argue that the peoples of the Alaskan peninsula are descendants of these lost tribesmen, some that the indigenous Native Americans are descendants, and some, the peoples of the Indian continent or China or Japan—as well as other groups (e.g., Vikings). The historical reality of that loss is, however, the following: defeat in battle on earth mirrored defeat in battle in the realm of the gods, who, themselves, entered the fray. Those who survived, willingly or unwillingly, surrendered their systems of belief, embraced those of the victors, and were assimilated into the societies of the conquerors. Thus, the God of Israel was seemingly defeated by the gods of the Assyrians, as were the people themselves, and the northern tribes, within a few generations, assimilated themselves and their unique identity out of existence, never more to be seen or heard from again.

Indeed, the import and impact of the second later destruction as formative to the maintenance and future survival of Judaism and the Jewish people—not without its difficulties—remains out of all proportion to its historical reality, as Tero Alstola writes:

> Nebuchadnezzar II's [d. 562 BCE] deportations from Judah were only one of numerous population transfers in the ancient Near East, but their legacy is unparalleled. The catastrophe of Jerusalem's destruction and deportation is reflected throughout the Hebrew Bible, and Christian Europe learned to know Babylon as a place of splendour, decadence, and oppression. The terms "Babylonian exile" came to describe the period from the deportations until the alleged return in the early Persian period. The terms "exile" and "exilic period" are also used in biblical scholarship, but this is problematic as the terms convey the idea of a period which had a clearly defined beginning and end. The Judean presence in Babylonia did not end in a mass return to Judah in the early Persian period. Moreover, the term "exile" is loaded with images of oppression and does not do justice to the different experiences among the Judeans in Babylonia.[1]

Even earlier, however, Alstola notes:

> The end of the kingdom of Judah and the destruction of the temple in Jerusalem was a catastrophe which required theological explanation. The deportations and exile started an interpretive process that contributed to the birth of Judaism and biblical literature, and, indirectly, to the emergence of Christianity and Islam.[2]

THE AGE OF THE PROPHETS

For the next approximately 135 years, until the destruction of Solomon's Temple by the Babylonians in 586 BCE, the Southern Kingdom—the tribes of Judah and Benjamin (and their Levites of course)—struggled to maintain its existence, deflected enemy attacks, entered treaty-alliances with its neighbors, and sought to create a nation-state of economic prosperity. Moreover, according to the prophetic texts found in the second section of the Torah/Hebrew Bible/Old Testament, the Israelites were reasonably successful in doing so—at a price.

Prophetic guilds in ancient Israel were not unique to the Hebrews. Both 1 Samuel and 2 Kings tell us of such Israelite groups—the so-called *b'nei nevi'im* ("sons of the prophets")—who lived communally and were given to states of ecstasy prior to their public utterances. Samuel (1071–1012 BCE), Elisha (~ 800 BCE?), and Elijah (900–849 BCE) may have initially been part of such groups.

The prophets of ancient Israel with whom we are most familiar, however—Isaiah, Jeremiah, Ezekiel, and "the Twelve," the so-called "minor prophets" (Hosea, Joel, Amos, Obadiah, Jonah, Micah, Nahum, Habakkuk, Zephaniah, Haggai, Zechariah, Malachi)—and who constitute the second section of the Torah/Hebrew Bible/Old Testament, were individuals of heightened moral sensitivity and devout religious sensibility who continually condemned their nation for what they regarded as catastrophically serious lapses of both ethical and religious responsibilities. Collectively, their goal was (1) to return their people and its leadership to the right path, and (2) to prevent the physical destruction of their country and the annihilation of its population. On both counts, they failed, but in so doing, they bequeathed to subsequent generations a religious-ethical literature that continues to inspire Jews and Christians today and challenges both groups to engage in *tikkun olam*, repairing a damaged world beneath divine sovereignty. Their concern for "the poor, the fatherless, the orphan, the widow," coupled with their critiques of both governmental and religious corruption, remain the yardstick by which we assess both religious communities and their faiths even today.

BABYLONIAN CAPTIVITY

In 586 BCE, the people of Judea found their very existence threatened by Babylonian invaders.[3] It was the Babylonians who would breach the walls of Jerusalem, raze the Temple of Solomon to the ground, and carry off into captivity its governmental, political, religious, social, economic, and military leaderships, leaving behind devastation unparalleled in the people's history, including the northern catastrophe. (The word *holocaust*—with a lower-case *h*—may, perhaps, be appropriately used here to mark destruction beyond compare, both physical and religious, not to mention psychological.) Those who remained, in truth the lower levels of their society, would literally have to confront the pieces of their shattered existence. If what happened in and to the Southern Kingdom was to parallel that of the Northern Kingdom, then the story of the Jewish people should have ended there, for obviously the God of Israel had now been defeated a *second* time. All that remained was for the people to abandon their commitment to their God and their identity and embrace that of the victors. However, such was not to be the case.

Significantly, the Babylonians proved gracious in victory and allowed the Israelites to settle in their own neighborhood (*āl-Yāhaūdu*), farm in assigned locales, and worship their own God—provided they themselves proved to be good captive citizens, paid their taxes, and did not engage in subversive military activities. They were even permitted to serve in a somewhat limited fashion in both the military and the governmental administrations. With their Temple destroyed, and their wounds still fresh and raw, scholars believe that, possibly, the origins of what would become the synagogue were born here: with no central sanctuary and no sacrificial cultic priesthood to oversee the rituals and ceremonies of worship, the Judeans reinterpreted their defeat as part of God's plan to spread the word of His singular sovereignty. In order to do so, they embarked on a threefold religious regimen that became the foundation of post-biblical Judaism. First, they told and retold their stories, myths, and legends as initially manifested in their sacred writings and wrote them down. (Scholars now believe that much of the Hebrew Bible/Old Testament was, in fact, *initially* written during the so-called "Persian Period," at a minimum, the Pentateuch [the Five Books of Moses, Bereshith/Genesis to Devarim/Deuteronomy] and possibly some of the earlier prophets.) Second, they communicated with their God directly, without the necessity of animal sacrifices (i.e., the "prayer process"). Third, they gathered regularly, especially on the Sabbath and the festivals, as a community in worship, an *ecclesia* (Greek, "religious assembly").

LIFE IN EXILE

The relative paucity of sources both Israelite/Judean and Babylonian limits our understanding of what life may have been like both for those who had experienced the trauma of captivity and exile and those born in Babylonia after relocation. As a captive people, we know that they tended to be resettled and grouped together in a specific geographic area, as the name *āl-Yāhaūdu* indicates, that they were primarily agriculturalists, farming limited plots of land to survive and contribute to the overall economy, and that some, over the course of their resettlement, moved up the socio-political-economic ladder to become reasonably successful merchants interacting with others, non-Israelites/non-Judeans, and others, less so, and even to achieve governmental and administrative posts in the empire. (Many scholars have tended to see and understand the decidedly Israelite-Judean names, both forename and surname, as indicative of that somewhat limited integration.[4])

RETURN TO PALESTINE

Approximately a hundred to a hundred and fifty years after settling in Babylonia and making uncomfortable peace with their reality (*c.* 538–440 BCE), *some* Israelites/Judeans, still stirred by longing to return to the land of their origins, began the journey home under the Aaronide priest, Ezra, and the man who would govern them, Nehemiah. It would fall to Cyrus the Great of Persia (d. 530 BCE), conqueror of Babylon, to enable them to do so. Their own books of the Torah/Hebrew Bible/Old Testament tell us of both Ezra's success in getting those already resident in Israel to divorce their non-Israelite wives, and Nehemiah's success in refortifying Jerusalem's walls and participating in the restoration and rededication of the Temple's foundations, although it would take several years before the completion of its rebuilding in 515 BCE. Yet, the texts themselves are strangely silent about whatever relationship, if any, existed between the two of them, and whether, in fact, they were there or not during the same period—it being understood, however, that Ezra's return did, in fact, precede Nehemiah's.

Legend has it that Cyrus was a follower of the Zoroastrian religious tradition which views the world as a conflict between the forces of good and evil and that he saw in a dream the God of Israel—Yahweh—as one of the "good gods." In that dream, he was commanded to allow the Judeans in Babylonia to return home and to rebuild/reconstruct their Temple; as one would thus conclude from reading both the books of Ezra and Nehemiah in the Torah/Hebrew Bible/Old Testament.

Reality, however, may have been somewhat different, though not necessarily in full disagreement. In 539 BCE, the so-called "Edict of Cyrus" was proclaimed, which permitted/allowed some conquered peoples to return to their lands of birth and origin (repatriation and restoration)—though no references are specifically made to Israelites, Judeans, the land of Israel, or Jerusalem, but rather to Mesopotamia itself, as recorded by the "Cyrus Cylinder", inscribed sometime after 539 BCE. (Ezra 1:2–4, however, includes the people of Israel and Yahweh in its own telling.) It was done for administrative reasons rather than religious ones and more of a military necessity to undermine potential insurrections and rebellions, though a commitment to the religion of these displaced people could further serve to bind them to the empire. (His conquered kingdom may, in fact, have been far too large to have been governed any other way.[5]) Interestingly, the Cyrus Edict and Cylinder may have been similar to ones that preceded them, for example, that of Marduk-apla-iddina II (d. 702 BCE) in 722 BCE and Sargon II (d. 705 BCE) in 710 BCE.

One simply cannot discuss that return from exile in Babylonia, no matter its historical controversies and disagreements, however, without first acknowledging the important and significant roles played by Ezra the Scribe and Nehemiah the Administrator.

EZRA AND NEHEMIAH

Ezra, no matter the actual number of returnees, led them back to the land of Israelite/Judean birth, specifically to the holy city of Jerusalem and the site of the destroyed Temple. The impetus for that return was the supposed acknowledgment that Artaxerxes I's (465–424 BCE) Judean residents were ignorant of the laws of the God of Israel. Upon Ezra's return, he gathered the inhabitants therein, read to them and interpreted for them the laws of Moses, had them renew their *B'rith*/Covenant with God, and, consequently, enabled (forced?) them to divorce their non-Israelite wives. (Ezra was said and understood to be fluent in both Hebrew—the language of the sacred writings—and Aramaic—the *lingua franca* of the time—which made his task thus somewhat easier.) As David Bossman writes:

> While the role of the scribe-priest was to preserve tradition, the new code was characterized by significant creativity in its reinterpretation of the tradition in areas such as literature, religious thought, and cultic organization. Ezra's law introduced the public reading of the law (Neh. 8), public confession (Ezra 9–10; Neh. 9), the enforcement of the sabbath (Neh. 13:15–21), the form in which the Succoth festival was to be observed (Neh. 8:13–18), and the statutes against intermarriage as they were to be applied in the new post-exilic community (Neh. 13:23–28; Ezra 9).[6]

Nehemiah—acknowledged as a real historical figure—was said to have been the governor of Persian Judea under Artaxerxes I and thus a member of the royal administration. Learning of the sad physical state of Jerusalem and its environs, he successfully petitioned Artaxerxes I to be allowed to return and commence a rebuilding and restoration of the area several years later, Ezra being already there. Among those projects was the refortification of the walls around Jerusalem itself.

Of textual and sacred importance, modern scholars believe that the books of Ezra and Nehemiah were originally one text, later divided by an unknown Christian editor of editors. Of even more significance, it is further believed that the original texts of the Pentateuch (Five Books of Moses) and possibly some but not all of the prophetic texts were preliminarily "canonized" before Ezra left Babylonia. As Alexander Fantalkin and Oren Tal of Tel Aviv University write:

> Traditionally, the canonization of the Pentateuch is associated with the "mission" of Ezra, who, according to the book of Ezr-Neh (hereafter: EN), presented the Torah of Moses to the inhabitants of Judah gathered in Jerusalem in the seventh year of Artaxerxes [I] . . . the majority of modern scholars consider it an integral part of the Ezra traditions, originally placed between Ezr 8 and 9 . . . .
>
> It is quite likely that the gathering of different law codes and narratives into one book with five parts, the Pentateuch, goes back indeed to the time of Ezra's mission in Jerusalem . . . *this activity should not be confused with the attempts of establishing the canonical version of the Torah, which corresponds to the time of Ezra's mission* [and which will be discussed in the early rabbinic period later] . . . .
>
> The canonization of the Torah—or better the pro-canonization under the authority of Ezra and his circle—should not be considered as the final redaction of the Torah that miraculously survived to these days, but rather as an initial attempt at canonization, with certain modifications made after Ezra's time . . . a conscious response to the Judahite priestly circles to a new geopolitical reality that characterized the first half of the fourth century BCE, when Egypt was no longer a part of the Achaemenid Empire.[7]

Assessing Ezra's contribution, more so than Nehemiah's, Klaus Koch writes:

> The role of Ezra in post-exilic history can hardly be overestimated. He was one of the greatest men within a people which was truly not deficient in great men! He had succeeded in moving the apparatus of a huge empire for the sake of a people, a small one in number and an unimportant one in political and economic regards. Even if his final intention did not last and the united people of twelve new tribes was not realized, his work was probably as far-reaching as that of Moses.[8]

RETURN TO ZION: YEHUD MEDINATA

Those who returned—a minority of those former Israelites who were resident in Babylonia, although the books of Ezra and Nehemiah estimate that highly doubtful number as 40,000 plus people—as well as those who had never left—the vast majority and decidedly from the lower classes—found themselves in a vassal-state with limited self-government within the Achaemenid Empire. (Coins unearthed from that period have imprinted on them Y–H–D.) Those who returned and in whom memories of a pre-exilic past were prominent saw and understood themselves to be the heirs and descendants of the tribes of both Judah and Benjamin with Levites and *cohanim* (high priests) sprinkled throughout.

Be that as it may, the Southern Kingdom would reconstitute itself and remain viable until the Roman debacle and its end, beginning in 66 CE and concluding in 70 CE (though its final gasp would not be realized until the defeat of Bar Kokhba in 135 CE). Prior to this, however, this "reborn" people would, again, confront a crisis of monumental proportions not only with the conquest of the then-known world by Alexander the Great (356–323 BCE), but with a religious, cultural, and philosophical system we today call "Hellenism" whose very ideals were perceived as direct threats to Jewish survival. It is to this crisis of enormous impact to which we now turn.

NOTES

1 Tero Alstola, *Judeans in Babylonia: A Study of Deportees in the Sixth and Fifth Centuries* BCE (Leiden and Boston, MA: Brill, 2020), 24.
2 Ibid., 1.
3 Tero Alstola reminds us (ibid., 16) that:

Babylonia is the later Greek name of Southern Mesopotamia, and it is never used in Neo-Assyrian or Neo-Babylonian sources to describe the region around the cities of Babylon, Borsippa, Sippar, Nippur, and Uruk, located on the alluvial plain of the Euphrates and the Tigris between present-day Baghdad in the north and the Persian Gulf in the south.

4 Among the important volumes attempting to assess what life was like for Judeans during their exile are the following: Alstola, *Judeans in Babylonia*; Jonathan Stökl and Caroline Waerzeggers (eds.), *Exile and Return: The Babylonian Context* (Berlin: de Gruyter, 2015); Oded Lipschits and Joseph Blenkinsopp (eds.), *Judah and the Judeans in the Neo-Babylonian Period* (Winona Lake, IN: Eisenbrauns, 2003); Oded Lipschits and Manfred Oeming (eds.), *Judah and the Judeans in the Persian Period* (Winona Lake, IN: Eisenbrauns, 2006); Oded Lipschits, Gary N. Knoppers, and Rainer Albertz (eds.), *Judah and the Judeans in the Fourth Century B.C.E.* (Winona Lake, IN: Eisenbrauns, 2007); Oded Lipschits, Gary N. Knoppers, and Manfred Oeming

(eds.), *Judah and the Judeans in the Achaemenid Period: Negotiating Identity in an International Context* (Winona Lake, IN: Eisenbrauns, 2011); and James W. Watts (ed.), *Persia and Torah: The Theory of Imperial Authorization of the Pentateuch* (Atlanta: Society of Biblical Literature, 2001).

5 Lester Grabbe, in his conclusion to "The Reality of the Return: The Biblical Picture Versus Historical Reconstruction," in Stökl and Waerzeggers (eds.), *Exile and Return*, 307, summarizes the significant differences between these two tellings.

6 David Bossman, "Ezra's Marriage Reform: Israel Redefined," *Biblical Theology Bulletin* 9, no. 1 (1979), 32, doi:10.1177/014610797900900105.

7 Alexander Fantalkin and Oren Tal, "The Canonization of the Pentateuch: When and Why? (Part 1)," *Zeitschrift für die Alttestamentliche Wissenschaft* 124, no. 1 (2012): 1 ff., doi: 10.1515/zaw-2012-0001; emphases added.

8 Klaus Koch (1974), "Ezra and the Origins of Judaism," *Journal of Semitic Studies* 19, no. 2 (1974): 195–6.

6

THE SECOND TEMPLE PERIOD AND THE CONFLICTS WITH "HELLENISM" AND "ROMANISM"

With the advancing legions of Alexander the Great, son of Philip of Macedon (382–336 BCE), the hegemony of the Persians came to its end. After his own death, and without a designated successor, Alexander's conquered kingdom was divided between the Ptolemies of Egypt and the Seleucids of Syria, with Judea under the reign of the Ptolemies. They enforced their own pattern of city governance as they understood it, affecting both social and political life, with Judea ruled by a high priest who served both religious and political functions. Constantly fought over for dominant control, Judea changed hands and came under the rule of the Seleucids about a century after Alexander's death. Initially, little change was evident for the people and leadership of Judea, until the ascension to the throne of Antiochus IV (215–163 BCE), named *Epiphanes* ("The Great One") by those who supported him and *Epimanes* ("The Mad One") by those who opposed him. He saw his responsibility as the imposition of all that was Greek on his subjects, forbidding Israelite religious practice on pain of death and desecrating the Holy Temple of Jerusalem.

PHILIP AND ALEXANDER

At the time of Philip's rise to power, Macedon was a relatively small and insignificant city-state. His genius in restructuring its military ultimately led to the defeat of both the city-states of Athens and Thebes at the Battle of Chaeronea in 338 BCE and the consolidation of his power. His proposed unification of all Greek peoples, with himself at the helm, and his planned attack on the Achaemenid Empire of Persia were both cut short by his assassination in 336 BCE, which resulted in his son Alexander taking the throne at age twenty. A brilliant military tactician and strategist, his successful defeat of the Persians after a ten-year conflict resulted in an Asia Minor now under full Greek control militarily, governmentally, politically, economically, and, for our purposes, culturally and, to a lesser degree, philosophically and religiously as well. His controversial embrace of Persian cultural practices, such as the wearing of Persian garments, did not endear him to his followers, while, at the same time, his restoration of Egyptian temples and the erection of additional statues to Egyptian gods furthered his agenda of consolidating his own power. The city of Alexandria, named after him, would become something of a mecca, in which Egyptians and Greeks would live side by side, comfortably interacting with each other. Both, however, would regard the Jews in their midst as something of an anathema.

THE CONFLICT WITH "HELLENISM"

During my graduate student years, I have a memory of a professor characterizing the conflict as one of opposites. For the Greeks, the ideal may best be understood as that of the "holiness of beauty," as evidenced by the nude statuary of both men and women and the Olympic games themselves, fought as they were in the nude. For the Jews, the ideal may best be understood as that of the "beauty of holiness," as evidenced by the entire Torah but, particularly, the Book of Leviticus and the early rabbinic post-biblical writings and including physical modesty.

While that understanding/characterization is, to some degree, reasonably accurate, the historical reality is much more complicated and uneven, and a distinction must be drawn between "Hellenism" and "Hellenization." "Hellenism" with the broadest of brushstrokes was the pervasive dominance of Greek culture in all its myriad expressions—the arts, literature, philosophy, and, yes, religion—the result of the military successes of both Philip initially and then his son Alexander. "Hellenization" was the embrace of that culture by various conquered peoples, including the Jews of Judea and more so the elites and upper classes, but filtering downward, more positively than negatively. (Rome, too, both before and after its own defeat of the Greeks was itself the recipient of Greek cultural influences.)

It should also be noted that, when speaking of both Hellenism and Hellenization, we must speak not only of the Jews of Judea who were influenced by the former and embraced the latter, but also the Jews of the Diaspora (Hebrew *t'futzah*, i.e., those living outside the land of Israel), especially, and particularly the Jews of the largest diasporic community, Alexandria in Egypt.

Equally important to keep in mind is Lee I. Levine's comment in his Epilogue to *Judaism and Hellenism in Antiquity*:

> At any specific stage in its history, Jewish civilization may be viewed as an array of traditions and institutions, many of which had been forged through contact with non-Jewish cultures whose influence had become part and parcel of the Jewish enterprise. . . .
>
> The Jews as a people have survived precisely because of their openness to change—in light of new conditions and circumstances—in such areas as dress, professions, languages, literary genres, political, social, and cultural institutions, methods of learning, *and even religious ideas and practices.* Without this ability to change and adapt, Jewish civilization might well have atrophied long ago. The dynamic interplay between cultures—its own and others—is an essential feature of the Jewish historical experience.[1]

Thus, John J. Collins could write the following regarding the Jews of the Diaspora but equally applicable to the Jews of Judea:

> It is evident from the literature of the Diaspora that at least some Jews were educated, by whatever means, in Greek literature and philosophy. The open attitude of the Diaspora Jews to their Hellenistic environment is amply shown by their use of Greek names and their recourse to Hellenistic law. The struggle of the Jews of Alexandria for parity with Greek citizens typifies the aspirations of the Hellenistic Diaspora. The Hellenistic Jews were not reluctant exiles. They were attracted to Hellenistic culture, eager to win the respect of the Greeks and to adapt their ways.[2]

Equally and summarily so, he reminds us that "much Judean literature was translated into Greek and circulated in the Diaspora."[3]

PHILO AND THE SEPTUAGINT

Despite the tensions in Alexandria with respect to both the native Egyptians and the resident Greeks, nowhere is this embrace of Hellenism and the influence of Hellenization more apparent than in the person of Philo and the translation of the Torah into Greek, the Septuagint.

Philo Judaeus ("Philo the Jew" or "Philo the Judean," *c*. 20 BCE– *c*. 50 CE) is best remembered for his philosophical writings and biblical commentaries saved and preserved by later Christians rather than Jews, as well as for leading a delegation of Alexandrian Jews to Rome to meet with Emperor Caligula (12 CE–41 CE) to petition him to ameliorate the tensions between the Greeks and the Jews in Egypt. Philo wrote in Greek but there appears to be little evidence that his Hebraic knowledge of the Torah was either substantial or proficient. As regards his philosophical writings, they are by and large syncretistic, merging his knowledge of both Greek Stoicism and Greek Platonism with his reading of the Torah, and, ultimately, arguing that Greek ideas were already embedded in the Scriptures themselves. Among his more well-known and important works were *On the Life of Moses, On the Jews, On the Contemplative Life, On the Eternity of the World, On Animals, On Providence,* and *Every Good Man is Free.* He also wrote verse-by-verse commentaries on both the Books of Genesis and Exodus.

According to the historically questionable *Letter of Aristeas* by an Alexandrian Jew of that name in the third or second century BCE, said to be from Marmora, to his brother Philocrates, and explaining the rationale for the Greek translation, Egyptian emperor Ptolemy Philadelphus II (308 BCE–246 BCE) honored a request by the director of the famous Library of Alexandria, Demetrios of Phalerum (350 BCE–280 BCE), that seventy-two Hebraic scholars—six from each of the twelve tribes—come from Palestine to Alexandria to translate the Pentateuch (First Five Books of Moses, Bereshith/Genesis to Devarim/Deuteronomy) into Koine Greek. All did so, and after examination, all the translations were the same. Scholarly consensus is that, however it came about, it was already available and in use by the third century CE during the Second Temple period, if not earlier, in both Palestine and the Diaspora. (Philo, Josephus, the Babylonian Talmud, the Tractate Megillah, all refer to the letter.) It is usually designated by Roman numerals LXX (seventy rather than seventy-two) and was increasingly accepted by the growing body of early Christians, while by and large rejected by those Jews and later rabbinic tradition for whom only the Hebrew Bible is sacred. (That some Jews, Philo included, were more familiar with their own sacred text in Greek rather than in Hebrew—both in Judea and outside—should not be rejected out of hand, just as today there are Jews more familiar with the Torah in their own native languages—especially English—than Hebrew.) Christian translations today of the "Old Testament" are more often accepted and based on the Septuagint rather than the original Hebrew text.[4]

HASMONEAN REVOLT AND RULE: THE MACCABEES

In 165 BCE, guerilla warfare broke out against the Seleucids, led by a family of Hasmonean priests from Modi'in, under the leadership of a father Mattityahu (Mattathias) and his eldest son Yehuda (Judah), nicknamed *Ha-Maccabee* ("The Hammer") due to his and his followers' guerrilla tactics (strike and pull back). One year later, they had achieved victory over their hated enemies and reconsecrated and rededicated their Temple with, according to Jewish religious tradition, enough sacred oil to keep the eternal flame of God's presence burning for eight days until enough additional stores could be found. (This "minor minor" Jewish festival of Hanukkah emerges from this story.[5])

For the next 130 years, the Hasmoneans would remain central to the leadership of the peoples of Judea, with Aristobulus I (104–103 BCE) taking upon himself the restoration of the monarchy in 104 BCE. Prior to his ascension, however, his Hasmonean predecessors, to solidify their leadership, had entered into an alliance with Rome, and, by 67 BCE, Rome was very much in evidence in the region, and this ultimately undermined his and their sovereignty.

THE CASE OF THE SAMARITANS

Still in existence during this period of Graeco-Roman tension and Maccabean/Hasmonean political intrigue and uncertainty, the Samaritans were an early ethno-religious group of ancient Israelites who then and now regarded Mount Gerizim as the site of the God–Moses (God's only true prophet) encounter rather than Mount Sinai, and who, therefore, produced their own Pentateuch. Despite, or perhaps because of, their understanding, during the Hellenic period, they repudiated any connection whatsoever with the Judaism of the Second Temple and any connection with the Jews then in existence and no later than 163 BCE, the endpoint of the reign of Antiochus IV Epiphanes. They continue to regard themselves as *Shomrei Torah*, "Guardians" or "Keepers" of the "true" Torah and the most authentic evolution of historical Judaism. (Still in existence today primarily in the modern State of Israel in and surrounding the cities of Nablus and Holon, they remain something of a closed community, marrying within themselves, and numbering perhaps fewer than 1,000 souls.) Most famously, they are known to many today via the Parable of the Good Samaritan in the New Testament in the Gospel of Luke 10:25-37, which, likely, would have been written during the Roman period. They, too, represent yet another group in existence during this period in a land filled with varying and various religious, political, economic, and social groups, all attempting to survive under what would become an oppressive regime.[6]

THE CONFLICT WITH "ROMANISM"

Initially, Roman conquest and the defeat of the Greeks was not a defeat for the Jews both inside and outside Judea, of which there were already significant populations in both Alexandria, Egypt, and Rome itself. Though regarded with a somewhat bemused tolerance, Jews were seen as peculiar religionists with their unseen God, their dietary restrictions, the circumcision of their males, and their seventh-day Sabbath observance. Christians were viewed as a subset of these same Jews. What evidently turned the tide was the growing imposition of Roman political and military oppression, including increasingly heavier taxation as dissidents in Judea and elsewhere, but primarily there, began to increase their violent opposition to the Romans and their collaborators and their hardline refusal to accord any compromise on their own reading and practicing of what we can label "Torah Judaism."

OPPRESSION UNDER ROMAN RULE

At this time (the first century BCE), Judea was under the governorship of Syria, with limited autonomy and freedom to worship. Even the Roman political and military leader Julius Caesar (100–44 BCE), who would later become emperor, initially viewed the province and its inhabitants most favorably. History, however, began to repeat itself with his assassination in 44 BCE: without a designated successor, jockeying for power and position was the order of the day, with Judea buffeted about as a prize, until King Herod (74–4 BCE), the Idumean, assumed power in 37 BCE. His reign was marked by an iron fist, diminishing the power of both the *Sanhedrin*—the ruling religious council—and the high priesthood, despite the relative internal tranquility of the province. Most notably, however, prior to his death in 4 BCE, he had the Temple in Jerusalem rebuilt.

(Today's Western Wall in Jerusalem, Judaism's confirmed holiest site, is the last remaining structure of that ancient temple.)

Upon his death, Judea would be governed by a series of Roman procurators (including one of Judean origin, Tiberius Julius Alexander [r. c. 46–48 CE] [about whom little is known[7]], who would restore some measure of authority to both the *Sanhedrin* and the priesthood). It is only with the procurator Pontius Pilate (governing 26–36 CE) that things go from bad to worse, with Roman soldiers occupying the streets of Jerusalem, Roman supervision of Temple practices, oppressively heavy taxation, and military violence.

It is during this period of oppression, and slightly before, that a Jew is born, according to the New Testament text, to a poor family in Bethlehem. He becomes a carpenter by profession, grows up thoroughly grounded in his Jewish religious education, unusually adept at teaching through stories (i.e., parables), feels the pain of his people, and travels the region offering his wisdom and comfort, generating increasingly larger crowds and interest primarily among the lower socioeconomic classes of Judean society. Misperceived by the Romans as a political insurrectionist, he is arrested and dies by crucifixion, the favored and preferred form of Roman execution (though, tragically, Jews would be blamed for the Christ's death for 2,000 years for the crime of *deicide*/God-killing). That man, possibly named (in Hebrew) Yeshua, Yehoshua or Yeshu (all meaning "God will save"), son of Joseph (Hebrew, Yosef) and Mary (Hebrew, Miryam) is known to us today as Jesus (the) Christ (Anglicized for "Messiah," *Christos* in Greek from the Hebrew *mashiach*/"anointed one"). His death and subsequent theological understandings of him and his teachings will ultimately, give rise to Christianity, an initially nascent *minority* Jewish religious movement that will split from its parent centuries later and mark a 2,000-year journey of tragedy for both Jews and Christians.[8]

Questionably central to the evolution of the Jewish religious tradition, even taking into consideration such biblical writings as Isaiah, Daniel, and post-biblical/rabbinic writings (e.g., 1 Enoch, Dead Sea Scrolls)—but at the heart of what would become Christianity—remains, however, this idea of the Messiah who would redeem the Jewish people/collectivity from their oppressors and restore theocratic Jewish sovereignty in the Holy Land of Israel including the building of the Third Temple and the gathering of the exiles.

Writing centuries after the canonization of the Torah/Hebrew Bible/ Old Testament and summarizing the thoughts of the past, the great

Jewish sage Moses ben Maimon (1138–1204 CE), better known as Maimonides, included this affirmation as Principle Twelve of his Thirteen Principles of the Jewish Faith: "I believe with perfect faith in the coming of the Messiah, and even though he tarries, I will wait for him each day that he will come."[9]

Significantly as well, in his Mishneh Torah, chapters eleven and twelve, he provides us with the criteria for evaluating/judging those who would claim the mantle of messiahship, either by themselves or by others. Examining both those criteria and the candidacy of Jesus Judaically and taking into consideration the writings of the New Testament, in chart form we find the following:

Maimonides' Messianic Criteria	Jesus' Candidacy
From the House of David	√
Studying Torah and observing *mitzvot*	√
Urging Israel to follow above	√
Strengthening Torah observance	√
Fighting the Lord's wars	X
To Be Treated as if He Is the Messiah	Possibility
Building the Holy Temple	N/A
Gathering the dispersed of Israel together	X
Bringing the world to worship the One God	X
Then He Is the Messiah of Israel!	≠

Thus, for Maimonides and for those Jews who still affirm and await a Messiah (noting that not all Jews do so), meeting four of his eight criteria suggests a possibility; meeting all eight would be an affirmation that the Messiah has arrived. (NB: Today, however, we would have to disregard rebuilding the Temple in Jesus' time as it was already in existence.) Moreover, while there are certainly those Christians who would argue that Jesus did, indeed, fight the "spiritual battles" of the Lord, both Maimonides and his predecessors and successors stand firm that he and they are literally talking of heading a Jewish military to defeat Israel's physical enemies.

Conclusion: The only Judaic statement that Jews can make and have made with certainty is that Jesus does *not* meet Judaic criteria for messiahship, noting the obvious, of course, that nowhere in Jewish literature is such a messianic claim predicated on one who is both fully human and fully divine, the very essence of the Christian claim.[10]

SADDUCEES, PHARISEES, ESSENES, AND ZEALOTS

Jesus and his growing followership in Judea were not the only contentious issue which confronted Roman-controlled Palestine, though Jesus would ultimately lose his life at their hands. Both Josephus (see below) and the rabbis acknowledge the divisive population that was resident in Jerusalem and beyond and see and understand them to divide into four main groups: Sadducees, supportive of and collaborating with the Roman leadership; Pharisees, representative of a more democratic community of Jews and rejecting priestly leadership as the only voice of the people; Essenes, both those in Qumran by the Dead Sea and elsewhere, who rejected all claims to the "true" understanding of Judaism and thus physically removed themselves from any interaction; and Zealots, the extreme militants doing whatever they could to foster and foment revolution. (Although questionable, was this last group those people whose Judaism Josephus labeled the "Fourth Philosophy"?)

Prominent among these groups were the religious-political, upper-class, aristocratic priestly elitists whom we label Sadducees (Zadokites), whose name in all likelihood was derived from a high priest known as Zadok (Hebrew root *tzedek*, "righteousness") and whom we ought to call "pietists" in the strictest of understandings—that is, those whose literalist readings of the Torah precluded any interpretive elaborations of either text or practice in their management of both Temple and state (under Roman hegemony, of course). They differed specifically with these other groups over such issues as free will (yes), the afterlife (no), Oral Torah [coming from Moses' no]), Hellenism (yes), and interpretation (rejection). After the Temple's destruction in 70 CE by the Romans, their status and influence waned, and, ultimately, they disappeared as a Jewish leadership cadre.

In rather dramatic opposition, we have the Pharisees, the "party of the people," who valued knowledge and commitment over lineage ("a kingdom of priests and a holy people," as Leviticus 19 would spell out). While the name may be derived from the Hebrew *perushim*, "separatists," we cannot claim certainty that it was given to them by others or one they took upon themselves and from whom, specifically, they were separating (Sadducees? Essenes, other Jews? non-Jew? Romans?). While there certainly were among them those of priestly descent, by and large, they were most likely in the socio-cultural-economic middle with representatives of both the upper and lower classes in fewer numbers. Thus, their popularity rested upon their inclusive standing rather than an appeal only to a priestly upper-class. Then, too, while, in a limited fashion, acknowledging the intrusion of Hellenistic ideas and practices into their community, they opted for a more "authentic" Judean Judaism. A central divide between them and the Sadducees was over resurrection of the dead: for them, it was a central tenet, claiming authority derived from Moses and Jewish law, but it was rejected by the Sadducees as having no foundation in the Pentateuch. Tragically, and somewhat ironically, their negative status today and even earlier is derived from their depiction in the New Testament gospels as the enemies of Jesus in their debates with him over the practices of Jewish ritual observances (e.g., their "hypocrisy" stridently condemned in Matthew 23). More accurately, however, their interpretive readings of religious Judaism and their inclusivity would lay the foundation for post-biblical rabbinic Judaism as it continues in the main to be observed as it was their leadership and followership which would survive the Roman debacle.

The Essenes resident in Qumran and away from Jerusalem and both Sadducees and Pharisees, though there may have been among them those who partially identified with both, we may best label as both "dissenters" from and/or "rejectionists" of both in favor of a monastic lifestyle suffused with piety, strict practice, and study. The scrolls and fragments found in the surrounding Dead Sea, which they hoped to retrieve after the Roman conflict and their own survival did not come to pass, testify to their orientation (e.g., the Copper Scroll). The name of their group, however, remains shrouded in mystery. (It is important to note that, while monasticism would come to occupy a prominent place in Roman Catholicism later, it never took hold in either earlier to later Judaism as a model of religious commitment, though biblically the Nazarites and their most famous representative Shimshon/Samson come as close to it as any in the past.)

Then, too, there were those known as Zealots (Hebrew *kana'im*, "ones jealous/zealous for God"), better labeled, perhaps as *Sicarii* (Latin, "daggermen") by virtue of the small daggers which they carried within their robes and used to murder both Roman soldiers and fellow Jews whom they regarded as turncoats or traitors; they were thus rightly regarded as extremists filled with revolutionary zeal. Ultimately, they would become the spark which would bring to a head the protracted conflict with Rome, the final resolution of which would be the destruction of Judean sovereignty and any semblance of political independence or quasi-independence for about 2,000 years.

DESTRUCTION OF THE SECOND TEMPLE

In 66 CE, open rebellion against Rome finally breaks out, one which Emperor Nero (37–68 CE) simply cannot afford to ignore. He sends his most trusted general Vespasian (9 CE–79 CE) to quell the revolt, but Nero dies in 68 CE. Vespasian will crown himself emperor in 69 CE, and task his son Titus (39–81 CE) with the subjugation of Roman-occupied Palestine. Titus besieges Jerusalem in 70 CE and, in his success, razes the Second Temple to the ground, and with it, ends all hopes for Jewish hegemony in the land until the birth of the Third Jewish Commonwealth—the modern State of Israel—on May 14, 1948. This First Jewish War would continue for three years until 73 CE but would not quell the unrest in Roman-controlled and Roman-occupied Judea. It would simmer for at least another approximately three decades until the Kitos War (the Second Jewish War), followed closely by the Bar Kokhba Revolt (the Third Jewish War), which would, ultimately, end whatever hopes existed for Jewish geographical and political sovereignty for nary 2,000 years, beginning a migratory journey primarily westwards across the Mediterranean towards the European continent, and laying the groundwork for what would essentially become a reconstituted and reconstructed Diasporic Judaism still incredibly viable today.

JOSEPHUS

Long regarded by historians as a—if not the—primary source of information regarding the period of Second Temple Judaism, the Roman destruction of the Temple, and the Jewish-Roman Wars, Yosef ben Mattityahu (37–100 CE), wealthy son of a priestly family, is better known to us today as Josephus, or, more fully, Flavius Josephus after his adoption of the name of his Roman benefactors. His fame, if not his infamy, rests on: his initial military leadership against the Romans until his defeat at Yotapata in 67 CE at the hands of Vespasian, who as emperor granted him his freedom; his defection to Rome itself where he would become a Roman citizen; his friendship with Vespasian's son Titus, who, in turn, would sack Jerusalem and destroy the Second Temple (though Josephus would try to ameliorate the destruction by pleading for the rebel holdouts' surrender). The writings for which he is best known, thought at times self-serving and slanted to present the Jews favorably to Roman audiences and to the Jews themselves, include: (1) *The Jewish War*, seven volumes written in 78 CE; (2) *Jewish Antiquities*, twenty-one volumes written 93/94 CE; (3) *Against Apion*, two volumes written in 94 CE; and (4) *Autobiography of Flavius Josephus*, written in 99 CE. All his texts were written in Greek. Today, scholars and others continue to mine his works for information about those times—including his references to Sadducees, Pharisees, Essences, Qumran, and, possibly, Jesus himself—and are reasonably comfortable with the understanding that, even discounting his obvious biases and historical inaccuracies, there is much we can learn about what transpired 2,000 years ago in those tumultuous times in Judea/Palestine.

LEGEND OF YOHANAN BEN ZAKKAI

An equally intriguing figure/personage during this same period of tragic destruction is Rabbi Yohanan ben Zakkai, who, even today, may be regarded as the perhaps unsung and perhaps little-known in some quarters savior of Judaism, and who laid the foundations of what would evolve into post-biblical and rabbinic Judaism, upon which present-day Jewish religion, practice, and tradition rest. Though originally resident in the Galilee, after almost two decades he moved to Jerusalem, believing it more conducive to his rather strict interpretation of Judaism. Finding himself and his students trapped during the Roman onslaught, he is believed to have advocated for peaceful surrender, but to no avail. According to the much later Aramaic text *Avot* [Fathers] *of Rabbi Nathan* (composed somewhere between 700 CE and 900 CE), and now included with the minor Tractates of the Babylonian Talmud (see below), it tells the following story:

> When Rabbi Yohanan ben Zakkai's repeated warning to surrender to the Romans went unheeded, he asked two of his students Rabbi Eliezer ben Hyrcanus and Rabbi Yehoshua ben Hananiah to make a coffin for him and take him outside the city. The Roman soldiers he knew would not interrupt such a burial detail. Having done so, they then made their way to General Vespasian (which says a lot about Roman security!). Standing before him, he told the general he would soon become emperor, for which he was initially thrown into prison. But, according to the rabbi's prediction (prophecy?), shortly thereafter such came to pass. Rabbi Yohanan was released from his imprisonment and allowed three wishes (paralleling perhaps some later fantasy stories): (1) that the city of Yavneh (Jamnia) be spared destruction in order that he and others could be sent to found a school/academy to teach and preserve the legal and

religious traditions of Judaism (which would, ultimately, result in the composition of the *Mishnah* a generation later); (2) the saving of the family and descendants of Rabban Gamliel (d. 52 CE); and (3) medical help for Rabbi Tzadok—all of which were granted.

The ultimate upshot as it has come down to us is that having done so, Rabbi Yohanan would convene a council (historically, highly questionable), which would sanctify the final canonization of the Torah into its three parts, Torah (First Five Books; Pentateuch), prophets (twenty-one books), and writings (twelve books), but reject others which were also available to them.

Because of the doubtful historicity of both Rabbi Yohanan's story and the process of canonization of the Torah/Hebrew Bible/Old Testament, it is important to understand how the Torah of ancient Israel would become the Torah of the Jews today and how it would later be incorporated into the Bible of Christianity.

THE QUESTION OF CANONIZATION

As I have written previously, scholarly consensus is that the rudiments of the first five books of the Torah (Bereshith/Genesis to Devarim/ Deuteronomy) were written during the Persian period of Judean domination and Babylonian exilic residence, prior to the return of Ezra and Nehemiah and the reconstruction of Jewish civil and religious life in a still-dominated Judea. Obviously, the words/sermons/writings of the fifteen prophets now included (Isaiah, Jeremiah, Ezekiel, and "The Twelve") would come later, composed possibly by 200 BCE, as would the various literary works (Psalms, Proverbs, Job, Esther, Daniel, Ecclesiastes, etc.), composed in the main possibly by 100 CE, also now included. Today, scholarly consensus would have it that the books now included were canonized—"officialized"—no later than 200 CE, which would find them sanctified a bit earlier than Rabbi Yehuda Ha-Nasi's compilation of the Mishnah. To be sure, this latter understanding would not be in accord with the Torah's own telling of Moses' return from Mount Sinai with a shattered first set of Commandments and a second set of Commandments, which traditional Judaism understands as an account of his return with a full Torah.

Further complicating this whole process has been this author's theoretical understanding that the necessity of canonization was mandated by two, possibly competing, realities: (1) the destruction of Jerusalem and the Second Temple was a religious and psychological trauma of such proportions that the rabbis found themselves having to comfort their people and and to provide them with a kind of meaningful nourishment which would enable them both to remain intact and move forward as a collectivity under dire conditions; and (2) the ever louder noisy voices of a dissident minority, who would evolve into an initially Jewish but later gentilized Christianity who were actively campaigning that other books—the Jesus biographies, the Pauline and other letters (epistles), and the theological work known as Revelation—were equally worthy of community and leadership inclusion and sanctification.

DEAD SEA SCROLLS

Even further complicating this picture, we must also keep in mind that the "Hebraic Torah" was not the *only* Torah circulating in the ancient period. The Samaritans had their own Pentateuch which differed, at times substantively, from the Torah. The Greek Septuagint was itself accepted and embraced by Western Christianity. The Peshitta in Syriac— an Eastern Aramaic dialect—comprised of both the Old and New Testaments, was used by Eastern Christianity.

Then, too, we have the Dead Sea Scrolls of the largely Essene community in Qumran, who rejected the "Torah of Jerusalem," and, while many of their books are copies of those already in existence (the Book of Isaiah being the longest and the Book of Esther being absent), those texts also reflect textual variations.[11] Of note is that labeled the Temple Scroll (Hebrew, *Megillat Ha-Mikdash*) and about which this author wrote his doctoral dissertation.[12] The scroll itself is a detailed description of a future Temple whose regulations are far stricter than those already in existence: for example, natural bodily necessities, defecation, were not to be permitted within the sacred precincts. Somewhat unique, while the text itself is a reworking of material found in Exodus 34 to Deuteronomy 23, it is one continuous text and references God in the first person rather than the third ("I say" rather than "He said"). At least three copyists' hands are in evidence.

Every text and fragment have been examined in minute detail and this has resulted in a veritable library in a plethora of languages the world over. However, and contrary to initial expectations, the texts themselves have not dramatically altered our understanding of either early

Christianity or Second Temple Judaism, though they have, of course, modified that same understanding by revealing a more complex historical environment than was initially thought.

APOCRYPHAL AND PSEUDEPIGRAPHICAL LITERATURE

During this Second Temple period, there were to be sure any number of books written, produced, and published which never became part of the official canonized Torah/Hebrew Bible/Old Testament, some for obvious reasons (written in Greek rather than Hebrew), others less so (e.g., Book of Jubilees). Post-biblical, rabbinic talmudic literature nowhere spells out the criteria by which the third section of the Torah—*K'tuvim*, "Writings"—included the books it did and why others were excluded. Collectively, these works are labeled *Ha-Sefarim Ha-Chitzonim/*"Outer" or "External" Works for which we use the term *Apocrypha* but reserving the term *Pseudepigrapha* for those which claim a disputed or false authorship. Among the more well-known are: 1, 2, 3 Enoch; Testament of the Twelve Patriarchs; Joseph and Aseneth; Psalms of Solomon; 1, 2, 3 Baruch; 1, 2 Esdras; Wisdom of Ben Sirach; Book of Judith; Book of Tobit; 1, 2, 3, 4 Maccabees; and the *Letter of Aristeas*—which supplied the supposed rationale for the writing of the Septuagint.[13]

THE KITOS WAR: 115–117 CE

Far less well-known than either its predecessor the First Jewish War of 66–73 CE or its successor the Bar Kokhba Revolt 132–136 CE was the Kitos War. It was fought primarily outside Judea in Cyrenaica, Cyprus, and Egypt, and initially saw Roman garrisons, both soldiers and citizens, slaughtered by Jewish rebels and later Jews slaughtered by Romans. This diasporic rebellion was likely the result of continuing Jewish dissatisfaction and worse with Roman rule politically and economically and religious tensions between Greeks, Romans, and Jews. The Jewish rebels were at first successful in all three locales. However, later Roman success would result in Jewish exclusion from both Cyrenaica and Cyprus and diminished Jewish populations throughout Egypt, although Alexandria continued to remain the largest Jewish population center outside Judea. Judea itself felt the sting of defeat most noticeably in Lydda where its own population experienced Roman brutality, and the "slain of Lydda" are memorialized in the Talmud (BT Ta'anit 18b and YT Ta'anit 66b).

THE BAR KOKHBA REVOLT: 132–136 CE

Wounds would continue to fester throughout the Jewish world both politically and religiously, especially in Judea, in the aftermath of these two devastating defeats. In 132 CE, one Simon bar Kokhba ("Son of the Star," a possible messianic pretension) led an open revolt against Roman forces for four years until his death in 136 CE. The large and ever-present Roman military and its overarching and heavy-handed administration by all-too-often incompetent rulers only made matters worse. Then, too, the decision under Emperor Hadrian (76–138 CE) to completely reconstruct Jerusalem, which Jews were only permitted to enter once a year on Tisha B'Av (the ninth of Av), and to rename it "Aelia Capitolina" poured oil on an already combustible fire. Ironically, Hadrian had initially promised the Jews that he would rebuild their Temple only to deceive them with a temple to the Roman god Jupiter. After the crushing of the rebellion, Hadrian's policies became increasingly anti-Jewish, forbidding Jewish religious practices. The Ten Rabbinic Martyrs slain during this period are commemorated annually in Jewish religious tradition; their story is recalled in the midrash, *Eleh Azkarah*. The most famous among them was Rabbi Akiba (50–135 CE) who proclaimed bar Kokhba as messiah.

Initially successful, by the end of the fight, Jewish communities were severely diminished population-wise throughout Judea. In the aftermath of this unsuccessful revolt, Jewish political orientations became increasingly conservative and hesitant and Jewish leadership refocused its energies on religious Judaism, most particularly, as regards Jewish thinking on messianism. (It was only with Hadrian's death in 138 CE that some of the political and economic constraints were lifted.)

MISHNAH AND TALMUDS

After these two conflicts and almost a century later, we continue to find a devasted Jewish community in Judea/Palestine (from the Roman *Palestina*) and in need of religious and psychological "ammunition" to remain steadfast and move forward. Thus, it would fall to the recognized head of the Jewish community Yehuda Ha-Nasi (Judah the Exilarch, 135–217 CE) to assemble and organize the operative laws of the community into what has come down to us as the second great body of Judaic literature, the *Mishnah* (Hebrew, "Second Teaching," after the Torah), which would give rise to the third great compendium of Judaic literature, the *Talmud* (Hebrew, "Teaching") in both its Babylonian and Palestinian forms. Together with the Torah, the Babylonian Talmud, which includes the Mishnah, are the mainstays of today's religious Judaism.

The Mishnah is composed of six "Orders" (Hebrew, *Sedarim*) as follows: (1) *Zeraim* (seeds or agricultural concerns and various blessings); (2) *Moed* (Shabbat and festivals); (3) *Nashim* (women, marriage, and divorce); (4) *Nezikin* (civil and criminal law); (5) *Kodashim* (holy things including the Temple, sacrifices, and dietary laws); and (6) *Tohorot* (purities including food and body and contact with the dead). Included for teaching purposes are case examples and seemingly authoritative rabbinic resolutions (to the degree to which the Romans would allow the Jews to control their own affairs). Jewish tradition continues to hold in high regard many of these laws originating on Mount Sinai and the result of Moses' interactions with God, and rabbis exercise their best interpretive judgments as to the present and future implementation of these same laws.

Because case laws themselves do not cover every imaginable instance, there naturally arises the need for expansive thinking and additional conversations and clarifications—as was the case both in Judea/Palestine and Babylonia, the other large and flourishing Jewish community and home to the descendants of those who did not return with Ezra and Nehemiah but stayed behind and made their peace with their diasporic reality. Each community would give rise to their own commentary—the *Gemara* (Hebrew, possibly from g-m-r "to complete")—and would incorporate into all later published editions both the laws and their commentaries we know today as Talmud. Contained within both are veritable encyclopedias of information vis-à-vis everything one would want to know about life during the period of their composition (laws, stories, myths, fables, biblical insights, relations with non-Jews, economics, religious and civil issues, poetry, foreign words, etc.). Both would become multi-volume ventures: the Palestinian/Jerusalem less complete and thus with fewer volumes; the Babylonian fuller and more complete.[14] (Though usually referred to as the *Talmud Yerushalmi/* Jerusalem Talmud, that is somewhat inaccurate as it was not produced there. A more accurate label would be the Aramaic *Talmuda d'Eretz Yisra'el*/Talmud of the land of Israel.) By the fifth century, work on the *Talmud Yerushalmi* was finished; by the sixth century, on the *Talmud Bavli*/Babylonian Talmud.

THE QUESTION OF GRAECO-ROMAN ANTISEMITISM

Finally, before moving this story of Judaism and the Jewish people forward, there is one more issue worth noting: that of the plethora of books and authors in both the Greek and Roman periods whose anti-Judaism and anti-Jewish people could, perhaps, be labeled early antisemitism, or, if one prefers, scholar Peter Schäfer's term "Judeophobia."[15]

As John J. Collins in *Between Athens and Jerusalem* pointedly writes:

> In general, the Greeks of the Hellenistic age looked upon Judaism as a strange superstition. . . . Anti-Jewish polemic reached its apex in Alexandria in the first century C.E., where Apion drew together the various historical and moral allegations hostile to the Jews. This polemic is mainly preserved in selective quotations in Josephus's *Against Apion*. In Rome, much of the most hostile polemic comes from the period after the Jewish revolt of 66–73 C.E., and much of it is animated by Roman paranoia about the dilution of Roman culture and values by eastern cults.
>
> Much of the hostile propaganda focused on the "strangeness" of the Jews, their refusal to worship the gods of the land and their alleged hostility to other people.
>
> We should not, of course, conclude that the Gentile reaction to Judaism was entirely negative. . . . It appears, then, that there was a dimension of Judaism which was quite attractive to some people in the Hellenistic world. This was its philosophical dimension, its ethical code, and aniconic God.[16]

Collins is *not* suggesting that the Jews of the Graeco-Roman period brought this hostility upon themselves. As I read it, rather, he is suggesting that the natural human xenophobic response to the strangeness and otherness of those who were and are different—in this case, religiously—was (and remains) a significant factor which, at times, resulted and results in open hostility, violence, and worse both in the hands of those in power and those not. Tragically, this thread of anti-Judaism, anti-Jewish people, and antisemitism would remain interwoven into much of subsequent history up to and beyond the genocidal event known as the Holocaust/Shoah.

Jewish life, heretofore centered in Judea/Palestine would now move beyond, though the memories of past glories and nationhood would forever remain part of Jewish memory until the reborn State of Israel in 1948.

NOTES

1   Lee I. Levine, *Judaism and Hellenism in Antiquity: Conflict or Confluence?* (Seattle: University of Washington Press, 1998), 183–4; emphasis added.
2   John J. Collins, *Between Athens and Jerusalem: Jewish Identity in the Hellenistic Diaspora*, 2nd ed. (Grand Rapids, MI: William B. Eerdmans Publishing Company, 2000), 5. My late teacher, Samuel Sandmel (1911–79), in his 1961 presidential address to the Society of Biblical Literature would state:

On the one hand, it is true that the Greek civilization represents a cultural and religious complex different from the Hebraic and Jewish; on the other hand, when Greek civilization penetrated Palestine and when Jews moved into the Greek dispersion, the Greek civilization began to penetrate the Jewish, revoking both a conscious rejection and also an acceptance and adaptation, whether conscious or unconscious.

Samuel Sandmel, "Parallelomania," *Journal of Biblical Literature* 81, no. 1 (1962): 6.
3   Collins, *Between Athens and Jerusalem*, 17.
4   For those further interested in this fascinating story, see Karen H. Jobes and Moisés Silva, *Invitation to the Septuagint* (Grand Rapids, MI: Baker Academic, 2000), and Natalio Fernández Marcos, *The Septuagint in Context: Introduction to the Greek Version of the Bible*, trans. Wilfred G.E. Watson (Atlanta, GA: Society of Biblical Literature, 2000).
5   Jewish holy days may be divided into five groups: (1) major—those which trace their origins to the Pentateuch (first Five Books of Moses); (2) minor—those which trace their origins to the Torah/Hebrew Bible/Old Testament but outside the First Five Books; (3) minor minor—those which are not part of the Hebrew Bible/Old Testament, of which the story of the Maccabees from the book(s) of that name is the most obvious; (4) rabbinic—those crafted by the rabbis in the postbiblical era; and (4) modern—only two: *Yom Ha-Shoah*/Holocaust Commemoration Day, and *Yom Ha-Atzmaut*/Israel Independence Day (though the State of Israel itself has designated others important to the nation-state). More on this later in this text.
6   They remain a fascinating look-see into the past of ancient and early Israelite and Judean history. See, for example: Anderson and Giles, *The Keepers*; Robert

T. Anderson and Terry Giles, *The Samaritan Pentateuch: An Introduction to Its Origins, History and Significance for Biblical Studies* (Atlanta, GA: Society of Biblical Literature, 2012); Knoppers, *Jews and Samaritans*; and Pummer, *The Samaritans*.

7   Writer Daniel M. Friedenberg has written a wonderful novel entitled *Tiberius Julius Alexander* (Amherst, MA: Prometheus Books, 2010).

8   The question of when historically Christianity separated itself from Judaism remains a complicated and contested one, though scholarly consensus would seem to be that, during the reign of Emperor Constantine the Great (d. 337 CE) and the establishment of the Holy Roman Empire, coupled with the now largely gentilized, formerly so-called, "Jewish Christianity," connections were rent asunder. Until then, apparently, some "Jewish Christians" in some locations found themselves worshipping in synagogues even if they are regarded by most Jews as dissident voices and thinkers. See, for example: Adam H. Becker and Annette Yoshiko Reed (eds.), *The Ways That Never Parted: Jews and Christians in Late Antiquity and the Early Middle Ages* (Minneapolis, MN: Fortress Press, 2007); James D.G. Dunn (ed.), *Jews and Christians: The Parting of the Ways* A.D. *70 to 135* (Grand Rapids, MI: William B. Eerdmans, 1992); Annette Yoshiko Reed, *Jewish-Christianity and the History of Judaism* (Minneapolis: Fortress Press, 2022).

9   The others, included in traditional prayerbooks are: (1) God as Creator; (2) God as Unity; (3), God as incorporeal (without bodily form); (4) God as First and Last; (5) God as object of prayer; (6) the words of the prophets are true; (7) the prophecies of Moses are true; (8) the Torah given to us is that given to Moses; (9) the Torah is unchangeable; (10) God knows all our actions and thoughts; (11) God rewards those who keep the Commandments (*mitzvot*) and punishes those who do not; and (13) resurrection of the dead.

10 See, for example: Steven Leonard Jacobs, "Teaching Jesus at the University of Alabama," in Zev Garber (ed.), *Teaching the Historical Jesus: Issues and Exegesis* (New York, NY, and London: Routledge, 2015), 48–58; and Steven Leonard Jacobs, "Two Takes on Christianity: Furthering the Dialogue," *Journal of Ecumenical Studies* 47, no. 4 (2012): 508–24.

11 The story of their finding in the caves surrounding the Dead Sea is well-known: an Arab shepherd boy looking for a lost sheep threw rocks into the various caves to ascertain its whereabouts and discovered preserved containers housing numerous manuscripts and fragments, which would later be collected by the pre-state Israeli authorities in 1946/1947, and which, today, are housed in the Shrine of the Book in Jerusalem.

12 Steven Leonard Jacobs, *The Biblical Masorah and the Temple Scroll: An Orthographical Inquiry* (Lanham, MD: University Press of America, 2002).

13 Importantly, see, for example: James H. Charlesworth (ed.), *The Old Testament Pseudepigrapha*, 2 vols. (Peabody, MA: Hendrickson Publishers, 1983); John J. Collins, *The Apocalyptic Imagination: An Introduction to Jewish Apocalyptic Literature*, 2nd revised ed. (Grand Rapids, MI: William B. Eerdmans, 1998); Michael D. Coogan (ed.), *The New Oxford Annotated Bible with Apocrypha*, 5th ed. (Oxford and New York, NY: Oxford University Press, 2018); David A. DeSilva, *Introducing the Apocrypha: Message, Context, and Significance* (Grand Rapids, MI: Baker Academic, 2018); Daniel M. Gurtner, *Introducing the Pseudepigrapha of Second Temple Judaism: Message, Context, and Significance* (Grand Rapids, MI: Baker Academic, 2020); and Jonathan Klawans and Lawrence M. Wills (eds.), *The Jewish Annotated Apocrypha* (New York, NY: Oxford University Press 2020).

14 This author's Jerusalem Talmud consists of four oversized volumes, and his Babylonian Talmud twenty oversized volumes.

15 Peter Schäfer, *Judeophobia: Attitudes toward the Jews in the Ancient World* (Cambridge, MA: Harvard University Press, 1998). See, also, for example: Bezalel Bar-Kochva, *The Image of the Jews in Greek Literature: The Hellenistic Period* (Berkeley: University of California Press, 2010); and Menahem Stern (ed.), *Greek and Latin Authors on Jews and Judaism*, 3 vols. (Jerusalem: The Israel Academy of Sciences and Humanities, 1976).

16 Collins, *Between Athens and Jerusalem*, 6 ff.

7

AFTERMATH OF THE ROMAN WAR TO THE SEVENTH CENTURY

The religious and political devastation to the Jews wrought by the Roman destruction of Jerusalem and its Temple were initially incalculable, as Jews now came to grips with horrors previously unknown. The Babylonian Talmud suggests that there were so many crucifixions and other deaths that "the streets of Jerusalem ran red with the blood of those killed." Here again it appears that the God of Israel and his chosen ones had been thoroughly vanquished yet a third time.

The wonderful tale of quasi-historical accuracy (and according to popular tradition) of Rabbi Yohanan ben Zakkai and the founding of the rabbinical academy at Yavneh (Jamnia) will come to support not only the canonization of the Hebrew Scriptures—about which process we know almost nothing and originally believed to have occurred in the year 90 CE (more likely later than 200 CE)—but also the dramatic change from that of a cultic priestly ritual into a more democratic Judaism, in which all, though initially only males, would participate. (It should be said, however, that changes were already occurring prior to the Roman debacle under the leadership of the Pharisees—perhaps the most misunderstood group in all of Judaic history.) Thus, even after the restoration of the Temple now a *second* time, the sharing of the scriptural/textual tradition, the "prayer process," and the further development of ethical norms would remain in effect.

As already noted, after the Bar Kokhba Revolt, under the patriarchal leadership of the charismatic third-century Rabbi Judah in 220 CE, the internal laws governing the Jewish people were brought together, organized, and codified in a document known as the Mishnah. Thus, we already see in microcosm the outlines of what would become post-biblical or rabbinic Judaism as a worshipping religious tradition.

RISE OF RABBINICAL ACADEMIES

Though terribly significant in the formative development of post-biblical Judaism, the Mishnah itself marked the end of Palestine as the center of Judaic life, and the scene shifted to Babylonia, where the Jewish population has been estimated to have been as high as ten percent of the total population, with political autonomy, religious freedom unrivalled by their compatriots in Palestine, and economic success far more than their southeastern relatives. As the Jewish population grew, its rabbinical academies, especially those at Nehardea, Sura, and Pumbedita, and the learning itself became more and more advanced. Its own codification of Mishnah and Gemara (Talmudic commentaries), the Babylonian Talmud provided the foundation on which all subsequent Jewries would come to depend as the authoritative source of information, both religious and secular, for all Jewish communities, up to and including our own day. Both the Babylonian and the Palestinian communities would continue to develop their own variations of religious Judaism in both thought and practice, with Palestinian Judaism ultimately declining in significance.

At the start of this period, the Jewish communities of both Babylonia and Palestine were relatively large, the former more so than the latter, and flourishing economically as well. Jews were also well represented in the Roman cities of Alexandria in Egypt, Antioch in Greece, and Rome itself. As the destruction of the Second Temple receded somewhat into history, westward Jewish migration became more and more of a reality.

CONSTANTINE, CHRISTIANITY, AND THE EDICT OF MILAN

Fortunes began to change significantly, however, in the year 313 CE, when Emperor Constantine (232–337 CE) affirmed the Edict of Milan, which favored the growing religion of Christianity in his empire, and entered an alliance with Christian leadership in what today we now refer to as the "Holy Roman Empire." While early on, both emperors and church leaders behaved ambivalently toward their Jewish populations, some supportive and well-intentioned, others restrictive and mean-spirited (e.g., the bishop of Syria and Constantinople, the great orator

John Chrysostom [*c.* 349–407 CE], who attacked the Jews, and the intellectual giant Augustine, bishop of Hippo [354–430 CE], who had initially supported the Jews), the alliance saw Jewish communities increasingly impoverished, their religious and political freedom restricted, and their now-diminished existence proof of the "truth" and "superiority" of Christianity. Jews would, however, survive and, in many, if not all, cases, thrive in many of these same European lands and nation-states despite the continuing animus of antisemitism that would rear its ugly head all too often.

EMERGENCE OF ISLAM

In the East, in the area known as the Arabian Peninsula, Jewish tribal communities had also lived reasonably well and successfully, interacting with the non-Jewish tribes in the region. In the seventh century, Muhammad (570–632 CE) came forward in response to what he (and his followers) accepted as a divine mandate, attempting to unite these tribes into a loose confederation, and to share with them a revelation known as the Qur'an. Initially favorably disposed toward both Jews and Christians—to whom he gave the title "peoples of the [Sacred] Book" (i.e., both Torah/Hebrew Bible/Old Testament and New Testament)—when the Jews rejected both his political leadership and his newer understanding of God's plan, he engaged them militarily, wiping out the Jews of Banu Qurayza, for example, in 627 CE. From that point on, both Jews and Christians would be classed as *dhimmis* ("protected ones"), with Jews, however, occupying a somewhat higher status than that of Christians. (The uneasy and ongoing relationship between all three groups remains problematic even today, further exacerbated by events in the Middle East vis-à-vis the State of Israel, its own history, and that of its neighbors.)

MIZRAHIM AND SEPHARDIM: A LESSER-KNOWN STORY TO ASHKENAZIM[1]

First the terms themselves: *Mizrahim* means "Easterners" or "Orientals," and, somewhat generally, refers to Jews of the Middle East, Western Asia, and North Africa (the *Maghreb*, "Westerners")[2]—Iraqis Jews, Kurdish Jews, Syrian Jews, Turkish Jews, Yemenite Jews, Iranian Jews, Egyptian

Jews, Libyan Jews, Tunisian Jews, Algerian Jews, Moroccan Jews. (At times, the term has also been used to include Dagestani Jews, Azerbaijani Jews, Uzbekistani Jews, and Tajikistani Jews.[3]) While many religiously follow Sephardic practices, this term is not equivalent, as Sephardic Jews (from the Hebrew *Sepharad*, "Spain") were and are initially most identified with Jews from Spain, Portugal, and Greece (which, however, also divided itself between other Sephardim and Romaniote Jews, an earlier and distinct sub-group). Linguistically, languages written and spoken were and are primarily Arabic, Aramaic, and a mixed Judeo-Arabic (incorporating Hebrew words).[4] Ashkenazic Jews (from the Hebrew *Ashkenaz*, "Germany"), today's largest population of Jews, are traditionally understood to be "Western" Jews from Germany, Poland, Russia, France, Great Britain, Scandinavia (and, of course, the United States, a later migration). Often in the past, but less so today, historians—Jews and others—telling the "Jewish story," tended to write more about these Ashkenazim, with only occasional nods (footnotes) to these other important populations.

Historically and collectively, however, these various groups of Jewish people, while largely resident in the land of ancient Israel/Palestine, tell us that migration, both forced and voluntary (Babylonia and Egypt being excellent examples) was the norm rather than the exception.

Scholars believe that this migratory journey began with the Babylonian exile/captivity (586 BCE), unlike that of the Assyrian exile/captivity of 721 BCE which resulted in the assimilation and disappearance of the Northern Kingdom of Israel and its tribes. However, far less well-known is the reality that ancient Israelite traders may very well have traveled *and settled* in outlying areas for economic reasons, having little to do with political or military realities, and whose own stories are difficult if not impossible to ascertain due to the paucity of evidentiary records other than contractual documents both in cuneiform and papyrus.

For hundreds of years, beginning perhaps in the period after the Second Temple's destruction, these communities would thrive in such places as Khaybar, Medina, and Mecca, interacting with their neighbors, establishing themselves primarily as merchants and craftspeople and achieving a level of economic success we would perhaps associate with a middle-class existence, some achieving great wealth and others remaining at the bottom of the socio-economic ladder. Like their fellow Jews "back home" in *Eretz Yisrael*, the Land of Israel, their organizational structure was initially that of patriarchal tribal groups, among whom the most populous were the Banu Nadir, the Banu Qainuqa, and the Banu Qurayza.

That reasonably harmonious existence would change with the appearance of Muhammad and the rise of Islam in the seventh century.

Appropriate to Muhammad's rise is to understand it in both its political and its religious aspects. Politically, he was born into a world—Arabia—of competing and all-too-often warring tribes lacking any reasons whatsoever for unification. His gift of God's revelation and the text of the Qur'an became that unifier. His military strategic success together with that of his followers brought about a time of reasonable peace. Religiously, he fully expected the conversion of the Jewish tribes, with whom he initially had positive relationships, and their full and total political subjugation and therefore support under his leadership. Such was not to be the case, however, and thus war with all three (and some lesser and smaller Jewish tribes as well, though not all) resulted in their destruction, ofttimes with their men put to death and their women, wives, and children enslaved and forcibly converted.

During the so-called "Middle Ages" (in Europe better understood perhaps by Jews as the "Dark Ages" of ignorance, intolerance and illiteracy stirred up by Christian religious fervor), Jews would exist throughout the Arab/Islamic world, tolerated as *dhimmi* (second class, protected class), free to practice their Judaism, but subject to the *jizya* (payment, tax) as non-Muslim, and, all too frequently, subject to pogrom-like mob violence. The bright star would come later with the *Convivencia* (Spanish, "co-existence") during the Muslim hegemony in Spain (900–1200 CE), when Muslim, Jewish, and Christian scholars and litterateurs would interact, and all three populations would seemingly maintain a delicate balancing act of harmony and tolerance.[5]

However, with the *Reconquista* (Spanish, "reconquest") achieved by Christians in 1492 CE, and the assertion of Christian dominance and power in Spain and Portugal, Muslim/Arab power would return to the East and lands under their control, coupled with a more conservative tradition of Islamic religion and a further diminution of Jewish status under subsequent caliphates. Jews and Jewish communities, however, would survive and flourish even if somewhat less so than previously.

Notably, under the Ottoman/Turkish Empire (c. 1300–1922), Jews would flee their exile from both Spain and Portugal (1492) to find a reasonable welcome among their already-resident brethren and a reasonably hospitable welcome from the Sultanate itself—albeit one that would still suffer political and economic restrictions and even occasional violence. Their uneasy existence would be the norm until the birth of the modern State of Israel in 1948, when the collective population of Jews—perhaps as many as 850,000—would largely flee to the new Jewish nation-state and those left behind would find themselves severely diminished in numbers, political and economic access, and, at best, a tolerated minority.[6] The First World War and the secularist takeover of the Ottoman Empire by the Kemalists under Mustafa Kemal Atatürk (1881–1938) would not change that reality for those left behind.[7]

A particularly tragic example of modern tensions was the case of the *Farhud* (Arabic, "violent dispossession") of Baghdadi Jews in Iraq in 1941 with 180 killed and more than 1,000 injured.[8] Equally tragic in both his antisemitism and his anti-Zionism was Mohammed Amin al-Husseini (1897–1974), who allied himself with Adolf Hitler (1889–1945), living in Berlin, delivering hateful messages to Arabs on Berlin radio urging them to kill the Jews of Palestine and hoping to bring Nazi-style extermination there, and who used his position as Grand Mufti of Jerusalem (1921–48) to thwart and worst all attempts at Jewish nationalism and Jewish-Arab/Islamic reconciliation.

The rebirth of the Third Jewish Commonwealth—the State of Israel—on May 14, 1948 has further exacerbated whatever historical tensions existed and exist between Jews and Arabs and Judaism and Islam now that Jews are again governing their own land with a sizeable Arab population, and viewed by Israel's enemies as a blight on the *ummah* (Arabic, "community") and one which must be either excised or destroyed. (NB: Not all Arabs are Muslims; some are Christians, e.g., the Copts in Egypt.) Israel's military successes in 1948, 1967, 1973, and 1982, and its ongoing confrontations with both Fatah and Hamas, who themselves jockey for power both inside and outside its own borders, as well as its occupation of its own Palestinian citizenry, have made the road to peace in the region a difficult and at times a seemingly impossible one to travel.

Religiously, to further round out this picture, one must realize and respect that theologically, Islam and Judaism share an outlook closer possibly than that between Judaism and Christianity, but perhaps less so in the West, for example: God/Allah is One (singularity) rather than Christianity's triune God (Three in One); Jewish prayer is offered three times a day (*Shacharit, Mincha, Ma'ariv*) and Islam's five times a day (*Fajr, Dhuhr, Asr, Maghrib, Isha*); the two faiths share Kashrut and Halal (dietary restrictions); and circumcision.[9]

Returning to the West, we turn back to Europe and the Middle Ages during the eighth and ninth centuries, including the Crusades, the "Golden Age," and the various expulsions and diasporas.

NOTES

1 Three excellent overviews are: Martin Gilbert, *In Ishmael's House: A History of Jews in Muslim Lands* (New Haven, CT, and London: Yale University Press, 2010); and, earlier, Norman Stillman, *The Jews of Arab Lands: A History and Source Book* (Philadelphia, PA: Jewish Publication Society, 1979), and *Jews of Arab Lands in Modern Times* (Philadelphia, PA: Jewish Publication Society, 2003).

2 One also finds the contested term in the literature "Arab Jews" or even "Jewish Arabs." This designation is both accepted by some within these communities but rejected by others.

3 Each of these Jewish populations are more than worthy of their own stories, historically, politically, economically, socially, and religiously, and would, quite obviously, result in many volumes.

4 The great Jewish scholar Maimonides, who lived in both Spain and later Egypt, wrote his major neo-Aristotelian philosophical text, *Moreh Nevuchim* ("Guide for the Perplexed"), in Arabic; it was translated into Hebrew by the ibn (Arabic for ben, "son of") Tibbon family of translators. Even earlier, Saadia Gaon (892–942 CE) wrote his own philosophical text, *Emunot v'Deot* ("Beliefs and Opinions"), in Arabic. Judah Halevi (1075–1141 CE) wrote his dialogical text, *al-Kuzari* ("On the Khazars"), in Arabic. The text tells of a Jewish teacher, who has been asked to present his philosophy to the Khazar king, after the king has heard those of a Christian and a Muslim, in order for him to decide to whom he should commit himself and his people. Of course, the rabbi wins, and the king and his people convert. Regarding this last text and the larger story, see Kevin Alan Brook, *The Jews of Khazaria*, 2nd ed. (Lanham, MD: Rowman & Littlefield, 2006).

5 Darío Fernández-Morera, however, disputes this assessment in his *The Myth of the Andalusian Paradise: Muslims, Christians, and Jews under Islamic Rule in Medieval Spain* (Wilmington, DE: ISI Books, 2016), especially chapter six, "The Truth about the Jewish Community's 'Golden Age,'" 177–203.

6 Lyn Julius, *Uprooted: How 3000 Years of Jewish Civilization in the Arab World Vanished Overnight* (Portland, OR: Vallentine Mitchell, 2018).

7 See Steven Leonard Jacobs, "The State and Fate of the Jews in the Ottoman Empire and the Early Republic during World War I: A *Necessary* Part of the Conversation," in George Shirinian, ed., *Armenians, Assyrians, and Greeks in the Ottoman Empire* (New York, NY and Oxford: Berghahn Books, forthcoming).

8 See Edwin Black, *The Farhud: Roots of the Arab-Nazi Alliance in the Holocaust* (Washington, DC: Dialog Press, 2010); Shmuel Moreh and Zvi Yehuda (eds.), *Al-Farhūd: The 1941 Pogrom in Iraq* (Jerusalem: Hebrew University Magnes Press, 2010).

9 See Bernard Lewis, *The Jews of Islam* (Princeton, NJ: Princeton University Press, 1984).

8

THE EIGHTH TO THE FIFTEENTH CENTURIES: THE MIDDLE AGES

The continuing success of Islam saw Arabs extending their empire from India to Spain and, as a by-product, encompassing by the year 712 CE approximately ninety percent of the Jews then alive. (Jerusalem had already been retaken from the Christian West by 638 CE.) Increasingly, Jews under Muslim hegemony gravitated toward cities and towns, away from their former occupation as farmers, and became traders, merchants, and craftspeople. Nowhere was their successful integration into the life of the empire more evident than in Spain in the lives of three truly remarkable individuals: Hasdai ibn Shaprut (915–970), physician and diplomat; Samuel ibn Naghrillah (993–1056), Talmudist poet, soldier, and diplomat; and Solomon ibn Gabirol (1021–58), poet and philosopher.

To the degree that "the exception proves the rule," these three somewhat singularly unique individuals should remind us what was possible in a world where Jews were sometimes welcomed, sometimes tolerated, and sometimes even permitted to contribute to the larger societies in which they lived.

Hasdai ibn Shaprut was born in Córdoba, Andalusia, and would go on, by virtue of his medical skills, knowledge, and affable personality, to become confidant and counselor to Caliph Abd-ar-Rahman III (emir, 912–929, then first caliph until his death in 961), becoming in the process something of an unofficial vizier and minister of foreign affairs. He would retain his status under Rahman III's son and successor al-Hakam II (915–976). Importantly, he was active in the Jewish community, supporting Jewish learning and cultural activities wherever possible, and advocating through government channels for the release of Jewish captives.[1]

Samuel ibn Naghrillah, born in Mérida, Andalusia, would go on to become perhaps the most influential Jew in Muslim Spain, despite the Pact of Umar which forbade Jews holding political office.[2] That he achieved the public rank and acknowledgment of both vizier and general in the army of Grenada speaks for itself. Tragically, however, the same could not be said for his son Joseph (1035–66), who succeeded his father but whose arrogance precipitated both his own death and the massacre of Granada's Jews in 1066.

Solomon ibn Gabirol, in some ways perhaps, remains the most fascinating of the three. His intellectual influence as a neo-Platonic philosopher was felt in both Christian and Islamic circles (both of which falsely regarded him as one of their own) rather than Jewish circles, largely the result of his text, *Fons Vitae* (non-Hebraic, "Source of Life"). His most well-known Hebrew poem, however, *Keter Malchut* ("Royal Crown"), set to verse his philosophical understanding of the relationship of God to creation as reflected in his narrative text.[3] His ethical tractate, "The Improvement of the Moral Qualities" (translated into Hebrew as *Tikkun Midot*), has been compared to that of the premier Jewish ethicist of the day, Bahya ibn Paquda (1050–1120), *Hovot Ha-Levavot* ("Duties of the Heart"). Ibn Gabirol also wrote more than one hundred poetic prayers for Sabbaths, festivals, and holy days, many of which have been included in the prayerbooks of both Sephardic and Ashkenazi Jews and even Karaites as well.

Communally, during this same period, two movements seemingly competed for the souls of the Jews: (1) the larger and more dominant one—which we may call "Rabbinism" or "Talmudism"—grounded in the Talmudic texts stretching back to the time of the Mishnah of the third century; and (2) its smaller opposite—"Karaism" (see below)— more conservative, more biblically literalist, rejecting the authority of the rabbis and their texts, and not unlike their Palestinian predecessors, the Sadducees in their controversies with the Pharisees, though they never claimed lineal descent from them.

THE FIRST CRUSADE AND TOO MANY MORE

In the Christian West the situation of the Jewish communities continued to deteriorate; they experienced a worsening of attitudes, economic impoverishment, increasing isolation, and forced ghettoization. As Christians under the imprimatur of Pope Urban II (1042–99) prepared to launch the First Crusade (1096–99), whose objective was to recapture the city of Jerusalem and all the Holy Land—and which succeeded shortly before his death—Jewish communities in the path of the Crusaders found themselves particularly vulnerable. The rallying cry *Hep! Hep! Hierosolyma est perdita!* (Latin, "Jerusalem is/has been lost!") galvanized Western Europeans to action. Led by knights and priests, the bulk of those who sallied forth to battle were largely illiterate peasants who needed little reminder and encouragement that the Jews found in their way were the descendants of those who supposedly killed their Christ, and, thus, were infidels like the Muslims of Palestine. Jewish communities were devastated, their populations decimated—including women and children—and their synagogues destroyed. Those who survived these onslaughts either fled to other locales or feebly attempted to reconstruct their lives, not always successfully.

Yet, even despite this picture of darkness and gloom, Jewish cultural and religious creativity did not diminish. The light of Jewish learning shone no more brightly than it did during this period in the person of Rabbi Solomon ben Isaac (1040–1105) of Troyes, France, where he established his own *yeshiva*, or academy of rabbinic and higher learning, in 1070. Better known by his acronym, Rashi, his almost-complete commentaries on both Talmud (thirty of thirty-nine tractates) and Torah/Hebrew Bible (except 1 and 2 Chronicles, Nehemiah, Ruth, Song of Songs, and Ecclesiastes) remain authoritative even today and are published together with those texts. His commentarial gift was his ability not only to master a wide variety of Jewish and non-Jewish sources, but his ability to present his commentaries in a clear and lucid manner so that ordinary Jews could understand the more complicated texts under consideration. Three hundred of his Responsa (answers to Jewish legal and other questions addressed to him by both rabbis and lay persons) have survived. These include such topics as food, prayer, wine, sales, loans, communal affairs, legal partnerships and oaths, Sabbath responsibilities, and the like. Perhaps more as a tribute than actual history, the semi-cursive script known as "Rashi script," in which his commentaries are printed in both Talmud and Torah (fifteenth century), remains the norm in all printed editions of both.

LATER CRUSADES AND JEWISH OPPRESSION

The Second Crusade (1147–49) and the Third Crusade (1189–92)—the latter under the imprimatur of Pope Innocent III (1161–1216)—saw a repeat of the very same reprehensible behavior against Jews that marked the First Crusade a generation before: destruction of Jewish communities and the murder of their inhabitants. As initiated, confirmed, and later accepted by the pope, the Fourth Lateran Council (1215) now saw the Jews (and Muslims) required to wear distinctive clothing to set them even further apart and lessen the contact between themselves and Christians (shades of later Nazism and the *Judenstern*/Jewish star!). Also, during this period, the notorious antisemitic charge of "blood libel"—supposedly using the blood of innocent Christian children during the Passover season in the making of the *matzot* or unleavened cakes required in celebration— slowly began to surface, first vis-à-vis the disappearance and murder of a boy apprentice, William of Norwich in Great Britain, in 1144. In addition, Jews found themselves expelled from England in 1290 and France in 1306.

On the continent, primarily in Italy, Jews again found themselves in an uncomfortably ambiguous position. The Christian church publicly condemned the charging of interest on loans ("usury") but, with the rise of mercantilism and commerce, secular society saw increasingly the need for larger and larger amounts of speculative capital and turned to the Jews for such monies.[4] Equally, Jews saw such monies not only as a form of safety and security, should quick exit from their place of residence be required, but also, as opportunities to ingratiate themselves with the larger society and make contributions to its growth and development, ideally this would reflect on them with goodwill from their hosts. Sadly, however, such was not to be the case, and usury was now added to the litany of deicide (i.e., killers of God/Christ) and blood libel/ritual murder in the antisemitic cacophony that marked the times.

DEICIDE AND BLOOD LIBEL/RITUAL MURDER

Important to keep in mind as we continue our story and the journey of Judaism and the Jewish people are these two most pernicious forms of antisemitism (i.e., hatred of the Jews and Judaism) and which saw their fullest flowering during this period. Thus, from a Judaic standpoint, it is not incorrect to regard the Middle Ages as the Dark Ages for this and other reasons when it comes to this tragic period.

Deicide

Deicide exists in numerous cultures (Norse, Japanese, Hawaiian, and Aztec), but has particular resonance in a Judaic antisemitic context, where it refers to the New Testament charge that the Jews in Roman-occupied and Roman-controlled Palestine were the *primary* culprits responsible for the murder of Christ Jesus, the "son of God." It is found in the Gospel of Matthew, chapter 27, in which the Jews are assembled in the courtyard outside the home of Roman procurator Pontius Pilate (d. *c.* 36–39 CE) prior to the festival of the Passover. Pilate, in a supposed expression of goodwill toward his subjects, offers to release one of two captives, either Barabbas (in Aramaic, Bar Abbas, "son of the father") or Jesus:

> Now it was the governor's custom at the festival to release a prisoner chosen by the crowd. At that time, they had a well-known prisoner whose name was Jesus Barabbas. So, when the crowd had gathered, Pilate asked them, "Which one do you want me to release to you: Jesus Barabbas, or Jesus who is called the Messiah?" For he knew it was out of self-interest that they had handed Jesus over to him. While Pilate was sitting on the judge's seat, his wife sent him this message: "Don't have anything to do with that innocent man, for I have suffered a great deal today in a dream because of him." But the chief priests and the elders persuaded the crowd to ask for Barabbas and to have Jesus executed. "Which of the two do you want me to release to you?" asked the governor. "Barabbas," they answered. "What shall I do, then, with Jesus who is called the Messiah?" Pilate asked. They all answered, "Crucify him!" "Why? What crime has he committed?" asked Pilate. But they shouted all the louder, "Crucify him!" When Pilate saw that he was getting nowhere, but that instead an uproar was starting, he took water and washed his hands in front of the [deicide] crowd. "I am innocent of this man's blood," he said. "It is your responsibility!" All the people answered, "His blood is on us and on our children!" Then he released Barabbas to them. But he had Jesus flogged and handed him over to be crucified. (Matthew 27:15–26)[5]

(The accounts found in the Gospels of Mark and Luke are modifications, but this scenario does not appear in the Gospel of John, although the latter does provide the rationale for the Romans putting Jesus to death by arguing that the Jewish leaders had no power to do so [John 18:31].) The important Roman Catholic theologian St. John Chrysostom (349–407 CE), the archbishop of Constantinople—known far and wide for the power of his oratory—was the first to accuse the Jews of the murder of Jesus and incorporate it into his theology, arguing that no forgiveness or pardon was possible for this sin. The first time the word deicide appears in Latin—*deicidas*—was in a sermon by the bishop of Ravenna, Italy, Peter Chrysologus (380–450 CE). Subsequently, for the last two thousand plus years, especially in the West more so than in the East, Jews have been consistently vilified as the enemies of God and subjected to various forms of violence—murder, pogroms, ghettoization, expulsions, and forced conversions. Eastertide, particularly in Europe and especially during the Middle Ages, was particularly frightful, as largely illiterate crowds were whipped up to a religious frenzy as the priests retold the story of Jesus's death to dramatic effect, after which the angry peasants would break into the Jewish ghettos and murder the inhabitants therein. This charge of deicide has remained part and parcel of Christianity, especially Roman Catholicism and later Protestantism, since its inception and is still found today in some of the more fundamentalist/literalist Christian communities who regard the events depicted in Matthew as historically accurate. The year 1965 would, however, mark a significant change in this understanding with the passage of the Roman Catholic document, *Nostra Aetate* (Latin, "In Our Time"), in the closing days of Vatican II (1962–65), largely exonerating Jews for whatever participation in which they *may* have engaged (i.e., Sadducean complicity rather than Pharisaic), rejecting the idea of any passing on of the sins of the past to the present and future generations, and rejecting as thoroughly anti-Christian any and all forms of antisemitism. Various expressions of Protestant Christianity (e.g., Anglican, Methodist, Lutheran, Presbyterian) rather quickly followed suit, leading to a flowering of Jewish–Christian dialogue, especially in the United States.

Although there is no historical basis for this false charge—none whatsoever!—the Talmud in Sanhedin 43a maintains that Jesus was put to death by a Jewish court for sedition and sorcery. The "alternative biography" of Jesus known as *Toledot Yeshu* ("Generations of Jesus"), a satiric text, appearing as early as the fourth century, of unknown authorship and origin and possibly even written or edited by non-Jews and found in several different versions, maintains that Jesus was born of a Jewish mother and Roman father and a maker of miracles. Among those various texts were those that also maintained that the Jewish court of the time was responsible for his death. Both the Talmud and *Toledot Yeshu* would go on to become weapons in the arsenals of Jew-haters, despite all such fraudulent claims being thoroughly debunked by sound historical scholarship as well as public pronouncements by all religious denominations.[6]

Blood Libel and Ritual Murder

Blood Libel—also sometimes referred to as the Blood Accusation—remains, perhaps, among the most notorious of antisemitic charges against both the Jewish people and Judaism. It falsely purports to accuse both Jews and Judaism of requiring the blood of a *religious* Christian, usually a naïve, young, and innocent child (male more so than female), to be drained and used in the preparation of the *matzot*—the flat, unleavened squares—associated with the festival of Passover (in Hebrew, *Pesach*). Equally and perversely, it is also associated with the Easter celebration of the resurrection of the Christ in the destruction of the sacramental wafer (which, according to legend, spouts the blood of Jesus as Jews attempt its destruction) and further perpetuates the notion of the Jews as a deicide people, mocking the death of Jesus and symbolically desecrating his memory. Its falsity is easily called into question not only by the Torah/ Hebrew Bible/Old Testament and its strong avoidance of blood (e.g., Leviticus 3:17, 7:26, 17:10–14 and Deuteronomy 12:15–16 and 20–24) but also by the post-biblical rabbinic literature, both of which strongly advise against contact with human and animal blood, ritually and ceremonially.[7] Most historians date the beginnings of this vile charge to the murder of William of Norwich in England in 1144. Yet, already in the early twentieth century, scholars revisited such texts as Josephus's *Contra Apionem* (though the original text of the Egyptian antisemite Apion [30/20 BCE–45/48 CE] to which he was responding has been lost), those of the earlier Greek writer Democritus (460–370 BCE), Greek philosopher Socrates' (469–399 BCE) *Ecclesiastical History*, and the writings of bishops Agobard of Lyon (779–840 CE) and Bernard of Clairvaux (1090–1153), among others, all of which contain references, however false, to Jews wantonly murdering Christians for either ritual purposes or simply out of contempt and disrespect for Christians and Christianity. The 1906 *Jewish Encylopedia* (www.jewishencyclopedia. com) lists more than 120 such reported accusations between the years 1144 and 1900 (and more since!) throughout every country on the European continent, Russia included, which oftentimes resulted in mass violence against vulnerable Jewish communities. Sadly, and tragically, Jewish converts to Roman Catholicism throughout the Middle Ages aided in the perpetuation of this lie and further added to it a hateful litany of accusations of sorcery and licentiousness (sexual debauchery). Some secular rulers and some princes of the church, however, decried and rejected these accusations and attempted to protect "their Jews" from the mobs, often with little power or ability to do so.

Examples of such accusations of ritual murder and trials against Jews and Jewish communities include the cases of Hugh of Lincoln, England in 1255, Simon of Trent (Simonino de Trento), Italy in 1475,[8] and the

Holy Child of La Guardia (El Santo Niño de La Guardia), Spain, in 1491. The famed English litterateur and poet Geoffrey Chaucer (c. 1340–1400) told one such story of a child martyr supposedly killed by Jews in his "The Prioress's Tale."

In the first part of the twentieth century, the Nazis made propagandistic use of the blood libel, most notoriously in Julius Streicher's (1885–1946) newspaper, *Der Stürmer* ("The Stormer" or "The Attacker"), which was replete with graphic portrayals of Jews executing young German males and virginal young females and draining their blood. After the end of the Second World War, in Kielce, Poland, forty-two Jews were murdered and forty injured when an eight-year-old boy went missing and the Holocaust survivors living there were accused of the crime. Even the United States was not spared from this libel. In 1928, in Massena, New York, a four-year-old girl went for a walk and seemingly disappeared, only to return a day later saying that she had fallen asleep (though the rumor persisted that she had been rescued by an anonymous benefactor). The rabbi of the small synagogue and other Jewish communal leaders were interrogated by the police and questioned as to whether Jews had in the past used human blood for ritual purposes. Although the mayor of the town would ultimately apologize, there were citizens who remained convinced that only her "rescue" had thwarted an attempt at ritual murder. In January 2005, twenty members of the Russian Duma (the lower house of the parliament of the Russian Federation) publicly accused Jews of blood libels against the Russian people.

The blood libel remains a staple today not only of Western antisemites but Middle Eastern, primarily Arab, foes of Israel. On a regular ongoing basis, political cartoons appear in Arab nation-state newspapers depicting Israelis replete with Stars of David on military uniforms dripping with the blood of innocent Palestinians, especially children. Moreover, according to the Middle East Media Research Institute (MEMRI, https://www.memri.org/reports/antisemitic-cartoons-arab-and-iranian-press), supposedly reputable scholars and imams continue to perpetuate the lie of the blood libel. In 1983, for example, Mustafa Tlass (1932–2017), the former Syrian minister of defense (1972–2004), published his libelous *The Matzah of Zion*, which is replete with all the previously held antisemitic tropes, including this one, and attempts to address the notorious Damascus Affair of 1840, when thirteen leaders of that Jewish community were charged with the murder of a French Franciscan monk, Father Thomas, and his assistant and arrested, tortured, indicted, and imprisoned, with some being murdered. International pressure and negotiations secured the release and exoneration of nine of the leaders; four had already died as the result of their wounds.

The very longevity of this libel in the minds of many attests to the enduring antisemitic hatred of Jews and Judaism, regardless of locale, education, political leaning, economic standing, or religious affiliation. Its many virulent expressions testify to its crudity, its graphic appeal to violence, and the willingness of some to both believe and accept this most outrageous of accusations against this minority people and their religious faith.[9]

A GOLDEN AGE[10]

In Spain, the period from 900 to 1200 would become known among some Jews then and now as a "golden age," when literary, cultural, and religious creativity was at its highest. Two of its more noteworthy representatives were the philosopher and poet, and also physician, Judah Halevi, born in Tudela in 1075, and physician, rabbi, and philosopher, Maimonides, born in Cordoba in 1138—perhaps the greatest figure in all Jewish history, second only to Moses. (Apocryphal lore has it that that he once said of himself, "From Moses [of old] unto Moses [me], there is none like Moses!")

Initially, after the successful *Reconquista* of Spain during the twelfth and thirteenth centuries, Jews shared their knowledge of philosophy, science, mathematics, medicine, and even astrology with their old/new hosts. All was not well, however. In 1263, in Barcelona, for example, the apostate and convert Dominican monk Pablo Christiani (d. 1274) engaged in a public debate with Rabbi Moses ben Nachman, Nachmanides (1194–1270), in an unsuccessful attempt to humiliate the Spanish Jewish community. Earlier, in 1239, Pope Gregory IX (*c.* 1143/70–1292) and, again, in 1244, Pope Innocent IV (*c.* 1195–1254) called for the confiscation and burning of the Babylonian Talmud to destroy Jewish communities (as would Martin Luther [1483–1546] in Germany later on). Conditions continued to worsen in Spain, beginning with riots in 1391 and then the expulsion of the entire Jewish community (estimated at more than 300,000 persons) under the royal edict of King Ferdinand II of Aragon (1452–1516) and Queen Isabella I of Castile (1451–1540)—with the imprimatur of her father confessor, the Dominican and Grand Inquisitor Tomás de Torquemada (1420–98), who was himself responsible for a bloody attempt to root out all "insincere and false Christians" in the realm. (The Edict of Expulsion of 1492, known as the Alhambra Decree, was revoked by the Vatican in 1968 at the Second Vatican Council.) To incompletely round out the story of Spanish Jewry, other Jews of note during this period include: grammarian, poet and biblical commentator, Dunash ibn Labrat (*c. 920–c. 990*); philologist Menahem ibn Saruq (*c. 920–c. 970*); the already-mentioned philosopher and ethicist, Bahya ibn Paquda; rabbinic scholar and teacher Joseph ibn Migash (1077–1141); the biblical commentator and philosopher, Abraham ibn Ezra (1089–1167)[11]; Talmudist Shlomo ibn Aderet (1235–1310); the Talmudist and teacher, Yom Tov ben Abraham of Seville (1260-1314); Talmudist Nissim Gerondi (1320–76); and statesman, philosopher, financier and biblical commentator, Isaac ben Judah Abarbanel (1437–1508).

Other Disputations

The disputation at Barcelona was not the only infamous one during this period. Earlier in Paris in 1240, the Talmud itself was subject to attack when converted Christian Nicholas Donin persuaded Pope Gregory IX to agree with his spurious claims of Christian defamation which resulted in the burning of twenty-four wagonloads of Talmudic texts and more than 10,000 volumes of Hebrew manuscripts.

After Barcelona, in Tortosa, Spain, during 1413 and 1414, an attempt was made at forced conversion and the censoring of Talmudic materials and teaching. Although with limited success, nevertheless, Jewish texts remained under the scrutiny of Roman Catholic censors and aggressive attempts at the conversion of the Jewish population continued.[12]

As a sidebar, a rather unusual idea has surfaced about this period with regard to the rather mysterious Christoforo Colombo of Italy and Spain, known to us today as Christopher Columbus (1451–1506). Because his initial voyage across the Atlantic coincided with the expulsion of the Jews, and his first interpreter and cartographer/mapmaker Luis de Torres (d. 1493) was known to be a Jew, and some financial support for his voyages came from wealthy members of the Jewish community, some, including famed Nazi hunter and Holocaust survivor Simon Wiesenthal (1908–2005),[13] have suggested that his true mission was *not* a route to the East for spices and other values, but, rather, a mission to discover a safe haven for the departing Jews. He himself further sweetened that speculation by referring to himself in a preserved letter as "a worthy son of [King] David."

THE INQUISITIONS—SPAIN AND PORTUGAL

The Spanish Inquisition (*Tribunal del Santo Oficio de la Inquisición*), established in 1478, was not initially and originally intended as an antisemitic persecution of Jews within the Spanish realm. Rather, it was an attempt to ferret out insincere Catholic Christians—both born and *conversos* (converts) or *marranos* (forced converts), the so-called "New Christians" (originally Jews and Muslims)—who had either lapsed in their practice of the faith, or, in the case of the latter, who secretly practiced their Judaism or Islam. Additionally, with the political control of the inquisitional courts and their overseers, especially Tomas de Torquemada, confessor to Queen Isabella I of Castile, and the opportunities to enrich the royal coffers and wrest power away from papal authority, King Ferdinand II of Aragon saw the potential to solidify his hold over his kingdom and further unify both Aragon and Castile. Portugal, like its neighbor, also engaged in these activities and only ceased doing so in 1821. Italy, too, fell under the power of the Inquisition, but it remained under papal control. (It should also be noted that Moors [Muslims forced to convert to Christianity, though now labeled as *moriscos*], too, came in for inquisitional terrors but to a somewhat lesser extent than converts or later Jews, though one of the fears on the part of the Inquisition was that the Muslims were secretly attempting to regain power and control for the Ottoman Empire.) For both Jews and Muslims, their alternatives were, initially, either conversion or expulsion, and a significant number of both chose the latter. According to the 1906 *Jewish Encyclopedia* article "Inquisition (called *Sanctum Officium* or Holy Office)," the following acts, for example, merited the attention of the Inquisition in the case of converts:

- Celebrate the (Saturday) Sabbath by engaging in practices associated with Judaism
- Wear a clean shirt or better garments on Saturday
- Light no fire
- Eat the food which had been cooked overnight in the oven
- Perform no work on that day
- Eat meat during Lent
  Take neither meat nor drink on the Day of Atonement [Yom Kippur]
- Celebrate the Passover with unleavened bread or eat bitter herbs
- Celebrate the Feast of Tabernacles [Sukkot] using green branches or send fruits as gifts to friends
- Marry according to Jewish customs or take Jewish names

- Circumcise their sons
- Eat no pork, hare, rabbits, or eels
- Give Old Testament names to their children, or bless the children by laying on of hands
- Women not attending church within forty days after confinement [childbirth]
- Turning the dying toward the wall [i.e., eastward toward Jerusalem]
- Recite psalms without concluding "Glory to the Trinity"

Those brought up on such charges were typically thrown into prisons under hellish conditions, where food was meager and poor and punishments included various forms of torture, including hanging by the wrists, "waterboarding," the rack, and, ultimately, death.

Less well-known, however, is the fact that the Inquisition spread its tentacles to the New World of the Americas under Spanish control, especially Mexico. Between 1581 and 1776, 129 acts of public penance and condemnation (*autos-da-fé*) took place, including fifty-nine people burned alive and eighteen in effigy. British Jewish scholar and historian Cecil Roth (1899–1970), writing in the *Encyclopedia Judaica* (2007, second edition), summarizes the Inquisition thus:

> Whatever the true reasons for the establishment of the Inquisition were, it cannot be denied that social, economic, racial, and political reasons nourished the trials of the Inquisition and the anti-Converso attitude that existed in Christian society. According to many Old and New Christian sources the hatred of the Conversos was due to the envy their economic and social achievements aroused in society in general. Many of them were able to translate their economic and social strength into political power which added to the antagonism they aroused among many Old Christians.

In that same article, Roth suggests that the number of deaths, public humiliations, and other indignities resulting from the Inquisition in Spain amounted to more than 340,000 people of all ages and more than 30,000 individuals in Portugal.

On July 15, 1834, the Spanish Inquisition was finally abolished. The Polish-Israeli scholar Benzion Netanyahu (1910–2012)—the father of current Israeli Prime Minister Benjamin Netanyahu (b. 1949) and the late Yonatan ("Yoni") Netanyahu (1946–76), a hero of the raid on Entebbe Airport in Uganda (July 3/4, 1976) to rescue hostages held by the Palestine Liberation Organization (PLO)—in his magnum opus, *The Origins of the Inquisition in Fifteenth Century Spain,* argues that what transpired in Spain laid the foundation for the racialist antisemitism of Nazism that ultimately resulted in the Holocaust.[14]

JEWISH MYSTICISM: KABBALAH AND ZOHAR

Having its origins, perhaps, in the biblical prophet Ezekiel, especially the first chapter, perhaps even earlier, mystical traditions have long held a place within the Jewish religious enterprise for those whose goal is a far closer contact with and experience of the God of Israel than the vast majority of Jews. While that associated with Ezekiel has been termed *Merkavah mysticism* (Hebrew, "chariot mysticism"), most Jews—and Christians—today know it as *Kabbalah* (Hebrew, "received tradition," though commonly spelled in Christian circles with a "C" rather than a "K"). It finds its fullest flowering during this period of Spanish or Sephardic religio-literary productivity associated with its most well-known text, the *Zohar* (Hebrew, "Book of Splendor"), an expansive and decidedly mystical biblical commentary said to have been authored in the thirteenth century by unknown writers. Moses de León (1240–1305) claimed its original author was the was the second-century Tannaitic teacher, Shimon bar Yochai, but scholarship has all but discounted this attribution. An alternative "vision" was and is that of Rabbi Isaac Luria (the *Ari*, Hebrew, "lion"; 1534–72) and is known to us today as Lurianic Kabbalah. Rabbi Ari never wrote his texts down; they are the result of his students' written notes of his oral lectures and discourses. (The Ari Synagogue in Safed/Tzfat, Israel, was built in his memory.) Hasidic Judaism, beginning in the eighteenth century in Eastern Europe under the inspiration of Rabbi Baal Shem Tov (Hebrew, "Master of the Good Name [of God]"; 1698–1760), is a further expansion of this mystical tradition.

Kabbalistic tradition for those so inclined is an attempt to explain the relationship between the God of Israel who exists outside creation and the universe itself which is understood to be a divine creation. It does so by interpreting biblical material for the initiated through four "fruits" of the "PaRDeS" method. (*Pardes* is the Hebrew word for orchard.) They are: (1) *pshat* or simple method; (2) *remez* or allegorical method; (3) *drash* or midrashic method; and (4) *sod* or mystical method. According to its devotees, the acquisition of such knowledge builds upon that which was transmitted orally by the patriarchs (Abraham, Isaac, Jacob, Moses), the prophets, and earlier generations of sages and scholars. The modern academic study of Jewish mysticism and kabbalistic literature and its adherents is the work of the late scholar at the Hebrew University of Jerusalem, Gershom Scholem (1897-1982).[15] American university professor Daniel Matt (b. 1950) is engaged in a multi-volume translation of the Zohar into modern English, replete with notes and commentary.[16]

KARAITES AND KARAISM

As has been the case throughout Jewish history, the story of the Jewish people from the pre-biblical and biblical period up until the present moment is one of competing factions (e.g., Jerusalemites and "Qumranites", Sadducces and Pharisees, Maimonists and anti-Maimonists, Mitnagdim (Hebrew, "Opponents") and Hasidim, Orthodox and Reform). So, too, down through the centuries, different schools and advocates of Jewish religious thought have competed for the attention of the religiously faithful.

This period under discussion is no exception with the appearance of a movement which rejected "Rabbinism" and its Talmud (by then only the Babylonian version and not the Palestinian one) and favored only the written texts of the Torah/Hebrew Bible/Old Testament—from the God of Israel to and through Moses to his successors—as the sole authority in matters of Jewish law and theology. The movement, still alive today though greatly diminished, is known as Karaism (from the Hebrew word *likro*/to read, i.e., literalism) and its followers Karaites ("literalists"). Its major founder was Anan ben David (715–811 CE), who rejected rabbinical law as divinely inspired, and thus the so-called "Oral Law" (Hebrew, *Torah she-be'al peh*/"Torah from the mouth") given to Moses at Mount Sinai as well. Scholars now contend that between the years 900 and 1200—its own "golden age"—saw the publication of numerous Karaite texts, most noticeably Jacob Qirqisani's (890–960 CE) *Kitab al-anwar wal-Maraqib* (Arabic, "Code of Karaite Law"). The late Karaite religious leader, Abraham Firkovitch (1787–1874) was, in addition, a major collector of Karaite manuscripts many of which are again being studied by scholars of Judaism today. While many of its practices are compatible with Rabbinic Judaism (e.g., *Kashut*/Jewish dietary observance—but do mix milk and meat; prayer more than once a day, though done in full prostration; wearing of tzitzit/fringes but differ on color scheme; both permit divorce, though Karaite law does not require the husband's affirmation), many are not (e.g., Karaite Jewish men do not wear *tefillin*/phylacteries; do not put up *mezzuzot*/encased scrolled Torah passages on their doorposts; and continue to follow biblical/ patrilineal descent). Today, it is estimated that 1,500 Karaites live in the United States, 30,000 in Israel, 1,200 in Ukraine, and far fewer numbers in such places as Istanbul, Turkey, Lithuania, and Russia. The Orthodox rabbinate in Israel and abroad, following matrilineal post-biblical tradition, maintains that the children of Karaite mothers are themselves Jews according to *Halakhah*/Jewish law.[17]

JEWISH EXPULSIONS AND DIASPORAS

During the period of the so-called Black Death (i.e., bubonic plague) of 1348 to 1349, which saw the death of millions of Europeans, the Jews were, again, seen as guilty of making it happen, part of a conspiratorial plot to destroy their hated enemies. Because in their ghettos Jews died in fewer numbers proportionately, the illiterate peasantry, observing this, attributed their own misery to the Jews. The truth, however, was quite different: because Jewish ritual behavior required both symbolic and literal handwashing before meals and full-body immersion at sacred times (pre-marriage for both men and women, conversion, at the conclusion of one's menstrual cycle, less so for a male after an nocturnal emission though encouraged), these simple religious acts may possibly have had a somewhat prophylactic effect, decreasing disease among the community, even if minimally.[18] However, for those without such knowledge, for whom Jewish religious practice was first and always a dark magic and mysterious other, their reading of such things was negatively different.

Thus, by the end of the fifteenth century, continuing into the sixteenth century, Jews had experienced expulsions from England (1290), France (1306), Italy (1524 and 1540), Spain and Portugal (1492 and 1493), and sporadically from Germany and Bohemia-Moravia. Only in Poland was the situation reversed.

NOTES

1   The "redemption of captives" (Hebrew, *pidyon shevuyim*) is among the highest of Jewish moral and ethical responsibilities and is reflected in numerous biblical (e.g., Vayikra/Leviticus 19:16 and 18; Devarim/Deuteronomy 15:7) and rabbinic texts (e.g., BT Bava Batra 8b), and elevated importantly in the Jewish legal tradition (*Halakhah*: *Shulchan Aruch*, Yoreh De'ah, 252:4 and 253:3). Historically, taking the form of a bribe (Hebrew, *kofer*) is not allowed under Jewish law. However, the modern state of Israel found itself addressing this reality over the issue of prisoner exchange, the most well-known example is soldier Gilad Shalit, captured by Palestinian militants in 2006, whom the Israeli government "swapped" for 1,207 Palestinian prisoners to gain his release in 2011.

2   Though questions remain as to its dating, locales of implementation, authorship, authority, and authenticity, its various iterations include: (1) prohibitions against the building of new synagogues; (2) the raising of Jewish voices at Muslim

prayer times; and (3) the requirement to wear distinctive garments (belts and turbans) to distinguish Jews (and others) from Arabs and Muslims.

3   A beautiful translation of *Keter Malchut* is that by David R. Slavitt, Solomon ibn Gabirol, *A Crown for the King* (New York, NY, and Oxford: Oxford University Press, 1998).

4   An important early book on the subject is that of Benjamin N. Nelson, *The Idea of Usury: From Tribal Brotherhood to Universal Otherhood* (Princeton, NJ: Princeton University Press, 1949). See, also: Charles R. Geisst, *Beggar Thy Neighbor: A History of Usury and Debt* (Philadelphia: University of Pennsylvania Press, 2013); and Rowan Dorin, *No Return: Jews, Christian Usurers, and the Spread of Mass Expulsion in Medieval Europe* (Princeton, NJ: Princeton University Press, 2023).

5   See Steven Leonard Jacobs, "Blood on Our Heads: A Jewish Response to Saint Matthew," in Tod Linafelt (ed.), *A Shadow of Glory: Reading the New Testament After the Holocaust* (London and New York, NY: Routledge, 2002), 57–67.

6   A serious scholarly examination of this text is that of Michael Meerson and Peter Schäfer (eds. and trans.), *Toledot Yeshu: The Life Story of Jesus* (Tübingen: Mohr Siebeck, 2014), Volume 1: Introduction and Translation, Volume 2: Critical Edition; and Peter Schäfer, Michael Meerson, and Yaacov Deutsch (eds.), *Toledot Yeshu: ("The Life Story of Jesus") Revisited* (Tübingen: Mohr Siebeck, 2011).

7   See, importantly, David Biale, *Blood and Belief: The Circulation of a Symbol between Jews and Christians* (Berkeley: University of California Press, 2007).

8   See R. Po-Chia Hsia, *Trent 1475: Stories of a Ritual Murder Trial* (New Haven, CT, and London: Yale University Press, 1992).

9   Much of this material, somewhat revised, is taken from the author's *Antisemitism: Exploring the Issues* (Santa Barbara: ABC-CLIO, 2020), 18–20 and 33–35.

10 Worth examining is Yitzhak Baer, *A History of the Jews in Christian Spain*, trans. Louis Schoffman, 2 vols. (Philadelphia, PA: Jewish Publication Society, 1961).

11 The English poet Robert Browning (1812–1889) composed a poem in tribute entitled "Rabbi Ben Ezra."

12 See, for example: Nina Caputo and Liz Clarke, *Debating Truth: The Barcelona Disputation of 1263: A Graphic History* (New York, NY: Oxford University Press, 2017); and Hyam Maccoby, *Judaism on Trial: Jewish-Christian Disputations in the Middle Ages* (Oxford and Portland, OR: Littman Library of Jewish Civilization, 1993).

13 Simon Wiesenthal, *Sails of Hope: The Secret Mission of Christopher Columbus* (New York, NY: Macmillan, 1973).

14 Jacobs, *Antisemitism*, 127–9. See, also: José Faur, *In the Shadow of History: Jews and Conversos at the Dawn of Modernity* (Albany: State University of New York Press, 1992); James Reston, Jr., *Dogs of God: Columbus, the Inquisition, and the Defeat of the Moors* (New York, NY: Doubleday, 2005); and Cecil Roth, *A History of the Marranos* (New York, NY: Sepher-Hermon Press 1974). For those who would wish to read fictional portrayals of these events, see: Marcos Aguinis, *Against the Inquisition*, trans. Carolina de Robertis (Amazon Crossing, 2018); Adam Gidwitz, *The Inquisitor's Tale, Or, The Three Magical Children and Their Holy Dog* (New York, NY: Dutton Children's Books, 2018); Noah Gordon, *The Last Jew* (New York, NY: St. Martin's Griffin, 2000); and Richard Zimler, *The Last Kabbalist of Lisbon* (New York, NY: Overlook Press, 2000).

15 For example, Gershom Scholem, *Major Trends in Jewish Mysticism* (New York, NY: Schocken Books, 1995).

16 Daniel Matt, *Zohar: Annotated and Explained* (Woodstock, VT: SkyLight Paths, 2002).

17 For a further look into Karaite Judaism, see: Yoseif Yaron, *An Introduction to Karaite Judaism: History, Theology, Practice, and Custom* (Troy, NY: al-Qirqisani Center for the Promotion of Karaite Studies, 2003); Daniel J. Lasker, *Karaism: An Introduction to the Oldest Surviving Alternative Judaism* (London: Littman Library of Jewish Civilization, 2022); and William Harris Rule, *History of the Karaite Jews* (London: Longmans, Green, and Co., 1870; reprint: Lexington: Loeb Classical Library, 2016).

18 See Joshua Trachtenberg, *The Devil and the Jews: The Medieval Conception of the Jew and Its Relation to Modern Anti-Semitism* (Philadelphia, PA: Jewish Publication Society, 2002 [reprint]), and Tzafrir Barzilay, *Poisoned Wells: Accusations, Persecution, and Minorities in Medieval Europe, 1321–1422* (Philadelphia: University of Pennsylvania Press, 2022).

9

THE SIXTEENTH AND SEVENTEENTH CENTURIES: THE MIDDLE AGES AND TRANSITIONS

With the expulsion of Jews from both Spain and, later, Portugal, Jews turned both East and West in their search for safe havens. In the East, in the Ottoman Empire, specifically Turkey and the land of Israel (Palestine), Jewish communities began to flourish both economically and religiously by the increase of their populations. In the West, in Germany, the Netherlands, and England (where in 1655 they were formally invited to return after having been expelled in 1290), Jewish communities began to thrive. In the Commonwealth of Poland–Lithuania, where Jews had by and large avoided the calamities of expulsions and resettlements, the Jewish communities continued their positive ascendancy. Prior to the time of the massacres initiated by the Hetman of the Ukrainian Cossacks, Bohdan Khmelnytsky (1595–1657) (in his successful attacks on the Polish aristocracy of the Commonwealth [1648–54] possibly as many as 100,000 Jews were murdered in 1648 and 1649), the Jews were sufficiently well-organized to convene the "Council of the Four Lands" (Hebrew, *Va'ad Arba Artzot*), dividing their lands of residence into four quadrants, with leaders from each sector meeting annually to discuss and finalize civil, political, economic, and religious matters.

INTERNAL JEWISH DYNAMICS

The Jews of the Netherlands also found a tolerant and safe port after fleeing Spain and Portugal. As the community began to grow and develop both economically and religiously, conservative parties began to assume control, such that, by the time of the philosopher Benedict (Baruch) de Spinoza, whose views were perceived as communally threatening, excommunication (Hebrew, *cherem*) was the only option.

WHY SO? BARUCH SPINOZA AND URIEL DA COSTA

Born into the Sephardic community of Amsterdam in 1632, Spinoza's rationalist turn of mind led him to reject the literalist understanding of the Torah as coming directly from the God of Israel through Moses rather than a humanly-crafted set of texts (though, Hebraically knowledgeable, he would write a valued text on Hebrew grammar), and to reject the historically traditional Judaic view of that same God as interacting with and parochially concerned with the Jews. Thus, for him, at least, the practices of Jewish ritual behavior became increasingly null and void. As regards his biblical views, one may, perhaps, rightly consider him the "father" of modern, objective, and secularized biblical or "higher criticism" (which British-American Judaic scholar Solomon Schechter [1847–1915] would go on to label "higher antisemitism"). As a consequence, he was excommunicated from both the Jewish community and his own family, which appears to have troubled him little, if at all— he relocated from Amsterdam to Voorburg. (On the "down low," however, he did manage to maintain some secretive contact with his family and they with him.) Interestingly and significantly, the harsh "ban of excommunication" against him, available to us in both its original language and appropriate translations, nowhere provides specifics with regard to his crimes, but, instead, refers only to "abominable heresies," and so we must conclude that both his actions and his writings, and, to a somewhat lesser degree, his public utterances, were perceived and understood as communally threatening to both its unity and potentially damaging to its reputation as relative newcomers. Both his masterwork, *Ethics*, especially Part I, and his *Theological-Political Treatise* would appear to confirm this assessment. In his *Ethics*, for example, he takes the position that good and evil are relative concepts, rather than intrinsic or divinely related and divinely revealed truths, and contingent on their own particularity (e.g., historical circumstance, locale, and/or community). Thus, for him, knowledge was threefold: experience or opinion, reason, and intuition (stemming from God), this last category refuting those who charged him with atheism even if his understanding differed from their own (i.e., a God who does not have personality and consciousness, nor intelligence, feeling or will, and one who does not engage in purposeful action).

By the time of his excommunication, Spinoza was seemingly already well-ensconced within a circle of like-minded persons who, perhaps, today we would characterize as radical Christian thinkers, writing and sharing their own ideas with him and others and he with them. It is to be noted, however, that formal conversion to Christianity was never part of Spinoza's agenda; although, ironically, he is buried in the churchyard cemetery of the Nieuwe Kerk ("New Church") in The Hague.

Rejecting both public adulation and university appointment, Spinoza preferred the ofttimes simple solitude of a lens grinder, and, quite possibly, it may very well have been glass dust which infected his lungs and precipitated his death at the early age of forty-four.

An equally tragic case is that of Portuguese philosopher, theologian and legalist, Uriel da Costa (1585–1640). Born a Roman Catholic, he learned of his Jewish roots and history, and began to take seriously *and literally* the words of the Torah. Living first in Venice, Italy, and later in Hamburg, Germany, he came to reject both the legalism and ritualism of the rabbinic leadership and community, which resulted in his excommunication before his arrival in Amsterdam, whose own rabbinic leadership found itself initially devoid of options and affirmed the *cherem*. Finding this exilic punishment too much to bear, he formally underwent a publicly humiliating ceremony of reconciliation (thirty-nine lashes and having members of the community literally walk on and over him) and was accepted back into the community in 1633. It would ultimately prove too much for him, as he wrote in his autobiography, *Exemplar Humanae Vitae* ("Example of a Human Life"), and would ultimately lead to his suicide seven years later.[1]

YOSEF KARO AND MOSES ISSERLES

In the East, in the land of Israel (Palestine), however, two significant events took place in the mountain city of Safed (Hebrew, Tzfat), "the city of the mystics." Rabbi Yosef Karo (1488–1575), born in Turkey, had begun a reorganization with commentary of the legal materials of Judaism, *Beth Yosef* (Hebrew for "House of Joseph"), which he completed and published in 1559. Also realizing the need for an abstract of his text for those whose education did not permit them the time to pore over such materials, he produced the *Shulchan Aruch* (Hebrew for "Set/ Prepared Table") of the laws themselves, topically arranged, and which remains even today *the* code of Jewish laws among the devout. His larger work, however, was criticized by the leading Polish rabbi of the day, Moses Isserles (1532–72), who regarded its commentaries as reflecting only a Sephardic or Spanish bias without taking into consideration the differences in customs and traditions of the Ashkenazic or Germanic communities. He was also concerned that Karo's *Shulchan Aruch* code of Jewish laws reflected only this same Sephardic orientation as well. Thus, he would go on to write notes and glosses to many of Karo's laws, which became known as *Hamapah* ("The Tablecloth"). Today, and for the last five hundred years, all Hebrew, English and other language editions of the *Shulchan Aruch* are published with both the work of Karo and the additions of Isserles and thus provide both Sephardic and Ashkenazic Jews with an invaluable resource in their practices of Judaism, despite, at times, their differences (e.g., Sephardic Jews eat rice and beans during Pesach/Passover; Ashkenazic Jews do not).

Because of the profound respect with which he was held as a Talmudic authority and his legal/halakhic authority, Isserles was also a member of the governing Council of the Four Lands.

THE COUNCIL OF THE FOUR LANDS

From approximately 1650 until 1764, the Jewish communities (Hebrew plural, *kehillot*; singular, *kehillah*) of "Greater Poland" (including Lithuania), "Lesser Poland," Galicia (and Podolia), and Volhynia were governed by a delegate-elected and appointed authority which met annually (and, if necessary, semi-annually) to set the parameters for such things as internal and external taxation and other civil, legal, and administrative matters, such as disputes between various *kehillot*, ritual and other religious matters of concern, especially dietary issues relating to *kashrut*, political issues, and the like. Especially noteworthy was its ongoing combat against antisemitism and, most especially, the false accusation of the blood libel addressed in the previous chapter. Within the spectrum of broader authoritative Polish governing and state structures, it was reasonably self-governing and autonomous. In 1764, however, its failure to deliver the requisite, agreed-upon taxes led to calls for its dissolution in the Polish diet (parliament) and it was dissolved.

The famous/infamous Emden–Eybeschütz controversy in the aftermath of Sabbatei Sevi came to the fore during this period, as did the expressed concerns regarding Jacob Frank and his followers and Frankism as a religious movement (more of which below). (Many of the latter would convert to Roman Catholicism as a result of what they saw and experienced as persecution and harassment.) The council was also the scene of early debates vis-à-vis Hasidism and its seeming encroachment on rabbinic authority.

THE KHMELNYTSKY MASSACRES

Having already endured the past traumas of Egyptian slavery, the Assyrian incursion, the Babylonian exile, the Roman destruction of the Second Temple, the Jewish people is confronted yet again with a major holocaust-like event: the destruction in 1648 and 1649 and afterward of perhaps as many as 100,000 Jews throughout Poland, Lithuania, and Ukraine as a result of the Ukrainian cossack and serf uprising led by Hetman Bohdan Khmelnytsky. (The actual number of deaths is, however, debated, with a lowest figure of "only" 18,000–20,000, most likely, to a middle figure of 40,000–50,000—still far too many innocent Jewish lives unnecessarily murdered to be a source of comfort to any reader.) The uprising itself was not initially a Jewish pogrom, despite an antisemitic history which viewed Jews as rapacious oppressors contemptuous of Orthodox Christianity, but, rather, one seeking the political and economic overthrow of a Polish landed and governing aristocracy which exploited its own population and cared little, if at all, about the lives of its subjects. Its impact, however, upon its Jewish victims continues to resonate today, with some religious Jews continuing to argue that it was a form of divine punishment, while others regard it as a prelude to the Holocaust/Shoah of the twentieth century. Significantly, despite the horrific memories of what had transpired in the not-too-distant past, by the 1800s, this same area saw a densely populated Jewish population unrivalled anywhere else in the world.

In Ukraine itself, Khmelnytsky continues to be viewed by the majority as a national hero, even if his legacy remains contested, to the dismay of Jews resident there and worldwide. His portrait appears, for example, on the five hryvnia banknote and a massive statue of him was erected in 1905 in Kyiv.

FURTHER CHRISTIAN PERSECUTIONS

The Protestant Reformation of the sixteenth century, which ultimately resulted in a reduction in the political and religious power of the Roman Catholic church and its splintering into various non-Catholic sects (e.g., Calvinists, Anabaptists, Anglicans, and Lutherans), equally saw these various communities and their leaders ambivalent both about their relationship with Jews and the role, place, and function of Jewish communities and persons in this new European world. The case of Roman Catholic monk, priest, and professor, Martin Luther (1483–1546)—said to be the "father" of the Reformation with his protest of "Ninety-five Theses" supposedly nailed to the church door in Wittenberg, Germany, in 1517—is an excellent case in point. Initially, his attitude toward Jews was positive, attacking his own Catholic church for its hateful and demeaning approach to the conversion of Jews in his lesser-known text, *That Jesus Was Born a Jew* (1523). Fully expecting them to convert when a hand was proffered in love, his attitude toward them changed dramatically when they did not. In 1543, he published *Von den Juden und ihren Lügen* (*On the Jews and Their Lies*), considered today among the most antisemitic texts ever written, second only to that of Adolf Hitler's *Mein Kampf*, and rivalled perhaps by the nineteenth-century Russian forgery, *The Protocols of the Learned Elders of Zion*, which scurrilously attacked not only Jews but religious Judaism, the Talmud, and synagogue buildings as well.

MARTIN LUTHER AND THE JEWS

Luther, the "Father of the Protestant Reformation" and, more specifically, the founder of what would later be called the Lutheran religious tradition ("Lutheranism"), was a German Roman Catholic professor of theology, a priest, a monk, and a composer of liturgical hymns. Propelled by his sharp intellect, coupled with a confrontational personality, his initial agenda may be said to have been threefold: (1) winning those who were not yet committed to the Christ to become so; (2) reforming what he regarded as a major violation of Catholic morals and ethics, the selling of indulgences by priests and bishops (payments to the church to purchase exemptions from punishment [penance] for some types of sin); and (3) reaching out the hand of friendship and love to Jews with the desire to convert them to Christianity. His unrelenting critiques of the Catholic church ultimately led to his excommunication in 1521, largely the result of the publication of his "Ninety-five Theses," the original title of which was the "Disputation of Martin Luther on the Power and Efficacy of Indulgences." (The historicity of Luther supposedly nailing the theses to the front door of the church at Wittenberg, Germany, cannot, however, be supported.)

Luther's continuing failure to convert Jews—even after the publication of his favorable text, *That Jesus Christ Was Born a Jew*—resulted in two overtly antisemitic texts, *On the Jews and Their Lies* (a 65,000-word treatise) and *Of the Unknowable Name and the Generations of Christ*, in 1543, three years before his death. Although he had hoped for their ultimate conversion, he had long believed the Jews guilty of the death of the Christ and thus, in his eyes, deserved their history of suffering and worse, though his personal contact with Jews, including rabbis, was minimal. The former text has served as a hateful source for antisemitism ever since, up to and including the period of Nazi terror and the Holocaust during the Second World War.

After its initial publication, *On the Jews and Their Lies* evoked both popular support and scholarly condemnation. His final sermon series, delivered three days before his death, also included an attack on the stubbornness of the Jews and his call to have them expelled from German lands; it was entitled *Admonition against the Jews*. Those who continue to reject this idea of Luther's antisemitism as foundational to all subsequent expressions of it argue regularly that his strong disagreements with Jews were theological and not the racial hatred into which antisemitism would evolve.

The most well-known excerpt of *On the Jews and Their Lies* remains his seven recommendations:

- First, to set fire to their synagogues or schools and to bury and cover with dirt whatever will not burn so that no man will ever again see a stone or cinder of them.
- Second, I advise that their houses also be razed and destroyed.
- Third, I advise that all their prayer books and Talmudic writings, in which such idolatry, lies, cursing and blasphemy are taught, be taken from them.
- Fourth, I advise that their rabbis be forbidden to teach henceforth on pain of loss of life and limb.
- Fifth, I advise that safe conduct on their highways be abandoned completely for Jews.

- Sixth, I advise that usury [the action or practice of lending money at unreasonably high rates of interest] be prohibited to them, and that all cash and treasure of silver and gold be taken from them and put aside for safekeeping.
- Seventh, I commend putting a flail, an ax, a hoe, a spade, a distaff, or a spindle into the hands of young, strong Jews and Jewesses and letting them earn their bread in the sweat of their brow, as was imposed on the children of Adam. [Genesis 3:19: "By the sweat of your brow will you have food to eat until you return to the ground from which you were made."]

As a thinker strongly committed to his faith, Luther's belief was that salvation through faith in the Christ was an act of grace, and no work, no matter how positive or benevolent, could alter that reality. One consequence of that commitment was his rejection of the pope as the only authoritative interpreter of the Old and New Testaments. For Luther, neither the pope nor the church was infallible. In 1525, he found himself in opposition to the Peasants' War and wrote *Against the Murderous, Thieving Hordes of Peasants* because of their numerous acts of violence. That opposition caused him to lose the support of many, even as his notoriety as an important religious person was growing. That same year he married former nun Katharina von Bora, having long condemned celibacy. In 1522, he had published his German translation of the New Testament, and the year after, along with his collaborators, he published his translation of the Old Testament, acknowledging all the while that his Hebrew language skills were rather poor at best and his Greek little better, forcing him in both cases to rely on others as collaborators. Since the 1980s, however, the various international Lutheran denominations have repudiated Luther's antisemitism and sought both forgiveness and reconciliation with Jews for his sins, noting consistently that his hateful rhetoric has never been part of official Lutheran theological or liturgical texts.[2]

FALSE MESSIAHS

Into the gloom, depression, and darkness of the Jewish communities of this period came those who offered a seeming way out, falsely, however. It is no accident that Jewish and other historians refer to this period as the "Age of the False Messiahs," the two most well-known being Sabbatai Sevi (1626– 76) and Jacob Frank (1726–91). The former was said to have been born in

Turkey and hailed by both Sephardic and Ashkenazic Jews as the long-awaited Messiah. Many of them surrendered their earthly goods to join him on his trek back to the Holy Land of Israel. Arriving back in Turkey, he was first welcomed by the Sultan as leader of the Jews, but, when informed that his supposed "true agenda" was the Sultan's overthrow—most likely by a dissident in Sevi's own ranks—he was cast into prison where he languished until given the choice of conversion to Islam or the sword. He chose Islam and wrote himself out of Jewish history. (Many of his followers saw the "hand of God" in his decision and followed him into Islam while retaining many of their Jewish religious practices. Their followers are said to have existed in the Crimea until the 1800s.)

SABBATAI SEVI, SABBATEANS, AND DÖNME

Sevi (or Tzvi or Zevi) was born into the Ottoman Empire in 1626 and thought to be of Romaniote origin, a Sephardic subset of Jews with a different historical tradition. Proclaimed by himself and others to be the long-awaited Jewish messiah by both Sephardic and Ashkenazic Jews during a difficult time for both communities, he would initially amass a large following who were prepared to surrender their earthly belongings and be led triumphantly back to the land of Israel. (According to one mystical understanding, the Messiah would be the seventh son of a seventh son born on the Sabbath; Sevi met that criterion.) His proclamation of the four-lettered Holy Name of God (the Tetragrammaton), historically reserved for the high priest in the Temple in Jerusalem on Yom Kippur (the Day of Atonement), and other pronouncements—including his ability to fly and see visions of God—led to his excommunication. It did not deter him or his followers.

Arriving back in Constantinople (Istanbul) in 1666 after unsuccessful stays in Jerusalem and Salonica and a contentious stay in Smyrna, he was initially welcomed by the Sultan Mehmed IV (1642–93). However, a disgruntled follower was able to convince the Sultan's inner circle that Sevi was plotting an insurrection and the Sultan's overthrow and he was imprisoned for three years, after which the Grand Vizier Köprülüzade Fazil Ahmed Pasha (1635–76) gave him the choice of conversion to Islam or death, and he, wisely or not, chose the former. Approximately three hundred families—seeing the work of God in this decision—followed him into Islam, instituted a merged religious tradition and became known as Sabbateans, many of whom would become known as Dönme

149

("Converts," better "Apostates"), themselves later splitting into three sub-communities. Most of his followers were, however, devastated by his decision and found themselves ridiculed by both Christians and Muslims in the Empire.

The original Sabbateans kept largely to themselves; some practicing Islam in public, while secretly retaining Jewish religious practices in private. In many Jewish communities, both inside and outside the Empire, there were calls for their excommunication as rabbinic authorities regarded these groups and their practices as heretical. For example, in 1725, the Ashkenazic Beit Din (Rabbinic Court) of Amsterdam issued such a *cherem*.

THE EMDEN–EYBESCHÜTZ CONTROVERSY

In 1751, Rabbi Jacob Emden accused Rabbi Jonathan Eybeschütz of Altona, Hamburg, and Wandsbek of being a Sabbatean vis-à-vis a reading of certain amulets or mystical/magical charms he was issuing, which Emden claimed were validating Sevi's messianic pretentions. He went so far as to call for Eybeschütz's excommunication and that of his followers, including Eybeschütz's own younger son, Wolf Jonas Benjamin (1740–1806), who would later publicly affirm his own Sabbateanism. Eybeschütz initially denied this attack, although the latest scholarship has validated that Emden's attack and assessment may have been correct.

Today, the Dönme continue to exist in Turkey, although actual numbers are hard to obtain. As regards their practices and beliefs, they remain something of a "closed society," marrying within their own ranks and practicing a merged Judaic-Islamic religious tradition with elements of both Jewish Kabbalistic and Islamic Sufi mystical traditions as well. Their very closedness has led to harassment akin to antisemitism, especially among those Islamists who continue to call for a re-Islamization of modern Turkey.

JACOB FRANK, EVE FRANK, FRANKISTS, AND FRANKISM

More ignominious, however, was Polish-born Jacob Frank (Jakub Józef Lejbowicz), the son of a self-professed Sabbatean, who convinced some that he was the reincarnation of both Sevi and King David as well as the biblical patriarch Jacob. Offering an interpretation of both Judaism and

Christianity, he tried to merge them, attempting to incorporate the New Testament into the world of the Jews, and, together with his followers, suggested that the way to God was through sin, most prominently sexual excesses. Encouraging his followers to have themselves baptized, he himself did so in 1759. (By 1790, one year before his death, approximately 26,000 Jews were baptized in Poland.) Excommunicated by the rabbinic authorities, his followers were later absorbed into the Roman Catholic church after his death. His followers would practice a religious tradition that today we would label "Frankism," and, at its height, would claim approximately 50,000 followers in Poland, Central and Eastern Europe.

Arrested in 1760 on charges of heresy, Frank spent the next thirteen years in prison. Upon his release he lived first in Brno, Moravia, then Vienna, Austria, and, finally, Offenbach, Germany, where his followers supported him and where he lived quite regally, assuming the title "Baron of Offenbach." Upon his death, his daughter Eve (1754–1816) assumed the mantle of leadership, but following the Napoleonic Wars (1803–15) her fortunes dwindled considerably, and she died in penury.

Rounding out this chapter, we would be remiss were we to argue that Sevi and Frank were the only contenders for the title of Jewish Messiah (Hebrew, *mashiach*, "anointed one") in Jewish history. Throughout history, many such claimants have appeared—some so designated by themselves, others by others. Among them are the following:

- Jesus of Nazareth (4 BCE–30/33 CE), proclaimed as such by his followers
- Simon bar Kokhba (d. 135 CE), proclaimed as such by Rabbi Akiva (50 CE–135 CE)
- Moses of Crete (fifth century CE), proclaimed by others
- David Alroy (d. 1160), self-proclaimed
- Abraham ben Samuel Abulafia (1240–1291), proclaimed by himself and others
- David Reubeni (1490–1541), proclaimed by others
- Mordecai Mokia (1650–1729), self-proclaimed
- Jacob Querido (d. 1690), proclaimed by others
- Abraham Miguel Cardoso (*c.* 1626–1706), self-proclaimed
- Menachem Mendel Schneerson (1902–1994), proclaimed today by some of his Lubavitch Hasidic followers as the Messiah.[3]

* * *

By the end of this period, various Western nations, to the degree to which the "plight of the Jews" was part of their political agenda, began to

Steven Leonard Jacobs

address issues of toleration and interaction with those Jewish communities resident in their midst. In France, Germany, England, and the Netherlands, conversations were beginning to take place about the Jews as the movement towards modernity continued.

NOTES

1 Suicide remains a difficult concept in Judaic religion. A true suicide has desecrated the body as "holy vessel" (biblically understood as having been created "in the image of God") and thus cannot be buried in a Jewish cemetery, although a case of questionable or doubtful suicide can, but only by the outer fence of the cemetery. Talmudically, the rabbis attempted to create a barrier against proclaiming true suicides, arguing that one must state one's intentions to do so publicly in the presence of at least two knowledgeable witnesses who inform him/her that it contravenes Jewish law and thus its consequences. The candidate would, again, publicly reject such overtures and proceed towards his/her death. The case of martyrdom—those who die by their own hand rather than profane their faith, *al kiddushat ha-Shem* (for the sanctification of the Holy Name of God)—especially during the Middle Ages throughout Europe and even earlier (the case of the Zealots at Masada under Eliezer ben Yair [d. 73/74 CE] during the Roman period) and later during the Holocaust/Shoah—remains problematic religiously.

2 Largely taken from Jacobs, *Antisemitism*, 81–83, it has been edited somewhat for this text. See, also: Mark U. Edwards, *Luther's Last Battles: Politics and Polemics, 1531–46* (Ithaca, NY: Cornell University Press, 1983); Eric W. Gritsch, *Martin Luther's Anti-Semitism: Against His Better Judgment* (Grand Rapids, MI: William B. Eerdmans, 2012); Thomas Kaufmann, *Luther's Jews: A Journey into Anti-Semitism*, trans. Leslie Sharpe and Jeremy Noakes (Oxford: Oxford University Press, 2017); Robert Michael, *Holy Hatred: Christianity, Antisemitism, and the Holocaust* (New York, NY: Palgrave Macmillan, 2006); William Nichols, *Christian Antisemitism: A History of Hate* (Northvale, NJ: Jason Aronson, 1995); Heiko A. Oberman, *The Roots of Anti-Semitism in the Age of Renaissance and Reformation* (Philadelphia, PA: Fortress Press, 1984); Christopher J. Probst, *Demonizing the Jews: Luther and the Protestant Church in Nazi Germany* (Bloomington: Indiana University Press, 2012); Richard Steigmann-Gall, *The Holy Reich: Nazi Conceptions of Christianity, 1919–1945* (Cambridge: Cambridge University Press, 2003); and Neelak S. Tjernagel, *Martin Luther and the Jewish People* (Milwaukee, WI: Northwestern Publishing House, 1985).

3 And there were others! Christianity, too, has had its share of "false messiahs" following the death of the Christ.

10

THE EIGHTEENTH AND NINETEENTH CENTURIES: PRE-MODERNITY TO MODERNITY

A simple division of Jewish history is the following: (1) the pre-biblical and biblical period (to 70 CE); (2) the post-biblical or rabbinic period (to 1791); and (3) the modern period (1791 to the present). Why so? Because the year 1791, coincident with the French Revolution (1789–99), saw the Jews of France granted the right to vote, and, with it, their status as citizens for the first time since leaving their ancestral homeland dramatically changed. A revolution in the West, even if not of their own making, had truly begun.

Citizenship, however, did not equate with either *integration* (successfully maintaining one's parochial identity) or *assimilation* (surrendering one's parochial identity), though the latter remains worrisome even today for Jews of all persuasions in enlightened democratic societies, i.e., the question of the preservation of a unique identity versus participation in the larger society and the loss of that identity.

In 1806, Emperor Napoleon Bonaparte (1769–1821) convened an "Assembly of Jewish Notables" out of which grew the Sanhedrin convened in 1807, both of which effectively rendered null and void any notion of Judaism as a *national* identity rather than a *religious* identity and enabled the Jews of France to see themselves as fully part of the French Republic, even if less than fully accepted by their post-ghetto neighbors. Other Jewish communities in both Europe and the United States—and elsewhere—would and continue to follow this model.

Steven Leonard Jacobs

FRANCE AND THE ASSEMBLY OF JEWISH NOTABLES:
THE GRAND SANHEDRIN

Twelve questions were presented to those assembled. After a somewhat lengthy "Declaration" addressed to "the sacred person of His Imperial and Royal Majesty" (Bonaparte), they responded:

1. Is it lawful for Jews to have more than one wife? Answer: *It is not lawful for Jews to marry more than one wife; in all European countries they conform to the general practice marrying only one.*
2. Is divorce allowed by the Jewish religion? Is divorce valid, although pronounced not by courts of justice but by virtue of laws in contradiction to the French code? Answer: *Repudiation* [of marriage] *is allowed by the law of Moses, but it is not valid if not previously pronounced by the French code.*
3. May a Jewess [*sic*] marry a Christian, or may a Jew marry a Christian woman? Or does Jewish law order that the Jews should only intermarry among themselves? Answer: *The law does not say that a Jewess cannot marry a Christian, nor a Jew a Christian woman; nor does it state that the Jews can only marry among themselves.*
4. In the eyes of Jews are Frenchmen not of the Jewish religion considered as brethren or as strangers? Answer: *In the eyes of Jews Frenchmen are their brethren and are not strangers.*
5. What conduct does Jewish law prescribe toward Frenchmen not of the Jewish religion? Answer: *The line of conduct prescribed towards Frenchmen not of our religion is the same as that prescribed between Jews themselves; we admit of no differences but that of worshipping the Supreme Being everyone in his own way.*
6. Do Jews born in France, and treated by the laws as French citizens, consider France their country? Are they bound to defend it? Are they bound to obey the laws and to conform to the dispositions of the civil code? Answer: *Men who have adopted a country, who have resided in it these many generations . . . cannot but consider themselves as Frenchmen in France; and they consider as equally sacred and honorable the bounded duty of defending their country.*
7. Who names the rabbis? Answer: *Since the revolution, the majority of the chiefs of families name the rabbi, wherever there is a sufficient number of Jews to maintain one, after previous inquiries as to the morality and learning of the candidate.*

8. What police jurisdiction do rabbis exercise among the Jews? What judicial police power do they enjoy among them? Answer: *The rabbis exercise no manner of police jurisdiction among the Jews.*
9. Are these forms of election, and that police jurisdiction, regulated by law, or are they only sanctified by custom? Answer: *Neither such jurisdiction, nor the forms of the elections, could be said to be sanctioned by law; they should be attributed solely to custom.*
10. Are there professions which the law of the Jews forbids them from exercising? Answer: *There are none.*
11. Does the law forbid the Jews from taking usury from their brethren? Answer: *The Hebrew word neshekh has been improperly translated by the word usury; in the Hebrew language it means interest of any kind, and not usurious interest. It cannot then be taken in the meaning now given to the word usury.*
12. Does it forbid or does it allow Jews to take usury from strangers? Answer: *We are generally forbidden, always on the score of charity, to lend upon interest to our fellow citizens of different persuasions, as well as to our fellow Jews.*

PERIOD OF JEWISH EMANCIPATION

With the ghetto walls down after many centuries of isolation and closed-off existence, Jews now found themselves admitted to universities and entering professions heretofore denied them. For some, the heady excitement proved too much, and, during the eighteenth century, it is estimated that as many as 200,000 Jews renounced the specifics of their Jewish identity in favor of the larger and largely Christian world of Western society.

Though emancipation of the Jews, hastened by the European Enlightenment of the eighteenth century, which was, in many ways, the final blow to the political power of the Roman Catholic church, would not come to Germany or England until the 1850s, one truly outstanding Jew who saw the possibilities of successfully bridging the gulf was the philosopher Moses Mendelssohn (1729–86) of Berlin. For him and others like him, it was possible to be a devout and religiously practicing Jew at home and an intellectual man of the world outside. Although somewhat deformed by his hunchback, the brilliance of his intellect and oratory caused those who interacted with him to pay it little mind. His own children, however, were unable to carry this dual torch; four of his six children converted to Christianity.

Steven Leonard Jacobs

MOSES MENDELSSOHN

By virtue of his own intellect coupled with both his philosophical leaning and framed by his Jewish commitments, Mendelssohn stands tall as the "herald" of the Jewish Enlightenment (*Haskalah*; began in Germany and spread quickly eastward to Poland and Russia) and, perhaps, equal in stature to Moses Maimonides generations earlier. Some non-Jews, it was said within the circles with which he interacted, even went so far as to call him "the Jewish Socrates" and/or "the Jewish Plato."

His contributions to the arrival of Jewish modernity were both significant and unique. First off was his translation of the Torah/Hebrew Bible/Old Testament into German (using Hebrew characters), thus moving Jews from their primary language of Yiddish into German and enabling them to interact with the larger society and culture. (Though he titled his translation *N'tivot Ha-shalom*/"The Paths to Peace," it was more widely known as *Bi'ur*/"Explanation" because of the accompanying explanations found on every page. His own cousin, Orthodox rabbi Samson Raphael Hirsch [1808–88], was highly critical of his translation.) Second was the publication in 1783 of his book, *Jerusalem, or On Religious Power and Judaism*, in which he argued that religious Judaism was compatible with good citizenship, was a rational religion, and thus compatible with the values of the Enlightenment as well. He also wrote that, as a faith community, Jews were not bound to a coercive religious authority, and that traditional Jewish law (*Halakhah*) was a highly moral code of conduct consistent in the main with the larger society's values. There were, however, among his most vocal Orthodox critics, those who argued that Mendelssohn's vaunting of the value of reason above all else denied the supremacy of faith, the Torah's eternality coming from the God of Israel, and God's direct involvement through its rabbinic spokesmen and their own understanding of Jewish law as God's interactive will made manifest in real and concrete terms for the Jewish people.

To some degree, because of his thinking and his own interactions with German society at large, Mendelssohn was committed to a certain brotherhood and universalism vis-à-vis the totality of humanity. This became real when the German playwright, Gotthold Ephraim Lessing (1729–81) wrote his famous play, *Nathan the Wise* (1779), and modeled his main character on Mendelssohn.

* * *

A DARK TURN

The great Jewish community of Poland–Lithuania would suffer from the breakup of the land by Austria in 1772, Czarist Russia in 1773, and Prussia in 1795. What had been a thriving and united population was now divided, its communal and organizational structure shrunk, and dramatically reorganized on a far smaller scale. Czarist Russia, which annexed the largest land area, also annexed the largest Jewish population, for which it was neither desirous nor prepared. Its monarchy, its peasantry, and its Russian Orthodox church vacillated between limited acceptance and outright hostility. Ultimately, hostility won out, and, by the end of the period, Jewish residence had become restricted to what became known as the "Pale of Settlement." Most of Russia's Jews found themselves unable to travel great distances for their livelihoods, occupationally restricted, and poor and threatened by an antisemitism that, by and large, they had not experienced in old Poland–Lithuania. They would later see the publication and wide dissemination of that most antisemitic of documents, *The Protocols of the Learned Elders of Zion* (1903).

THE PROTOCOLS OF THE LEARNED ELDERS OF ZION

As perhaps the world's most "successful" and notorious forgery, *The Protocols of the Learned Elders of Zion* supposedly describes a secret midnight cabal in an undisclosed Jewish cemetery somewhere in Europe, likely Prague, Czech Republic. In this alleged gathering, the unnamed chief rabbi informs his fellow rabbis of the "master plan" to subjugate the gentile world under Jewish monarchical hegemony and the twenty-four protocols that will enable them to do so (e.g., subverting the morals of gentiles, exercising economic and journalistic controls, destroying the religious basis of civilization, destroying the political and constitutional foundations of the various nation-states, and the like, which will all lead to the eventual coronation of a king in Jerusalem, a descendant of the Davidic line, to rule the world). In the main, scholars have concluded that the original text upon which the *Protocols* was based was French lawyer, Maurice Joly's (1829–78) 1864 satire, *Dialogue aux enfers entre Machiavel et Montesquieu ou la politique de Machiavel au XIXe siècle* ("The Dialogue in Hell between Machiavelli and Montesquieu"), about the French government under Louis Napoleon Bonaparte (1808–73), of whom Joly was a staunch opponent and severe critic. Additionally, a chapter of the 1868 novel *Der Schmuggler von Biarritz* ("The Smuggler of Biarritz") by German novelist Hermann Goedsche (1815–78), writing under the pseudonym Sir John Retcliffe, is also said to have contributed by providing the geographic locale for this supposed meeting and the actual "speech" of the rabbi. Both texts, not surprisingly, given the climate in Europe at the end of the nineteenth century, with conspirators and *agents provocateurs* everywhere, found their way to the attention of the Okhrana, the Russian secret police, and later became publicly available in *The Great within the Small: The Coming of the Anti-Christ and the Rule of Satan on Earth* by the dissident, and later disgraced, Russian Orthodox mystic, Sergei Nilus (1862–1929) in 1905. From these strange and perverse beginnings, the text as a stand-alone document has traveled the world. Translated into any number of languages, including Arabic and English (in 1919), the *Protocols* were discredited soon afterwards in 1921 by reporter Phillip Graves in *The Times* of London in three lengthy articles (August 16, 17, and 18) and later republished in booklet form under the title "The Truth about 'The Protocols': A Literary Forgery." The document itself would also be put on trial as a hate text in Berne, Switzerland, between 1934 and 1935, where the chief presiding judge termed the *Protocols* "ridiculous nonsense" and found them to be a forgery. Its most notorious English-language publication, however, appeared in the Henry Ford–owned newspaper, *The Dearborn Independent*, originally serialized between 1920 and 1922, and later published separately as *The International Jew: The World's Foremost Problem*, with a press run of 500,000 copies, which were distributed to Ford automobile dealerships throughout the United States (for which Ford, under coercion, later apologized and withdrew its publication). Adolf Hitler also included a reference to the authenticity of the *Protocols* in his political testament *Mein Kampf*:

> To what extent the whole existence of this people is based on continuous lies is shown incomparably by the Protocols of the Wise Men of Zion, so infinitely hated by the Jews. They are based on a forgery, the *Frankfurter Zeitung* moans and screams once every week: the best proof that they are authentic. What many Jews may do unconsciously is here consciously exposed. . . . Anyone who examines the historical development of the last hundred years will at once understand the screaming of the Jewish press. For once this book becomes the common property of a people, the Jewish menace may be considered as broken.[1]

Despite its obvious forgery, the *Protocols* remains a staple of the modern antisemitic world and is still available in a variety of languages and on the Internet as well. Most perniciously, it is still easily available in bookstores throughout the Arab world and is sometimes referenced: for example, in the 1988 Hamas Charter, it is called "the Zionist blueprint for a world takeover." Also, it is well known that the late king Faisal of Saudi Arabia (1906–75) used to present visiting dignitaries with leather-bound copies of the *Protocols* during their audiences with him.[2]

FOUR JEWISH MOVEMENTS

Yet, despite these various deprivations and antisemitic disturbances, four remarkable and remarkably unique movements arose during this same period: (1) *Hasidism*, an Eastern religious movement; (2) *Reform Judaism*, a Western religious movement; (3) *Haskalah*, an Eastern secular movement; and (4) *Zionism*, a Western secular movement. While these identifiers should not be understood as hard and fast distinctions, collectively, they established the foundational patterns for Jewish life today and set the stage for it tomorrow, both religious and secular.

In the late 1770s, traditional Jewish religious life and practice were perceived by many, especially the lower socioeconomic classes, as rigidly authoritarian (read "Orthodox") and joyless. Into this scene came a pietistic Polish rabbi named Israel ben Eliezer (1698–1760), whose approach to God was filled with joyous singing and (segregated) male dancing, respect for all, especially the lower classes, optimism for the future, embracing certain mystical aspects of the Jewish religious tradition, and a rejection of ascetic religious life. Though not without opposition from those already in authority—the so-called *Mitnagdim* (Hebrew, "Opponents")—he and his followers survived the challenge, and today different offshoots of his original understandings are known for their distinctive garb, modeled on the eighteenth-century Polish nobility, their primary use of Yiddish (a folk and literary language akin to Hebrew) as the language of discourse, as well as their self-imposed residence restrictions, and their different approaches to religious practice vis-à-vis other Orthodox Jews and Orthodox Judaism.

One half-century later, in 1810 to be exact, in Seesen, Germany, wealthy Jewish landowner Israel Jacobson (1768–1828) built a beautiful synagogue on the grounds of the school he had built a decade before, to which he added musical instrumentation and invited prominent liberal and university-educated rabbis to deliver sermons in the vernacular (i.e., German rather than Yiddish). From such a beginning came Reform Judaism, a liberal and progressive alternative to the perceived legalistic Orthodox Judaism of the day. Like many upstart movements, it initially went too far, and, in the 1850s, Positive-Historical Judaism (modern Conservative Judaism) also arose in Germany, not as a challenge to Orthodoxy but as a reaction to the too-liberal-fast-becoming-radical Reform Judaism, whose own initial goals were the *reforming* or changing of the liturgy, stemming the tide of assimilation, and integrating into the larger society while maintaining positive Jewish identity. (It is today in the United States, where it continues to flourish, the largest Jewish religious movement of all the denominations.) Thus, distinctions between Orthodox Judaism, Reform Judaism, and Conservative Judaism—and, somewhat later, especially in the United States, Reconstructionist Judaism and Humanistic Judaism—as regards the practice of religious Judaism remain ever present—and will be addressed, summarily, here.

Hasidism and the Ba'al Shem Tov

An honest historical assessment of the late seventeenth and eighteenth centuries compels us to recognize that religious Judaism was that of a divisive family: serious ritual practice, framed by intensive Talmudic study, dictated by an intellectual rabbinic elite largely in Eastern Europe, but Western Europe as well, and a "Judaism of the masses," which by and large found themselves disenfranchised from the centers of Jewish learning, somewhat ignorant of much Jewish knowledge, and with men intermittently engaging in Jewish practice when their economic circumstances permitted them to do so.

Into this seeming void stepped Israel ben Eliezer, who would come to be known as the Ba'al Shem Tov ("Master of the Good Name"), abbreviated to Besht. Something of a mystic and a healer, the essence of his teaching, coupled with his personality and respect for all Jews regardless of socioeconomic status, endeared him to many throughout his travels, and therefore elevated him to almost mythic importance and significance. For him and his followers, connections with God could be found not only in texts and prayers, but in all human activity. Among those followers, at least initially, were those who regarded him as a descendant of the biblical Davidic household. (Thus, because of early and later Jewish religious tradition linking the messiah of Judaism with

David's own lineage, it is not surprising that some Hasidic communities would see him as either the Messiah himself or a precursor to one to come later—e.g., Chabad Lubavitch in the person of the late Rebbe Menachem Mendel Schneerson.)

As the Hasidic movement began to grow and spread and itself divide into its own "courts," each with its own *rebbe* (rabbi), it is not surprising that opposition began to develop; those opponents were labeled the Mitnagdim, while the term *Hasidim* is perhaps best understood as "Pietists." At times, the disputes became so bitter and public that both sides appealed to the local non-Jewish authorities, who, reluctant to involve themselves at first, would be prevailed upon to imprison representative leaders on both sides. The most prominent opponent was the great Lithuanian, Elijah ben Solomon Zalman (1720–97), known as Vilna Gaon, who regarded the decrease in the study of the Talmud and the primacy of Torah study as a lessening of Jewish commitment. By the mid-nineteenth century, however, such debates and disputes had largely subsided, and, today, Orthodox Judaism may best be understood as encompassing both Hasidic and non-Hasidic forms and practices and all having equal standing. Noteworthy as well is the joy which the Hasidim bring to Jewish worship with innovative musical forms and a celebration of the holiday of *Simchat Torah* in the fall at the end of *Sukkot* early on in the new Jewish year unrivalled among other denominational expressions. Today there are numerous Hasidic groups not only in Israel and the United States, but throughout the world, and distinguished by variations of clothing initially worn by Polish nobility in an earlier epoch.[3]

Reform Judaism and Conservative Judaism

Equally in opposition to what was perceived, at least in the Germany of the same period, as the rigidity of Orthodox Judaism in the aftermath of the Enlightenment and the reluctant admission of Jews into the larger society, there arose a Western religious movement known as Reform Judaism. Though originally intended by both its university-educated rabbis and increasing lay leadership to reform what they regarded as an overlong liturgy with far too many repetitions of prayers on both Sabbaths and festivals, and a strong desire and attempt to stem the tide of assimilation and conversion to Christianity, it was, perhaps, the ultimate religious expression of Moses Mendelssohn's dream of being in two places at once: a Jew at home, comfortable with a uniquely separate religious tradition, and "a Jew in the street," so to speak, of the larger society. As it continued to evolve, like the Hasidim, Talmud study took a back seat to Torah study while the ethical imperatives of the prophetic tradition would loom large. While many in the past have attributed its founding to German-Jewish financier, philanthropist, and communal leader, Israel Jacobson, the noted American scholar, Michael A. Meyer (b. 1937) has called this assessment into question, arguing, instead, that Jacobson regarded himself throughout his life as comfortable within the boundaries of *Halakhah* (Jewish law), whose own innovations (mixed seating, instrumental music, and sermons in the German language rather than Yiddish or Hebrew) were more external and cosmetic than altering the direction of German-Jewish religious Judaism.

Today, in both Europe and South America, Reform Judaism is more comfortable with the label Progressive Judaism. It would, however, reach its fullest flowering in the United States with the immigration and guiding genius of Bavarian rabbi Isaac Mayer Wise (1819–1900), first to Albany, New York, and then to Cincinnati, Ohio, where he would establish the organizational pattern for so much of American Jewish religious life, founding the seminary the Hebrew Union College (1875),[4] the Union of American Hebrew Congregations (1873), and the Central Conference of American Rabbis (1890). Later on as it evolved in the United States, as evidenced by both the Pittsburg Platform of 1885 and the Columbus Platform of 1937, it merged its liberal religious Judaism with that of American liberal democracy and is still the largest Jewish religious denomination in the United States—evolving away from its initial anti-Zionist position in the aftermath of the Holocaust/Shoah and establishing its own seminary branch in Israel to ordain Israeli-born Reform rabbis and establishing congregations throughout Israel. (The first president of the Hebrew University in Jerusalem was Reform rabbi Judah Magnes [1877–1948], and among the most zealous champions for a reborn state were Reform rabbi Abba Hillel Silver [1893–1963] of Cleveland, Ohio, and Stephen Samuel Wise [1874–1949] of New York.)

The presidents of the Hebrew Union College–Jewish Institute of Religion have included: world-renowned biblical archaeologist, Nelson Glueck (1900–71; served 1947–71); Alfred Gottschalk (1930–2009; served 1971–96); David Ellenson (b. 1947; served 2001–13); Sheldon Zimmerman (b. 1942; served 1996–2000); Aaron Panken (1964–2018; served 2014–18); and Andrew Rehfeld, PhD (b. 1965), its first non-rabbinic president (2019).

Viewing itself somewhat as a "cutting edge" Jewish religious movement, it ordained the first woman rabbi in North America—Rabbi Sally Priesand

(b. 1946) of Cleveland, Ohio, and Tinton Falls, New Jersey in 1972—ordained the first openly gay rabbi Allen Bennet (b. 1946) in 1974, admitted to its congregational union congregations composed of largely gay persons, welcomed families of mixed Jewish/non-Jewish parentage into congregational membership through its outreach programs, and has taken controversial stands oft times in opposition to the larger society and/or other Jewish denominations (e.g., abortion, homosexuality).

Also arising in Germany, but not as a response to either Orthodoxy or Hasidism, but rather to the perceived excesses of Reform Liberal Judaism was Positive-Historical Judaism now known as Conservative ("Middle of the Road") Judaism, committed both to Jewish Law (*Halakhah*) but also open to changes and modifications based upon evolving historical and societal realities. It too would reach its fullest flowering in the United States with the founding of its flagship institution, the Jewish Theological Seminary, New York, its Rabbinical Assembly (founded 1901), and its United Synagogue (founded 1913) union. (As of this writing, 2023, both Reform and Conservative Judaism are seeing serious declines not only in membership but rabbinical school candidates as well, but Conservative Judaism more so.)

Historically, its origin is attributed to Rabbi Zacharias Frankel (1801–75) of Dresden, a moderate reformer, and the founder of the Rabbinical Conference of Frankfurt in 1841, and its Jewish Theological Seminary in Breslau in 1854 (and later in New York in 1886). As a Jewish denominational religious movement, it would remain viable throughout Central and Eastern Europe until the Nazi takeover in the 1930s, when immigration to the United States would build upon its original visionaries, Rabbis Sabato Morais (1823–97), Henry Pereira Mendes (1852–1937), Alexander Kohut (1842–94), Cyrus Adler (1863–1940), and the appointment of British scholar Solomon Schechter (1847–1915) as its seminary president, and, later, Louis Finkelstein (1895–1991) and Ismar Schorsch (b. 1935). (JTS of America would ordain its first woman rabbi, Amy Eilberg [b. 1954], in 1985.) Like Reform Judaism, it, too, would establish a small but growing religious presence in the State of Israel.

The Impact of Secularism and the *Haskalah*

By the late eighteenth century, Czarist Russia was in the throes of political and revolutionary chaos as movements sprang up that sought new forms of governmental models. Jews, too, participated in these calls for change, feeling that their participation could only redound positively on their discriminated-against communities. Internally, however, the impact of Western European secularism had already begun to intrude into those same communities. For the first time, Jewish thinkers and writers began to draw on the university education of themselves and others and their own thoughts to critically assess the Torah/Hebrew Bible/Old Testament, but, more importantly, to see the Hebrew language as a means of discourse not confined to the religious realm only, and, at times, in serious conflict with the Orthodox religious establishments in various locales. Plays, novels, short stories, essays, newspapers, all manner of written texts, began to pour forth. Among those associated with the Jewish *Haskalah* ("Enlightenment") movement were: Chaim Nachman Bialik, the "father of modern Hebrew literature"; Sholom Aleichem, writer of humorous stories; Saul Tchernichovsky, poet; and too, too many others to cite here. Unbeknownst to themselves, or perhaps prescient, nonetheless, their work set the foundation for the Jewish cultural life of the modern State of Israel and elsewhere, including the United States. Important to keep in mind, however, that the *Haskalah* began first in Germany with the founding in 1819 of an organization *Verein für Cultur und Wissenschaft der Juden* ("Organization for Culture and Scientific knowledge of Judaism and Jews"). Thus, summarily, we have a Jewish secular literary movement towards modernity whose authors would write in both Yiddish—the folk language of communication—and Hebrew, the historic language of the sacred. Somewhat ironically, Hebrew literary productivity continues to flourish—not only in Israel but worldwide—while Yiddish, though experiencing a small revival in the US, has largely fallen into disuse as its native speakers and writers die out.

CHAIM NACHMAN BIALIK

It is no exaggeration to suggest that Bialik was, indeed, the "poet laureate of the Jewish people." Born in the Russian Empire in 1873, he would die in Vienna, Austria, in 1934, the result of a heart attack after a prostate operation. Raised by his Orthodox Jewish grandfather in Zhytomyr, Ukraine, after his father's death, he was also exposed to European literature, as a result of which he convinced his grandfather to send him to the Volozhin Yeshiva in Lithuania. He would later move to Odessa, then the center of the Russian Jewish Enlightenment. The pull of Zionism and the return to the land of Israel also exerted a pull on Bialik, as well as increasing Russian antisemitism. His poems, in both Hebrew and

Yiddish, reflected all these influences. For example, *"HaMatmid"* ("The Yeshiva Student") tells of the loneliness of the student, while at the same time affirming the importance of classical Jewish education. His first poem *"El Ha-Tzipor"* ("To the Bird") is understood as that longing for Zion. In 1903, he was sent to Kishinev, Moldova, to report on the massacre of its Jewish inhabitants, but turned his report into, perhaps, his most famous poem *"BaIr Ha-Haregah"* ("In the City of Slaughter"), which later critics would view as prophetic of the Shoah/Holocaust. His growing reputation and career as both a poet and a translator would later take him to Warsaw, Poland, briefly, and later Berlin, Germany. Together with Yehoshua Ravnitzky (1859–1944) he would publish the three-volume collection *Sefer Ha-Aggadah* ("Book of Legends"), hailed as a masterwork. In 1924, Bialik moved to British Mandate Palestine, and reestablished his publishing house, Dvir.[5] His reputation as among those responsible for the revival of the Hebrew language remains untarnished today as "Israel's national poet."

SHOLOM ALEICHEM

Born in the Russian Empire in 1859, Solomon Naumovich Rabinovich would later die in New York in 1916, where he had moved to two years before his death. He would take the traditional Jewish greeting, *shalom aleichem* ("Peace be unto you") as his literary pseudonym and achieve fame as a writer of humorous stories, akin, perhaps, to the American writer, Mark Twain (Samuel Langhorne Clemens, 1835–1910), writing in both Hebrew and Yiddish. He is today most well-known, perhaps, for his stories of Tevye the Dairyman, which would become the long-running Broadway (and elsewhere throughout the world) musical, *Fiddler on the Roof.*

SAUL TCHERNICHOVSKY

The third literary figure of renown was the poet Tchernichovsky (1875–1943), whose poetry reflected the language of Greek culture and literature, but unlike that of Bialik, focused on nature itself. Born in Russia, he would die in British Mandate Palestine, achieving fame not only as a poet essayist and translator, but a medical doctor as well. He would go on to receive the Bialik Prize for Hebrew Literature in 1940 and again in 1942. His most well-known poem "In My Dream," among his first, remains his legacy:

Laugh, laugh at all my dreams!
What I dream shall yet come true!
Laugh at my belief in man,
At my belief in you.
Freedom still my soul demands,
Unbartered for a calf of gold.
For still I do believe in man,
And in his spirit, strong and bold.
And in the future, I still believe
Though it be distant, come it will
When nations shall each other bless
And peace at last the earth shall fill.[6]

FRANCE, *L'AFFAIRE DREYFUS*, AND ZIONISM

Captain Alfred Dreyfus of the French army was born in 1859 in Alsace to a wealthy Jewish family, highly assimilated into French culture and religiously nonobservant. A graduate of the École Polytechnique as an engineer, he entered the military and was attached to the general staff in Paris, the only Jew in such a position (though other Jews did achieve officer rank in the French army). In 1894, a supposedly treasonable document—the so-called *bordereau*—offering to give or sell weapons secrets to Germany was found in the wastebasket of the German military attaché. The handwriting on the spurious document was said to resemble that of Dreyfus, and he was brought to trial that same year, found guilty by a court of military conservatives and monarchists—in violation of standard legal protocols— stripped of rank, publicly humiliated, and sentenced to life imprisonment on Devil's Island, off the coast of South America. The hue and cry and protestations regarding his innocence—his own included—led to a second trial in 1899, where he was again found guilty. During the years in between, however, the French military intelligence officer Georges Picquart (1854–1914), who would himself suffer exile to Africa after an initial imprisonment, concluded that the forged document was the work of the French officer and adventurer Ferdinand Walsin Esterhazy (1847–1923), with additional forged documents by a Colonel Hubert-Joseph Henry (1846–98), who committed suicide in prison after his arrest rather than face trial. By the turn of the twentieth century, the case had become a *cause célèbre* not only in France but internationally as well, with many voices calling for yet another trial and Dreyfus's acquittal. Most notable among them was the premier French litterateur of the day, Émile Zola (1840–1902), whose scathing front-page editorial, "J'Accuse . . . !" in the newspaper *L'Aurore*, accused not only the military but the government and the Roman Catholic church of an orchestrated cover-up, forcing him to flee temporarily for his own safety. In 1906, twelve years after Dreyfus was first brought to trial and found guilty, he was finally exonerated, restored to rank, elevated to major, fought for France in the First World War, and retired with the rank of lieutenant colonel. He died in 1935. The consequences of this entire affair are notable. First, it exposed the deep-seated antisemitism of the French people, military, the Roman Catholic Church, and government, and saw the increasing prominence of journalist and antisemite Édouard Drumont (1844–1917), whose 1886 book, *La France juive* ("Jewish France"), went through numerous reprintings. Second, covering that trial was the Viennese journalist, Theodor Herzl (1860–1904), who was so appalled by the public spectacle of antisemitism already rife in France and elsewhere and daily outside the courtroom that, upon his return to Austria, he concluded that the only solution to this enduring problem of antisemitism was for the Jewish people to have a nation-state of their own. He would go on to write his tract *Der Judenstaat* ("The Jewish State") and, given both his charismatic personality and organizational abilities, became the "Father of Modern Political Zionism," predicting a Jewish state—Israel—fifty years hence. Third, and of equally important significance, it revealed to the world the power of political antisemitism not only to rally the masses but to accomplish whatever right-wing goals were important to both those in power and those aspiring to achieve it. The Nazis, under Adolf Hitler, would learn this lesson well and take it to its most perverse conclusion, which we know today as the Holocaust/Shoah.[7]

Sadly, and ironically, Herzl's ultimate dream has yet to be realized: with the creation of the State of Israel in 1948, the world has not yet accorded Jews equal status, antisemitism has not decreased, and the troubles and tragedies of the Middle East continue to play out on a far larger canvas as seen by its wars of conflict in 1948, 1956, 1967, 1973, 1981, and its ongoing engagement in terrorist activities and responses.

A Sidenote to *l'Affaire Dreyfus*

Shortly after Dreyfus was finally acquitted of all charges and fully readmitted to the French military, in Portugal, Artur Carlos de Barros

Basto (1887–1961), who only learned of his Jewish ancestry at age seventeen from his dying grandfather and began his own journey back, was dismissed from the army in 1937 because of his publicly acknowledged Jewish identity and his work on behalf of his fellow Jews—despite a distinguished military record during the First World War. He did not live long enough to see his own "rehabilitation," which occurred in 2012, largely the result of the efforts of his granddaughter, Isabel Ferreira Lopes, herself active in Jewish affairs in the town of Porto, Portugal. He died, at least from his own perspective, in disgrace; his case never formally reviewed.

ZIONISM AND THEODOR HERZL

Modern political Zionism is most associated with Viennese journalist Theodor Herzl, whose 1895 pamphlet, *Der Judenstaat*, came out of the trial of Dreyfus and the overt antisemitism of that event and elsewhere, including in his own nation-state of Austria. A nation-state for the Jewish people was his answer to the ongoing problem of antisemitism. Given both his oratorical and organizational expertise, not to overlook his commanding physical presence (6 feet 4 inches tall, ~ 260 lbs., coal-black piercing eyes), he was able to win Eastern European Jews to his banner, though less so Western European ones. Important to remember, however, the dream of religious Jews to return to their land of origin was and is part and parcel of the Jewish historical experience since the biblical exilic periods in both Babylon and Egypt. Then, too, there were those non-Jews/ Christians in the West who saw such a Jewish return as a precursor to the return of the Christ. Foremost among them, perhaps, was Arthur James Balfour (1848–1930) in Great Britain, who would send a letter to the head of its Jewish community, Lionel Walter Rothschild, second Baron Rothschild (1867–1937), in the aftermath of the First World War and the dissolution of the Turkish Ottoman Empire in support of Jewish aspirations but carefully avoiding a political commitment by his use of the phrase "national home," words which have no legal validity whatsoever.[8]

On May 14, 1948, the State of Israel comes into being—the Third Jewish Commonwealth— with its first prime minister, David Ben-Gurion (1886–1973) going on Tel Aviv radio to announce its creation to the world. Dancing would break out not only in Tel Aviv but throughout the new nation-state and world over. Shortly thereafter, the combined might of the surrounding Arab states would attack to try to put an end to its existence—unsuccessfully. They would again fail in 1956, 1967, 1973, and 1981, to say nothing of the ongoing terrorist attacks both inside and outside the state itself by disgruntled Palestinians and other Arab/ Muslim/Islamist militants who continue to view its very presence as an anathema within the Arab world—the *Ummat/Dar al-Islam*.

Tragically, the ongoing situation of the Palestinians within Israel and their second-class or lesser status, despite their citizenship and access to health care, education, and other benefits, has not been resolved, and there are those both inside and outside Israel, including members of the international community both Jews and non-Jews, who characterize it as the world's longest occupation, with everything negative that that implies. Calls for a two-state solution—a Jewish state and a Palestinian state— alongside each other or a newly reconstituted state with a different name and a decidedly non-Jewish minority remain ever-present in discussions worldwide. Be that as it may, today (2023) Israel remains a viable national entity with a growing economy, a military presence always at the ready, a technological marvel, and a growing Jewish population expected to pass, if trends continue, the American Jewish community and presently more than 7,000,000 children, women, and men.

TWO OTHER MODERN JEWISH RELIGIOUS MOVEMENTS

Reconstructionist Judaism

This American religious denominational movement was the result of the vision of Orthodox ordained rabbi, Mordecai Menahem Kaplan (1881– 1983), born in Lithuania, who taught at the Conservative Jewish Theological Seminary of New York until his retirement. Kaplan was also rabbi of the Society for the Advancement of Judaism, which he founded, and where he would celebrate the bat mitzvah of his daughter Judith (1909–96), both in 1922—the first such celebration in Jewish history. (Judith would later marry Kaplan's successor, Rabbi Ira Eisenstein [1906–2001].) Building upon his progressive understanding of Judaism as so much more than a religious community, rather a civilization with all the component parts that mark such an entity (language, culture, etc.), it is also the title of his magnum opus, *Judaism as a Civilization: Toward the Reconstruction of American–Jewish Life* (1934). Though the smallest of the three major American religious denominations, it too has a seminary, the Reconstructionist Rabbinical College in Philadelphia,

Pennsylvania, and the Reconstructionist Rabbinical Association, both founded in 1968, and the Federation of Reconstructionist Congregations and Havurot in 1955.

Humanistic Judaism

A non-theistic form of religious Judaism, this newest American denominational movement was founded by Reform ordained rabbi, Sherman Wine (1928–2007). He served a congregation in the Detroit, Michigan, area, before founding the Birmingham Temple in 1963, and would go on to found the Society for Humanistic Judaism in 1969, and the International Federation for Secular Humanistic Jews in 1986. He also created the International Institute for Secular Humanistic Judaism to train leaders and rabbis. His growing dissatisfaction with what he understood as the meaninglessness of theological words and understandings—God included—saw him express a different understanding of Judaism as the cultural and historical experience of the Jewish people and the foundation upon which to build contemporary meaning and practice. Equally, Wine's and his followers' commitment was and is to the primary of the individual and his/her conscience to interpret and understand Judaism in his/her own way and take from its vast resources that which gives life meaning. Wine's vision was and is a far more radical break from Orthodox, Conservative and Reform Judaism than Kaplan's, although both spring from a fertile American religious environment.

*   *   *

At the start of the twentieth century the world of the Jews seemed poised to advance positively, at least in the West, with an estimated population of more than 7,500,000 persons in pre-state Israel, British Mandate Palestine, and growing, and approximately the same number in the United States; the two largest Jewish population centers in the world. Such would, however, prove not to be the case.

NOTES

1   Adolf Hitler, *Mein Kampf* (New York, NY: Houghton Mifflin, 1939), 279.
2   See: Hadassa Ben-Itto, *The Lie That Wouldn't Die: The Protocols of the Elders of Zion* (London and Portland, OR: Vallentine Mitchell, 2005); Herman Bernstein, *The Truth about "The Protocols of Zion,"* reprint (Hoboken, NJ:

KTAV Publishing House, 1971); Stephen Eric Bronner, *A Rumor about the Jews: Reflections on Antisemitism and the Protocols of the Learned Elders of Zion* (New York, NY: St. Martin's Press, 2000); Norman Cohn, *Warrant for Genocide: The Myth of the Jewish World-Conspiracy and the Protocols of the Elders of Zion* (London: Eyre & Spottiswoode, 1967); John Shelton Curtiss, *An Appraisal of the Protocols of Zion* (New York, NY: Columbia University Press, 1942); Cesare G. de Michelis, *The Non-Existent Manuscript: A Study of the Protocols of the Sages of Zion* (Lincoln: University of Nebraska Press, 2004); Will Eisner, *The Plot: The Secret Story of the Protocols of the Elders of Zion* (New York, NY: W.W. Norton & Co., 2005); John Gwyer, *Portraits of Mean Men: A Short History of the Protocols of the Elders of Zion* (London: Cobden-Sanderson, 1938); Adolf Hitler, *Mein Kampf* (New York, NY: Houghton Mifflin, 1939), pp. 293–4; Steven Leonard Jacobs and Mark Weitzman, *Dismantling the Big Lie: The Protocols of the Elders of Zion* (Jersey City, NJ: KTAV Publishing House, 2003); Maurice Joly, *The Dialogue in Hell between Machiavelli and Montesquieu: Humanitarian Despotism and the Condition of Modern Tyranny*, trans. John S. Waggoner (Lanham, MD: Lexington Books, 2003); Richard Landes and Steven Katz (eds.), *The Paranoid Apocalypse: A Hundred-Year Retrospective on The Protocols of the Elders of Zion* (New York, NY: New York University Press, 2012); Göran Larsson, *Fact or Fraud? The Protocols of the Elders of Zion* (Jerusalem: AMI-Jerusalem Center for Biblical Studies and Research, 1994); Benjamin W. Segal, *A Lie and a Libel: The History of the Protocols of the Elders of Zion*, trans. and ed. Richard S. Levy (Lincoln: University of Nebraska Press, 1996); and Lucien Wolf, *The Myth of the Jewish Menace in World Affairs: Or, The Truth about the Forged Protocols of the Elders of Zion*, reprint (Calgary, AB: Theophania Publishing, 2011).

3   A fascinating look at some of these European communities prior to the First World War is the book, *Nine Gates: The Chassidic Mysteries*, trans. Stephen Jolly (Cambridge: Lutterworth Press, 2022), by the Czech Hebraist, poet, scholar, journalist, and teacher Jiri Langer (1894–1943).

4   In 1947, Hebrew Union College would merge with the Jewish Institute of Religion, New York, founded by the acknowledge champion of American Jewry Rabbi Stephen S. Wise (1874–1949)—no relation to I.M. Wise—and is today home not only to its rabbinic program with campuses in Cincinnati, Ohio, Los Angeles, California, New York, New York, and Jerusalem, Israel, but its graduate school (Cincinnati), its cantorial school (New York), and its school of Jewish communal service (Los Angeles).

5   For a further look at Bialik and his work, see Sara Feinstein, *Sunshine, Blossoms and Blood: H.N. Bialik in His Time: A Literary Biography* (Lanham, MD: University Press of America, 2005), and Steven Leonard Jacobs, *Shirot*

Bialik: A New and Annotated Translation of Chaim Nachman Bialik's Epic Poems (Columbus, OH: Alpha Pub. Co., 1987).

6 This English translation of the poem can be found at: https://www.poetrynook. com/poem/creed-2 (accessed May 19, 2023).

7 See Louis Begley, *Why the Dreyfus Affair Matters* (New Haven, CT: Yale University Press, 2009); Jean-Denis Bredin, *The Affair: The Case of Alfred Dreyfus* (London: Sidgwick & Jackson, 1986); Guy Chapman, *The Dreyfus Trials* (London: Batsford, 1972); and Alfred S. Lindemann, *The Jew Accused: Three Anti-Semitic Affairs: Dreyfus, Beilis, Frank, 1894–1915* (Cambridge: Cambridge University Press, 1993). Two novelistic retellings of the Dreyfus story are Michael Hardwick, *Prisoner of the Devil* (New York, NY: Pinnacle Books, 1990); and Robert Harris, *An Officer and a Spy* (New York, NY: Vantage Books, 2013).

8 Foreign Office

November 2nd, 1917

Dear Lord Rothschild,

I have much pleasure in conveying to you on behalf of His Majesty's Government, the following declaration of sympathy with Jewish Zionist aspirations which has been submitted to, and approved by, the Cabinet.

His Majesty's Government view with favour the establishment in Palestine of a national home for the Jewish people and will use their best endeavors to facilitate the achievement of this object, it being clearly understood that nothing shall be done which may prejudice the civil and religious rights of existing non-Jewish communities in Palestine or the rights and political status enjoyed by Jews in any other country.

I should be grateful if you would bring this declaration to the knowledge of the Zionist Federation.

Yours,

Arthur James Balfour

11

THE TWENTIETH AND TWENTY-FIRST CENTURIES AND BEYOND: MODERNITY

Already in the early 1800s, increasing antisemitism in Russia led her Jews to consider the option of mass emigration to either Arab-controlled Palestine (Herzl's Zionist movement would find a far more willing and receptive audience in the East than in the West) or the United States. By the 1880s, massive and continuous pogroms were no longer idle conversations but hard and tragic realities. More and more Jews fled, the clear majority leaving to join an American Jewish community already resident and successfully integrated over the centuries since the first Jews arrived in the Dutch colony of New Amsterdam in 1654. Spanish and Portuguese émigrés from Recife, Brazil, had arrived more than a century earlier, the descendants of those who originally fled Spain and Portugal.

IMMIGRATION AND EMIGRATION

The American Jewish story may be characterized historically as one of successive *waves* of immigration, though the first group was, in truth, more of a trickle than an actual wave. The Jews who did come, however, settled mainly in the larger cities, including the American South, and, by the time of the Revolutionary War of 1775–83, numbered approximately 200,000 persons, primarily Jews of Sephardic (Spanish-speaking) background rather than Ashkenazic (German and Russian-speaking) background. After that, and prior to the American Civil War (1861–65), and after, until the First World War (1914–18), the Jews who came and established the organizational pattern of American Jewish life were Ashkenazim, primarily from Germany and Austria. In the aftermath of both the First World War and the Russian Revolution of 1917, the Jews who came were Eastern European who brought with them their religious ways, especially Hasidism, which was something of an anathema to their co-religionists who had already established Reform Judaism as a very much Westernized American reinterpretation of traditional Jewish religious thought and practice. After the Second World War (1939–45) and Israel's War for Independence (1948), the Jews who came, primarily from a devastated Europe, were both Ashkenazim and Sephardim. Today, the Jewish communities of both the United States and the State of Israel are the largest in the world.

ANTISEMITISM IN EUROPE

During the early part of the twentieth century, Jews found themselves active in both the First World War on both sides of the battlefront and in the Russian Revolution. While antisemitism was a fixture of both, it would not truly rear its ugly head to any appreciable degree until both events were over. It what had become Soviet/Communist Russia, Jewish distinctiveness and parochial uniqueness remained a hindrance to universal identity. For both the Leninists (followers of Vladimir Lenin, 1870–1924) and the Stalinists (followers of Joseph Stalin, 1878–1953), more so the latter than the former, and especially Stalin himself, the Jews remained a cosmopolitan enemy, unassimilable and unable to be integrated. Liquidations and imprisonments of Jewish religious leaders and other professionals—for example, Stalin's infamous and notorious "Doctors' Plot" of 1953—and the destruction of Jewish religious and cultural life became the norm rather than the exception under the Communists. It was only in the 1970s, when cracks began to appear in the so-called "Iron Curtain," that the attempt to completely destroy Jewish identity was realized to have significantly failed. In the twenty-first century, the former Soviet Union—Communist rule ended in 1991—is experiencing a revitalization of Jewish life on many fronts, cultural as well as religious.

GERMANY, THE SECOND WORLD WAR, AND THE HOLOCAUST/SHOAH

This was not so for Germany, however, in the chaotic days after the First World War. Economic, political, and social dislocations were the order of the day as political parties on both the right and the left attempted to bring stability to a country made to pay heavily for its sins by the Versailles Treaty of 1919. Even the failed Weimar Republic (1919–35) could do little to stem the chaos, made more dramatic by the worldwide depression of 1929.

Into the breach stepped an unknown Austrian corporal, who had served in the German army, was temporarily blinded by mustard gas and hospitalized, remained in the army upon his discharge, only to quit, join, and reorganize the National Socialist German Workers' Party and become Chancellor of Germany on January 30, 1933.

Adolf Hitler was born in Branau am Inn, Austria, the son of Klara and Alois Hitler, who was a minor civil servant. According to his own account in his political biography, *Mein Kampf* (German, "My Fight" or "My Struggle"), he was underappreciated for his intellectual abilities at school, and later underappreciated for his artistic and architectural talents in Vienna, where he lived prior to the First World War. Absorbing both the public antisemitism and pan-Germanism that were rife in Austria, he would make use of both in his political ambitions as a skilled orator and organizer. Once in power, he was able to exploit both skills, first, to remilitarize Germany—despite violating the Versailles Treaty—and, second, to implement a master plan, nearly successful, to exterminate and annihilate the eleven million Jews of Europe.

The Holocaust, as it has come to be called in English (from the Greek, for "a totally burnt offering to God," and based on the cultic sacrificial system of the Hebrew Bible)—though the currently-preferred term is the Hebrew *Shoah* ("Devastation" or "Destruction")—saw the murderous deaths of *more than* 6,000,000 Jewish men, women and children (1,000,000 of whom were children of twelve years old and under, and 500,000 of whom were between the ages of twelve and eighteen) between the years 1939 (the start of the Second World War) and 1945 (Hitler's suicide, together with his mistress-wife, Eva Braun). The manner of these Jewish deaths in ghettos, rounded-up villages, and concentration and death camps is filled with horror and terror and well-known to most, if not all, readers of this text. The meaning and implications of those deaths, however, is yet another matter.

THE PROBLEM OF DEFINITION

In truth, there is no one single word to define the horrendous and murderous deaths of nonmilitary combatants by the Nazis and their allied minions during the Second World War, and largely the result of the implementation of a Hitlerian ideology that blamed the Jews not only for Germany losing the First World War—the so-called *Dolchstoßlegende* (the "stab-in-the-back" myth)—but also for all the supposed ills that afflicted Western civilization. The English word Holocaust, derived from the Greek word *holocaustos*—referring to animal offerings totally consumed by fire by the priests to the God of ancient Israel—indirectly suggests the religious aspects or dynamics of what transpired and, perversely, may even play into the justifications of those who would argue that the Nazi were doing the "will of God" as priestly agents of the divine. The Hebrew word *Shoah* ("Destruction" or "Devastation") only refers to Jews, as does the Yiddish word *Khurbn*. The Sinti/Roma word *Porajmos* ("Devouring") refers only to their tragedy. None of these words, however, addresses the fate of innocent civilians throughout Europe, who were subjected to Nazi tyranny, hegemony, or worse, nor homosexual persons, Jehovah's Witnesses, political dissidents, or so-called "asocials." The following two definitions—one by a recognized scholar of the Holocaust only recently posited and the second by the author—focus on different aspects of the event. The first is that of Michael Marrus (b. 1941), a retired professor at the University of Toronto:

> The brutalization of men, women, and children across Europe, in a sinister racially inspired scheme of wiping millions of Jews off the face of the earth; rounding them up everywhere they could be found, often after murderous attacks; exposing them to disease, cold, hunger, and other degrading conditions, robbing, torturing them, beating them, shooting them, and in some cases murdering them by gassings in trucks or in specially-built gas chambers, and by the killing of many hundreds of thousands, amounting to close to six million in all.[1]

The following definition is used in an undergraduate course taught by the author, entitled "The Holocaust in Historical Perspective," and has evolved over years of teaching and is further unpacked below:

> The Shoah/Holocaust is the historically validated, legalized, bureaucratic marriage of technology and death, directed primarily against the Jewish People and Judaism by the Nazis of Germany and their non-German allies on the European continent between the years 1939 and 1945, and which resulted in the murderous deaths of more than six million Jewish persons, children, women and men.

Thus, the keys to understanding and unpacking this latter definition are described in the following paragraphs.

Historically validated: Despite the claims of so-called Holocaust revisionists (more accurately described as "Holocaust denialists"), the overwhelming abundance of documents (official governmental materials), films and photographs, memoirs, and eyewitness accounts of both victims and perpetrators, and the like, situate the events within a historical context.

Legalized: With the passage of a whole host of discriminatory legislation and laws by the Nazi government of Germany, its allies, and those formerly independent and sovereign states that fell to its power and might, laws were put in place that disadvantaged (and worse!) the Jews within their ever-expanded orbit. Examples include the "Law for the Protection of German Blood and German Honor" and the "Reich Citizenship Law," both enacted Septembers 15, 1935.

Bureaucratic marriage of technology and death: To murder such large populations on so vast a scale required an organizational apparatus second to none, beginning in Germany itself, and integrated into its various structures (political, military, economic, academic, etc.), and its scientific implementation, the goal which was the extermination/annihilation of the Jews. Those organizations included the *Sturmabteilung* (SA, storm troopers), *Geheime Staatspolizei* (Gestapo, secret state police), *Schutzstaffel* (SS, protection squad), the *Sicherheitsdienst des Reichsführers SS* (SD, security service), and the various departments and branches of the German government and its ministries. In addition, one must also include German society as being either complicit in these crimes or indifferent to the fate of their Jewish friends and neighbors, and ofttimes their own family members, as numerous works indicate. Today, significantly, German governmental and citizen acceptance of the reality of the Holocaust/Shoah is officially and publicly acknowledged, and education about the Holocaust/Shoah is a mandated part of the national curricula.

By the Nazis of Germany and their non-German allies: The Holocaust/Shoah could not have been accomplished solely by the Nazis themselves. It relied on the willing complicity of populations found in those nation-states that came into the Nazi orbit: Poland, Lithuania, Latvia, the Baltic States, Romania, Czechoslovakia, and Ukraine, among others. Those already predisposed to implementing their antisemitic agendas now found themselves having the power to do so, and others, whether for personal or professional goals, were all too easily co-opted and complicit

177

in the murder of their Jewish friends, neighbors, family members, and those whom they did not know.

On the European continent: It is now the scholarly consensus that, had the Nazis been successful both in their military conquests throughout the period of the Second World War and the implementation of the Holocaust/Shoah on the European continent, they would have taken their two goals worldwide, opting for both political sovereignty on other continents (North America, South America, Australia, Asia, and Africa) and implementation of their "Final Solution to the Jewish Question" (*die Endlösung der Judenfrage*) to exterminate all Jews worldwide.

Directed primarily against the Jewish people and Judaism: The goal of the Nazis was not only the obliteration of the Jewish people physically but also the evisceration of their centuries-old religious tradition known as Judaism, its cultural production (books, music, newspapers, etc.), including its physical institutions (synagogues), and its plethora of communal organizations.

Between the years 1939 and 1945: Except for *Kristallnacht* (the pogrom of November 9–10, 1938), the Nazis and their allies commenced their journey to death and destruction with the beginning of the Second World War on September 1, 1939, and the invasion of Poland, and ceased their operations with V-E (Victory over Europe) Day on May 8, 1945 (after the apparent suicide of Adolf Hitler on April 30 or May 1). However, others have argued for a beginning date of January 30, 1933, with the assumption of Hitler's appointment as Chancellor of Germany and encompassing the entire twelve-year period of *das Dritte Reich* ("the Third Reich"). Still others have argued for an even earlier date, suggesting that, with the end of the First World War (November 11, 1918), the formation of the German Workers' Party (January 5, 1919), which would subsequently become the National Socialist German Workers' Party (NSDAP, acronym "Nazi") once Hitler claimed its leadership, and the signing of the Versailles Treaty (June 28, 1919), along with the onerous burden of financial restitution, the march to the Holocaust had begun.

More than six million Jewish people, children, women, and men: Conclusively accurate figures remain difficult to come by, and ranges of deaths appear more appropriate, as noted below. With the opening of the archives after the collapse of the Soviet Union in 1991, it now appears that, whatever understandings and figures were previously agreed upon, they will have to be revised upward rather than downward. However, this much is certain: more than one million of those murdered Jews were children up to age twelve, and five hundred thousand children were between the ages of twelve and eighteen. In total, whatever the number, the losses themselves represent more than one-third of all Jews alive at the beginning of the twentieth century (sixteen million to eighteen million), two-thirds in Europe alone, and are a net loss from which the Jewish people will never recover.

Additionally, the present demographic realities (Jews in Israel, ~ 6,000,000–7,000,000; in the United States, ~ 7,000,000 plus; in the former Soviet Union, ~ 3,000,000; and in the rest of the world, ~ 3,000,000) equate to a potential future growth and loss of approximately 50 percent of Jewry (i.e., victims included girls who never reached the age of maturity; girls and women who never married; those who married but were murdered prior to giving birth or were murdered with their children; and families who never achieved their desired number of children or were murdered with them or whose surviving children were less than the total number birthed). And yet, while this author's own definition addresses many salient concerns, it does not include the overall historical context(s), the locales of death and destruction, or the manner of those murders, which are discussed below.

Holocaust Historical Context, Locales, and Manner of Murder: Since the fall and destruction of the Second Temple by the Romans in the year 70 CE, two thousand years ago, the Jewish people have been a vulnerable, wandering minority throughout primarily Western Europe, a population whose very safety, security, and survival were dependent upon those holding the reins of political, economic, religious, and social power. The early rise of Christianity, which saw the destruction as payback for the failure of the Jews to recognize and accept their long-sought-for Messiah in the person of Jesus Christ, coupled with the alliance of Roman and later Protestant Christianity with the nation-state, up until the Enlightenment and Protestant Reformation—both of which severed the church-state marriage—only increased that vulnerability. With the power to restrict the Jews came the implementation to do so. Thus, a fertile ground was prepared for the active antisemitism upon which the Nazis were able to draw, given the reality of a negative Western assessment of the Jewish people and Judaism. That "journey of antisemitism" may thus be described as follows: (a) social-cultural dislike; (b) religious-theological dislike; (c) the merging of the two; and (d) racial-biological dislike, the Nazi contribution. In every historical period, Jews were subjected to discrimination, repression, and violence, and Judaism itself was subjected to various forms of discrimination.

Locales: Although places of Jewish internment were initially established in Germany, with Dachau being the site of the incarceration of more than 10,000 Jewish men after *Kristallnacht*, the primary locale for the construction and location of the *Konzentrationslagers* (concentration camps), *Arbeitslagers* (work camps), and *Vernichtungslagers* (extermination camps) was Poland; other Eastern European countries also found themselves home to such sites. In Poland, six primary killing centers were established: Chelmno (Kulmhof), Belzec, Sobibor, Treblinka, Maidanek, and Auschwitz. Additionally, the major concentration camps were Ravensbruck, Neuengamme, Bergen Belsen, Sachsenhausen, Gross-Rosen, Buchenwald, Theresienstadt, Flossenburg, Natzweiler-Struthof, Dachau, Mauthausen, Stutthof, and Dora/Nordhausen. More than 3,500,000 Jews met their end in these factories of death. All told, the actual number of these sites have been estimated to have been more than 40,000; for example, 30,000 slave labor camps in the occupied countries, one thousand concentration camps (with numerous subcamps), and one thousand prisoner-of-war camps.

Manner of murder: It is important to realize that the systemic murder of the Jews of Europe was an evolving process that included: the *Einsatzgruppen* (mobile killing squads), which consisted of four units of approximately up to 1,500 men following the invasion of the Soviet Union ("Operation Barbarossa," beginning June 22, 1941), who entered Eastern villages and then corralled and slaughtered more than 1,300,000 Jews; removing Jews from civil society through restrictive legislation (e.g., Nuremberg racial laws of September 1935); ghettoization; death from carbon monoxide poisoning in large vans with capacities of up to one hundred people (perhaps as many as 500,000 persons were murdered this way); and, finally, the various camps and subcamps leading to all manner of brutalities, starvation, disease, beatings, and, ultimately, death due to Zyklon B gas in gas chambers and body disposal in oven crematoria. Additionally, horrific pseudoscientific medical experiments were performed on any number of unwilling prisoners (disease injections, high altitude and seawater immersions, amputations, drug testing, sterilizations, infliction of simulated battle wounds, etc.) that regularly resulted in death. In terms of the number of murdered, the following numbers give some indication of the horrific scale of these crimes (80–90 percent of these victims were Jews): Auschwitz-Birkenau 1,000,000; Treblinka 870,000–925,000, including the author's own grandparents, Leo and Ella Jacob; Belzec 434,000–600,000; Chelmno 152,000–320,000; Sobibor 170,000–250,000; Majdanek 79,000–255,000; a total of 2,705,000–3,350,000.

Once the war ended, some perpetrators—but not all, including the Nazi leadership—were brought to various trials (e.g., International Military Tribunal at Nuremberg [1945–1946]; Doctors' Trial [1946–1947]; Dachau trials [1945–1947]; Auschwitz trial [1947]; and the Buchenwald trial [1945–1948]). Ultimately, only a relatively small number of perpetrators out of a total of perhaps 200,000 men and women were prosecuted and punished, including death for some, for their crimes. Many escaped punishment by hiding in Germany, the Middle East, especially Egypt and Syria, or South America (e.g., Argentina, Brazil, Paraguay, and Uruguay). Others returned home to be reintegrated into their respective societies without discrimination. For the Jewish survivors, however, including those who survived the death marches (estimated at more than 250,000), the trauma of the Holocaust/Shoah remains to this day. Many have shared their stories of survival with their immediate families and the public at large. Unable to return to their countries of origin—no longer in possession of their homes or assets—they left the graveyards of Europe to build new lives in Israel, the United States, Australia, Canada, and elsewhere, leaving behind much smaller and devastated populations in France, Britain, and Eastern Europe. It should also be noted that the great myth or lie of the Holocaust/Shoah remains that the Jews, willingly or unwillingly, went to their deaths "like lambs to the slaughter," when the reality was that various forms of resistance broke out in many of the places of their incarceration, including the ghettos (e.g., the Warsaw Ghetto uprising of April 1943) and the camps (the Sobibor uprising in October 1943). There was also active participation of somewhere between 20,000 and 30,000 Jews in partisan anti-Nazi insurgencies (e.g., the Bielski brothers and partisans in Poland beginning in 1941). Finally, with the passing of the survivors, the aging of the "Second Generation" (their children), and the coming-of-age of the "Third Generation" (their grandchildren), issues of memory and historically accurate retellings of the events appear to gain increasing prominence, as do questions of uniqueness versus unprecedentedness and the place of the Holocaust/Shoah within the larger discussions of genocide. Thus, there is no indication whatsoever that Holocaust/Shoah-related issues will disappear from the world stage anytime soon.[2]

For one thing, at the beginning of the Second World War, the Jewish population of the world was estimated to be approximately 16,000,000 persons. Among those who were murdered were young women who never married, those who married but had no children, and those who married and had children but not the number they had dreamed or planned. Using the statistical tool of the demographer, such deaths in total are said to *represent* a net collective loss of two and one-half times their number. Thus, the reality of the deaths of the Jews in the Holocaust/ Shoah equals 15,000,000 persons (i.e., ~ 6,000,000 x 2.5 = ~ 15,000,000). With a post-Second World War population of approximately the same as that before the war, the Holocaust/Shoah destroyed a present and future by approximately fifty percent, a loss from which Jews may very well never recover in terms of what could have been but will never be.

Second, as the revelations of what was done to the Jewish people by the Nazis and their allied minions became more and more public, it caused a frightening divide among religious Jews as to how to make sense of their Judaism in its aftermath. At the same time, it also caused a reappraisal on the part of some in the Christian world as to how such a thing could have happened at the very heart of a Christianized Europe. These latter investigations led to a rethinking of the relationship between Jews and Christians and Judaism and Christianity, not only Roman Catholics but by Protestants as well, which has not abated even today.

Third, the tragedy of the Holocaust/Shoah caused a reuniting and re-solidification of Jews worldwide, most often expressed in unswerving support for the nascent State of Israel, for, while the events of the Second World War did not bring about its rebirth—a myth exploited by its enemies—Jews have been politically active in realizing this dream since the late 1800s, it did cause the nations of the world to be more open and receptive to its possibility. Even this tragedy, however, has not caused the nations of the world, particularly Israel's neighbors, to welcome Jews into the world community of peoples and nations. Tensions and worse in that region continue to remain high; needless and wanton deaths throughout the region, stridently negative political decisions, and costly military operations on both sides remain the order of the day.[3]

HOLOCAUST DENIALISM

Perversely, "Holocaust denialism" is the antisemitic attempt by a minority of so-called scholars, the majority of whom lack proper academic credentials as historians or in related disciplines, to question the historical veracity of the Holocaust/Shoah by: (1) focusing on specific details that legitimate scholars continue to discuss (e.g., the lack of a specific document signed by Hitler to mandate the extermination of the Jews, dismissing his numerous speeches); (2) arguing that the figure of six million Jewish deaths is far more inaccurate than the 100,000 at most who (unfortunately) perished during wartime from incarceration, disease, or as collateral military damage (accurate figures, however, put those tragic murders at somewhere between 5,933,000 and 5,967,000, though with the opening of the Soviet archives these figures may very well be revised upward); (3) arguing that the concentration camps, labor camps, and extermination camps were constructed not to murder Jews but to save and protect them from various European populations who may or may not have been antisemitic; and (4) continuing to affirm that the "Holohoax" is a nefarious plot on the part of Jews worldwide—specifically American and Israeli Jews—to continue financially to ruin not only Germany and its Second World War allies through reparation payments, but also the West, in support of the nation-state of Israel. The French term for such pseudohistory is *négationnisme* (negationism). Those who advocate this distortion of history argue that they are "historical revisionists" in keeping with the sound academic practice of revising our understandings of the past as new documents and other materials (e.g., archaeological evidence) surface and mandate both revising and rewriting our knowledge. These ongoing efforts at Holocaust/Shoah denialism cannot be divorced from various antisemitic conspiracies theories against the Jewish people, most notably, *The Protocols of the Learned Elders of Zion* of the early twentieth century, which remains current. Such denialism obviously started with the Nazis. During the last days of the Third Reich, Heinrich Himmler (1900–45; the *Reichsführer* of the SS and a leading member of the Nazi Party)—the "architect" of the Nazi genocide—gave orders to destroy evidence of their crimes (e.g., unearthing bodies and reducing them to ash, destroying camp buildings and records, etc.). Even before, Himmler and others made much use of coded language and concealment about their crimes, the most obvious being *die Endlösung der Judenfrage* ("the Final Solution to the Jewish Question"). In the aftermath of the Second World War, American professor Harry Elmer Barnes (1889–1968), who taught at Columbia University in New York (1918–29), came to question the Holocaust, as did French political activist and author Paul Rassinier (1906–67), who, ironically, had spent time in both Buchenwald and Mittelbau-Dora as a member of the French Resistance. Rassinier is still considered by many today, both his supporters and critics, as "the father of Holocaust denial." In 1978–79, American antisemite Willis Carto (1926–2015) founded the Institute for Historical Review in California, as well as its publishing house, Noontide Press, and began to publish the *Journal of Historical Review*, all blatant attempts to foist Holocaust/

Shoah denialism on the unsuspecting by lending it an aura of supposed academic legitimacy, including a series of annual conferences at which speakers attempted to debunk historical scholarship on the Holocaust. Today, the ease of use vis-à-vis the Internet continues to provide numerous forums, websites, and the like, for such denialists worldwide to post unsubstantiated and false historical claims, including books and other documents. To combat Holocaust denialism online, the Nizkor Project (from the Hebrew for "we will remember," www.nizkor.org), for example, was founded by Ken McVay and gifted to B'nai B'rith of Canada in 2010.

In September 1996, David Irving (b. 1938) filed a libel suit in the British courts against American professor Deborah Lipstadt (b. 1947) of Emory University, in Atlanta, Georgia, and her publisher, Penguin Books, for her characterization of Irving as a Holocaust denier, falsifier of history, and bigot/racist in her book *Denying the Holocaust: The Growing Assault on Truth and Memory* (1994). Because British law—unlike American law—places the burden of proof on the defendant rather than the plaintiff, Lipstadt assembled not only an excellent legal team, but a group of scholars who thoroughly eviscerated Irving's protestations. Judge Charles Gray (b. 1942), finding for Lipstadt, ordered Irving to pay the publisher's costs, which amounted to more than GB £2,000,000 (US $3,000,000), causing Irving to file for bankruptcy and lose his home, but this did not prevent him from writing, traveling, and lecturing in support of his continuing denialist falsehoods. The case also became the subject of the 2016 film "Denial."[4]

Among the most well-known and infamous Holocaust denialists are the following:

Mahmoud Ahmadinejad (b. 1956): the sixth president of Iran (2005–13). During his term in office, he hosted the denialist International Conference to Review the Global Vision of the Holocaust (2006) and, after leaving office, he sponsored the International Holocaust Cartoon Competition (2015).

Austin App (1902–84): a German American professor of medieval English literature who taught at the University of Scranton and La Salle University. App defended Germans and Nazi Germany during the Second World War. He is known for his work denying the Holocaust, and he has been called the first major American Holocaust denier.

Andrew Anglin (b. 1984): an American neo-Nazi, white supremacist, and Holocaust denier who hosts a website and message board that continue to advocate for genocide against Jews.

Don Black (b. 1953): the founder and webmaster of the antisemitic, neo-Nazi, white supremacist, Holocaust denialist, and racist Stormfront Internet forum. He was a grand wizard in the Ku Klux Klan (KKK) and a member of the American Nazi Party in the 1970s.

Pat Buchanan (b. 1938): an American paleoconservative political commentator who has in the past unsuccessfully run for office. He is an author, syndicated columnist, politician, and broadcaster who continues to challenge accepted facts of Holocaust/Shoah history and make overtly antisemitic statements.

Arthur Butz (b. 1933): an associate professor of electrical engineering at Northwestern University and best known for his Holocaust denialist views and as the author of *The Hoax of the Twentieth Century*, a Holocaust denial publication that argues that the Holocaust was a propaganda hoax.

Roger Garaudy (1913–2012): a French philosopher, resistance fighter, and a prominent communist author who converted to Islam in 1982. In 1998, he was prosecuted for Holocaust denial under French law for claiming that the death of six million Jews was a myth.

Hutton Gibson (b. 1918): the father of the American actor Mel Gibson (b. 1956). In a 2003 interview, he questioned how the Nazis could have disposed of six million bodies during the Holocaust/Shoah and claimed that the September 11, 2001, attacks were perpetrated by remote control. He has also been quoted as saying the Second Vatican Council (1962–65), which rejected Jewish responsibility for the death of the Christ and repudiated antisemitism as anti-Christian, was "a Masonic plot backed by the Jews."

Michael A. Hoffman II (b. 1950): an American denier and conspiracy theorist and known for his attacks on Orthodox Judaism, the Talmud, and Zionism. Hoffman published one book on the Zündel trial in Canada, arguing that Zündel's case was that of free speech and that, legally, he should be allowed to publish whatever he chooses. He also worked for a time as the assistant director of the Institute for Historical Review in California, and his newsletter *Revisionist History* regularly publishes Holocaust-denying materials.

Fred A. Leuchter (b. 1943): an American Holocaust denier who is best known as being the author of the "Leuchter Reports," pseudoscientific documents that allege there were no gas chambers at Auschwitz-Birkenau. Leuchter's work is often presented by Holocaust deniers as scientifically based evidence for Holocaust denial, despite his research methods and findings having been widely discredited on both scientific and historical grounds.

Germar Rudolf (b. 1964): a German chemist and convicted Holocaust denier in Germany and the author of numerous publications attempting to repudiate the Holocaust.

Bradley R. Smith (1930–2016): the founder of the Committee for Open Debate on the Holocaust (CODOH). He attempted to place controversial advertisements in college and university newspapers under such titles as "A Revisionist Challenge to the US Holocaust Memorial Museum" and "The Holocaust Controversy: The Case for Open Debate." Under the guise of free speech, more than 350 student newspapers published the ads.

Ernst Zündel (1939–2017): the publisher of denialist literature in Canada. He was brought to trial in the 1980s and jailed several times both in Canada and in Germany. After his release, he remained in Germany until his death.

THE AMERICAN JEWISH STORY[5]

Dominating the "Jewish world stage," to be sure, are both the stories and the fates of its two largest Jewish communities, those of the United States and Israel, though a much more expansive text would encompass equally important communities as well (e.g., those of the former Soviet Union, Great Britain, France, Germany, South America, Australia). However, and somewhat more realistically and honestly, the future fate of the Jewish people worldwide may very well hinge upon the fate of these two largest populations of Jews and what the unknown future holds for both.

The American Jewish story is usually told in terms of "waves" of immigration: Spanish/Portuguese; Ashkenazic, first German then Polish/Russian; and, finally, post-Second World War/Holocaust, a mixing of all who survived. The reality, however, is that this "journey to freedom" began with something of a trickle rather than a wave.

In 1654, twenty-three (23!) Jews, descendants of those who survived the Spanish/Portuguese Inquisition of 1492, arrived at the port of New Amsterdam (later renamed New York), the Dutch colony of New Netherlands, under the governorship of Director-General Peter Stuyvesant (1610–72). After they were initially denied admission, Stuyvesant was prevailed upon to request confirmation of his decision from the Dutch West India Company, on whose board of directors sat

Jews. Request denied. Stuyvesant would try a second time in court to deny Jewish residents the right to bear arms as a badge of citizenship. Again, he lost, and thus we have the beginnings of the American Jewish community. In 1730, the first synagogue was built in North America: Congregation Shearith Israel ("Remnant of Israel") in New York City.

Between this rather small beginning and the Civil War ("The War Between the States," 1861–65), German Jews would arrive in droves. Well-educated and cultured, they would populate the country, originally arriving in the South (e.g., Charleston and Savannah, South Carolina, which saw the first liberal prayerbook, *The Sabbath Service and Miscellaneous Prayers Adopted by the Reformed Society of Israelites*) and the Northeast (New York and Boston, Massachusetts). In turn, they would establish the organizational pattern of American Jewish religious life most noticeably under the Bavarian-American rabbi Isaac Mayer Wise (1819–1900), who began his career in Albany, New York, but would move to and flourish in Cincinnati, Ohio, establishing the rabbinical seminary, the Hebrew Union College in 1875 (which would later merge with the New York Jewish Institute of Religion in 1947, and which, today, has campuses in Cincinnati, Los Angeles, California, New York City, and Jerusalem, Israel), the Central Conference of American Rabbis in 1889, and the Union of American Hebrew Congregations in 1873 (and now renamed the Union for Reform Judaism).

Though Wise envisioned all three as American umbrella organizations, such did not come to pass. The Positive-Historical movement, established in Germany by Rabbi Zacharias Frankel to counter what he perceived as the excesses of Reform Judaism, would become in the United States the Conservative movement with its flagship institution the Jewish Theological Seminary founded in New York in 1886, the Rabbinical Assembly in 1901, and United Synagogue in 1870. Mainstream centrist Orthodoxy would follow suit with the establishment of Yeshiva University (originally Yeshiva College in 1908), and its own seminary, the Rabbi Isaac Elchanan Theological Seminary in 1886, the Rabbinical Council of America in 1923, and the Union of Orthodox Jewish Congregations in 1898. Each of these movements has grown, flourished, and splintered somewhat in the open environment of the United States.

Jews would also participate in the American Revolutionary War (1765–83) as both soldiers and supportive citizens, freeing up the British colonists from British tyranny. Perhaps the most well-known today was the financier Hayim Solomon (1740–85), but other important figures include: Mordecai Sheftall (1735–97) of Savannah, Georgia; Reuben

Etting (1762–1848) of Baltimore, Maryland; Abigail Minis (1701–94) of Charleston, South Carolina; Aaron Lopez (1731–82) of Newport, Rhode Island; Rabbi Gershom Mendes Seixas (1745–1816) of New York, New York; and many others. Jews had, indeed, found a home on these shores and were willing to fight and die to preserve their freedom.

Prior to the twentieth century, increasing antisemitism in Czarist Russia and throughout Eastern Europe brought thousands of Jews to the United States. Unlike their German counterparts, they were not participants in the larger societies where they lived, leading restricted lives in terms of both residence (i.e., the so-called "Pale of Settlement" in Russia) and economic opportunities, ofttimes relegating them to the lowest classes for their own survival. Then, too, they brought with them a religious Judaism, primarily, Hasidic but, equally, far more narrowly Orthodox, and which was highly disturbing to those Jews who preceded them and saw their own Judaism— Reform and Conservative, less so Orthodox—well integrated into the fabric of America and American religious life. Then, too, many of those who came, some as young as twelve or fourteen years of age, were secularists and radical political activists, resulting from their years of oppression, and brought their own brand of politics with them. Despite these, at times stark, differences, the Jews who came before them would work hard to integrate these "new Jews" into American society, providing jobs, relief aid, schools, language instruction, fellowship organizations (e.g., B'nai B'rith, "Sons of the Covenant," founded in 1843), and the like. Today, whatever one's Jewish background and geographic heritage, Jews are Jews, and such historical distinctions matter little if all, with the important exception of religious differences—Hasidic vs. non-Hasidic Orthodox, Orthodox vs. non-Orthodox.[6]

Both the Russian Revolution (1917–23) and the First World War I (1914–18) would find Europe's Jews active in both, fighting on the side of the Bolsheviks in Russia, and fighting on both sides—Axis and Allies— in "the war to end all wars."[7] Perhaps the most infamous Jew in the Russian conflagration was Leon Trotsky (born Lev Davidovich Bronstein, 1879–1940), People's Commissar for Military and Naval Affairs (1918– 25), who would later be murdered in Mexico by agents of the Soviet Union leader Josef Stalin. The aftermath of both conflicts—especially the increasing antisemitism in now Soviet Russia—would find Jews emigrating to the safe haven of the United States.

The rise of Nazism in Germany under Adolf Hitler, his arrival as Chancellor (January 1933) and with him the Final Solution as the regime's vicious and murderous brand of antisemitism, coupled with initial miliary successes in Eastern Europe early on in the Second World War, found Jews precariously struggling for their own physical survival as, consistently, their hoped-for immigration plans increasingly turned to dust. The allied nations fighting the Nazis, however, reveal a consistent pattern of denial and legal barriers to those attempting to flee—including the United States.[8] American Jews did step up in the fight against Nazism and Germany and her allies in disproportion to their numbers and many saw first-hand the results of the Nazis unsuccessful attempt to erase a living population from Europe. The scars of the Holocaust remain ever present in American (and European and Israeli) memory, not only among those who survived and came to the United States after the war, their children and grandchildren, the American Jewish community, and the larger American society, as evidenced by the creation of the United States Holocaust Memorial Museum in 1980. One very real and concrete manifestation of this memory is, in the main, the overwhelming support of American Jews for the State of Israel and its own compatibility with the aims of Zionism as the successful establishment and return of Jews to their historic homeland. In 2004, the United States Congress established the Commission for Commemorating 350 Years of American Jewish History with the Library of Congress, the National Archives and Records Administration, the American Jewish Historical Society, New York, and the Jacob Rader Marcus Center of the American Jewish Archives on the campus of the Hebrew Union College-Jewish Institute of Religion, Cincinnati, Ohio.

Prior to the twenty-first century, American Jews, despite periodic flare-ups of antisemitism, have understood their residence in the United States almost in defiance of all past Jewish history, as unique unto itself, successfully integrating themselves into the larger community and nation-state, contributing to its economic, cultural, and political[9] productivity, disproportionately for a community of little more than 7,000,000 children, women, and men out of a "sea" of more than 360,000,000 persons. However, in the twenty-first century, after all their successes, American Jews still manifest their concerns for their own survival as increasing antisemitism continues to rear its ugly head, birth rates are stable or declining, exogamous marriage outside the Jewish community shows no signs of abating, religious involvement outside Orthodox circles appears to be waning, and philanthropic, organizational and institutional commitments also appear to be lessening on the part of younger generations. Neither crystal balls, nor other manners of prophecy will work. The future of American Jews and Judaism remain an ever-present source of debate and discussion among those for whom it is vitally important.

THE ISRAELI JEWISH STORY[10]

The story of modern Israel is rooted in the Torah/Hebrew Bible/Old Testament and the Jewish religious traditions, which have arisen from it, and which have sustained the Jewish people for the last several thousand years, epitomized, perhaps, in Psalm 137:1: "By the waters of Babylon, there we sat down and wept when we remembered Zion." Dating the Babylonian exile to 586 BCE, this means *in real and concrete terms* that Jews have longed to return and reestablish their political sovereignty for more than 2,600 years, until that dream was ultimately realized with David Ben-Gurion's proclamation on Tel Aviv radio, and dancing in the streets, declaring the reborn State of Israel on May 14, 1948.

At no point in all Jewish history, however, were Jews absent from the land, even if, at times, they were a decided minority. The rise of modern political Zionism—the longing to return—is attributed to the towering presence of Austrian assimilated Jew and journalist Theodor Herzl, who, after covering the infamous Dreyfus Trial in France and exposed to the daily occurrence of antisemitism there and elsewhere, returned home to conclude that the *only* viable solution to antisemitism was for Jews to have a nation-state of their own. (Although somewhat more flexible than those he drew to his banner—e.g., the suggestion of British-held Kenya as a *temporary* solution—he, too, would come to realize that *only* the Land of Israel would meet the needs and expectations of worldwide Jewry, especially those religiously motivated, Eastern European Jews.)[11]

Herzl would go on to meet with world leaders, including Turkey which held sovereignty of the land of Palestine, delicately implying that he represented world Jewry. In 1897, he convened the First Zionist Congress in Basle, Switzerland.[12] The year before, 1896, he published his pamphlet *Der Judenstaat* (either "The Jewish State" or "The State of the Jews") setting forth his vision. In that text, he concluded:

> Let me repeat once more my opening words: The Jews who wish for a State will have it. We shall live at last as free me on our own soil and die peacefully in our own homes. The world will be freed by our liberty, enriched by our wealth, magnified by our greatness. And whatever we attempt there to accomplish by our own welfare will react powerfully and beneficially for the good of humanity.[13]

He did not live long enough to realize his dream, though was said to have remarked on his deathbed in 1904, "Fifty years from now, there will be a Jewish state."

Jews throughout the world, inspired by Herzl and others—e.g., poet Chaim Nachman Bialik, essayist and litterateur Ahad Ha'am ("One of the People," born Asher Ginzberg, 1856–1927)—would gather, exercise whatever political and economic power they saw themselves possessing, and work diligently to realize their dream of a reborn State of Israel.

The First World War and its immediate aftermath would intrude but not necessarily interrupt that dream. As noted, Jews fought on both sides of the conflict and Zionists could be found in Germany, France, the United States, Russia, and, most importantly, Great Britain, which held governing responsibility over Palestine as a League of Nations mandated territory. (Turkey was forced to surrender its hold as payment/punishment for having sided with Germany.)

In 1917, Arthur Balfour, then British Foreign Secretary, had delivered to Lord Walter Rothschild, second Baron Rothschild, a letter which would subsequently become known as the "Balfour Declaration." Dated November 2, it read:

> I have much pleasure in conveying to you, on behalf of His Majesty's Government, the following declaration of sympathy with Jewish Zionist aspiration which has been submitted, and approved by the Cabinet:
>
> His Majesty's Government view with favour the establishment in Palestine of a national home for the Jewish people and will use their best endeavours to facilitate the achievement of this object, it being clearly understood that nothing shall be done which may prejudice the civil and religious rights of existing non-Jewish communities in Palestine, or the rights and political status enjoyed by Jews in any other country.
>
> I would be grateful if you would bring this declaration to the knowledge of the Zionist Federation.[14]

Carefully worded, Jews worldwide celebratorily misinterpreted and misunderstood the letter as British support for a Jewish nation-state. Its ambiguous phrase "national home" was delicately used, open to other possible understandings, but had no legal or international force or standing. Nonetheless, Jews, again worldwide, began increasing their efforts eventually to bring about such a nation-state. The European political upheavals after the First World War, coupled with the Second World War and the realization of the devastation of the Holocaust/Shoah only increased and intensified those efforts. Important to those efforts as well was the creation of the United Nations (UN) in October 1945, the successor to the League of Nations.[15]

Sensitive to both Jewish realities in the aftermath of the Holocaust/ Shoah, and Arab displeasure at the thought of a seeming Jewish majority in the region, the UN consistently tried fruitlessly to make peace between Jews, Arabs within Palestine, and the surrounding Arab states.

Oh May 15, 1947, the United Nations created the Special Committee on Palestine (UNSCOP) and submitted its report on September 3 of that year: Britain was to surrender mandate control, and the land itself was to be partitioned into a Jewish state and Palestinian state. The Jews accepted the report, the Arabs did not; and the "Arab/Palestinian-Israeli conflict" would grow in intensity with wars being fought in 1948 (which both Palestinians and other Arabs refer to as the *Naqba* — "The Catastrophe"), 1956 (the Suez Canal crisis), 1967 (the Six-Day War), 1973 (the Yom Kippur War), 1981 (the Lebanese incursion), and regular terrorist raids into Israel throughout up to the present day with both Fatah historically and Hamas contemporarily engaging in such acts.[16] In 2005, Israel withdrew from the Gaza region and repopulated and relocated formerly Jewish settlements within its own borders. That act, however, has not reduced tensions within the region. Israel's relationship with its neighbors—including Egypt with whom it signed a Peace Accord in 1978 (which, ultimately, would cause the assassinations of both Egyptian president Anwar el-Sadat [1918–81] and Israeli prime minister Yitzhak Rabin [1922–95])—is a "cold peace."[17] Nor have tensions reduced in Israel's governance over its own Palestinian population—who are themselves citizens of Israel, but decidedly second class and who are regarded by some as victims of the world's longest ongoing occupation.

Yet, despite these seemingly formidable and unresolved difficulties, the State of Israel continues to be a vibrant democracy in a region where democracy is not the political norm. Its Jewish population continues to grow and is expected to pass that of the United States by the beginning of the next century. Its economy and educational and technological expertise are second to none. Its cultural productivity is at an all-time high. Politically, however, its Jewish population appears to be turning more to the right and more conservative, and the recent 2022 election and return to office of former prime minister Benjamin Netanyahu (b. 1949) has caused Jewish concern outside the State of Israel. Additionally, the seemingly growing power of the religious right (read Orthodoxy, Sephardic, Hasidic, and non-Hasidic) has also caused concern. Important to note as well is the reality that American Jewish support for the State of Israel, perhaps, as a consequence of both the Holocaust/Shoah and Israel's repeated conflicts, has neither lessened nor wavered to any appreciable degree, even if not always unified.[18, 19]

* * *

In conclusion, the final decades of the twentieth century found Jews relatively safely ensconced in Western democratic societies such as the United States, Australia, and Canada, less so in Germany (the fastest growing Jewish population on the European continent), Great Britain (whose Jewish population is not increasing to any appreciable degree) and France (where antisemitism appears to be rife and its Jewish population is dwarfed by an Arab and Muslim population of immigrants ten times its size), and facing hostile enemies inside Israel and the nations under Arab and Muslim control. At the start of the twenty-first century, however, Jews remain troubled by their existence: too many continue to perceive themselves as the world's "pariah people."

The ongoing issues of safety and security and a meaningful survival continue to dominate the Jewish landscape worldwide and not just in locations of danger.

NOTES

1 Michael R. Marrus, *Lessons of the Holocaust* (Toronto: University of Toronto Press, 2016), 4.

2 See, for example: Jeremy Black, *The Holocaust: History and Memory* (Bloomington: Indiana University Press, 2016); David Cesarani, *Final Solution: The Fate of the Jews, 1933–49* (New York, NY: Macmillan, 2016); Debórah Dwork and Robert Jan van Pelt, *Holocaust: A History* (New York, NY: W.W. Norton & Co., 2002); Christian Gerlach, *The Extermination of the European Jews* (Cambridge: Cambridge University Press, 2016); Peter Hayes, *Why? Explaining the Holocaust* (New York, NY: W.W. Norton & Co., 2017); Peter Longerich, *Holocaust: The Nazi Persecution and Murder of the Jews* (Oxford: Oxford University Press, 2010); Marrus, *Lessons of the Holocaust*; Lisa Pine (ed.), *Life and Times in Nazi Germany* (London: Bloomsbury Academic, 2016); and Laurence Rees, *The Holocaust: A New History* (New York, NY: Public Affairs, 2017).

3 This material, somewhat rewritten, as well as that of Holocaust/Shoah denialism, is taken from Jacobs, *Antisemitism*, 56–63, 63–7.

4 See, for example: Richard J. Evans, *Lying about Hitler: History, Holocaust, and the David Irving Trial* (New York, NY: Basic Books, 2001); Ted Gottfried,

Steven Leonard Jacobs

Deniers of the Holocaust: Who They Are, What They Do, Why They Do It (Brookfield, CT: Twenty-First Century Books, 2001); Charles Gray, *The Irving Judgment: David Irving V. Penguin Books and Professor Deborah Lipstadt* (New York, NY: Penguin Books, 2000); D.D. Guttenplan, *The Holocaust on Trial: History, Justice and the David Irving Libel Case* (New York, NY: W.W. Norton & Co., 2002); R.A. Kahn, *Holocaust Denial and the Law: A Comparative Study* (New York, NY: Palgrave Macmillan, 2004); Deborah Lipstadt, *Denying the Holocaust: The Growing Assault on Truth and Memory* (New York: Plume; London: Penguin, 1994), and *History on Trial: My Day in Court with a Holocaust Denier* (New York, NY: Harper Perennial, 2006); Robert Jan van Pelt, *The Case for Auschwitz: Evidence from the Irving Trial* (Bloomington: Indiana University Press, 2016); Kenneth Stern, *Holocaust Denial* (New York, NY: American Jewish Committee, 1993); and John C. Zimmerman, *Holocaust Denial: Demographics, Testimonies, and Ideologies* (Lanham, MD: University Press of America, 2000).

5 Two excellent overviews are Howard Morley Sachar, *A History of the Jews of America*, reprint (New York, NY: Vintage, 1993), and Jonathan Sarna, *American Judaism: A History* (New Haven, CT: Yale University Press, 2019).

6 The classic work addressing the story of Eastern European Jews in the United States is Irving Howe, *World of Our Fathers: The Journey of the East European Jews to America and the Life They Found and Made*, annotated ed. (New York,NY: New York University Press, 2005).

7 On a personal note, the author's own two grandfathers American Samuel Buchler (d. 1929) and Polish-German Leo Jacob (murdered in Treblinka death camp, July 1942) each fought for their respective countries, and may, somewhat ironically, have faced each other in France, where both were stationed during the war.

8 Immigration historian David Wyman's (1929–2018) two books, *Paper Walls: America and the Refugee Crisis, 1938–1941*, reprint (Lexington, MA: Plunkett Lake Press, 2019) and *The Abandonment of the Jews: America and the Holocaust, 1941–1945*, reprint (Lexington, MA: Plunkett Lake Press, 2018), tell this sordid chapter in American history without minimizing what took place.

9 Perhaps the best example of political integration was the candidacy of Democratic senator Joseph Lieberman (b. 1942) of Connecticut, an Orthodox Jew, as US vice president, running mate to former vice president and US presidential candidate, Tennessean Al Gore (b. 1948) in their unsuccessful 2000 election.

10 A good overall telling of Israel's story is Howard Morley Sachar, *A History of Israel: From the Rise of Zionism to Our Time*, 3rd rev. and updated ed. (New York, NY: Alfred A. Knopf, 2007).

11 A fascinating look into other geographical solutions is that of Adam Rovner, *In the Shadow of Zion: Promised Lands before Israel* (New York, NY: New York University Press, 2014).

12 The "Basel Program" included the following points:

1. The promotion by appropriate means of the settlement in Palestine of Jewish farmers, artisans, and manufacturers.
2. The organization and uniting of the whole of Jewry by means of appropriate institutions, both local and international, in accordance with the laws of each country.
3. The strengthening and fostering of Jewish national sentiment and national consciousness.
4. Preparatory steps toward obtaining the consent of governments, where necessary, in order to reach the goals of Zionism.

13 Quote taken from the 1946 edition of *Der Judenstaat*, published by the American Zionist Emergency Council and translated from the German by Sylvie d'Avigdor. See, also, Henk Overberg, *The Jews' State: A Critical English Translation* (Northvale, NJ: Jason Aronson, 1997). Herzl's was not the only text to re-inspire Jews to actualize their yearning for Zion. In 1862, German-Jewish philosopher Moses Hess (d. 1875) published his *Rom und Jerusalem: Die letzte Nationalitätenfrage* ("Rome and Jerusalem: The Last National Question"), a socialist advocacy for return. In 1882, Russian-Polish-Jewish doctor Leo Pinsker (1821–91) published his own pamphlet, *Selbstemanzipation* ("Auto-Emancipation"), also arguing for Jewish self-rule and a national consciousness as a solution to antisemitism. Two important anthologies of Zionist thought are Arthur Hertzberg (ed.), *The Zionist Idea: A Historical Analysis and Reader* (Philadelphia, PA: Jewish Publication Society, 1997), and Gil Troy (ed.), *The Zionist Ideas: Visions for the Jewish Homeland—Then, Now, Tomorrow* (Philadelphia, PA: Jewish Publication Society, 2018).

14 See https://avalon.law.yale.edu/20th_century/balfour.asp (accessed 20 May 2023).

15 See, for example, Leonard Stein, *The Balfour Declaration* (New York, NY: American Council of Learned Societies, 2008), and Jonathan Schneer, *The Balfour Declaration: The Origins of the Arab-Israeli Conflict* (New York, NY: Random House, 2012).

16 Fatah was first called the Palestinian National Liberation Movement and remains a nationalist, social democratic political party. Founded in 1959, over the years it has engaged in terrorist activities. Hamas, founded in 1987, is a Palestinian fundamentalist, Sunni-Islamist militant organization with a strong social service component. It, too, engages in terrorist activities. The State of Israel engages in ongoing political discussions with Fatah, based in Ramallah. It does not do so to any appreciable degree with Hamas.

17 In 2020, Israel "normalized" its relationships with the United Arab Emirates (UAE), Bahrain, Sudan, and Morocco.

18 See, for example, Walter Russell Mead, *The Arc of a Covenant: The United States, Israel, and the Fate of the Jewish People* (New York, NY: Alfred A. Knopf, 2022), and Eric Alterman, *We Are Not One: A History of America's Fight Over Israel* (New York, NY: Basic Books, 2022).

19 Important to Israel's story as well are: Chaim Weizmann (1874–1952), its first president; Golda Meir (1898–1978), Israel's first and only woman prime minister; and Judah Magnes (1877–1948), the first president of the Hebrew University of Jerusalem.

12

THE TWENTY-FIRST-CENTURY MOMENT AND BEYOND AND CONCLUSIONS

Given the extraordinary historical journey of the Jews—the good with the bad; the ups with the downs—and the evolving creativity of its religious expression throughout its journey, at the beginning of this twenty-first century, only the most naïve reader would suggest a present and future free of difficulties (but certainly one also filled with promises and successes). This chapter will focus on the three issues that loom largest in Jewish thinking and consciousness, and that, in the process, have brought forth more publications and presentations, both within and outside Jewish circles, than others. They are: (1) American, Israeli, and worldwide Jewish survival; (2) antisemitism: hatred old and new; and (3) the Middle East: Israel and her neighbors.

AMERICAN, ISRAELI, AND WORLDWIDE JEWISH SURVIVAL

Jews throughout the world continue to share a common concern for their collective survival. Among the Jewish people worldwide, in the aftermath of the Second World War and the ongoing crises in the Middle East, there are those for whom their Judaic identity—religious and nonreligious—is central to their existence, those for whom it is central most of the time and peripheral at other times, and those for whom it is peripheral all the time. Coupled with the sociological reality that the longer one's period of education (a primary Judaic value), the later one marries and the fewer children one has, this all adds to other levels of anxiety. Moreover, in environments where Jews are increasingly welcomed and accepted—the United States being the prime example—

diminished Jewish commitments resulting from intermarriage/mixed-marriage increases that angst.

For those in the first category, issues and concern with the literal physical survival of Jews is paramount. For those in the second category, they, too, are somewhat concerned, if perhaps less committed, but are more willing to be on the receiving end of innovative programs to ensure such survival, rather than on the so-called "front line" addressing the question. For those in the third category, the accident of their birth is just that, neither a fortuitous nor a disadvantageous event, but a simple fact, one of questionable meaning in the working out of their own lives, and, following the normal human progression of plodding the path of least resistance, they are as likely as not to remain within the structures of the organized Jewish communities where they reside, but do not communicate to their own offspring the positivity of Jewish involvement. That is, they *may* join Jewish congregations, they *may* educate their children Jewishly, they *may* contribute financially to Jewish causes, and they *may* remain current in their knowledge of issues of Judaic concern. About this last group, there are no guarantees whatsoever.

Thus, surveying the worldwide communities of Jews, two opposite approaches appear to present themselves: organizations and communities that invest their energies and resources in programs and opportunities directed toward those who are already committed to Jewish life and Jewish survival, regardless of denominational affiliation; and others who direct their energies and resources in outreach towards those who are only marginally identified and marginally concerned.

AMERICAN JEWISH COMMUNITIES

Turning first to the American Jewish communities—the prevailing myth is that of unity—divisiveness is the norm rather than the exception, even on issues of agreed-upon concern (e.g., Israel and antisemitism). Yet, there is a strong feeling and sense of privilege at the opportunity to be Jews in a country still evolving its own relationships to its subpopulations, where overt discrimination is addressed legally, where governments are neither controlled by nor answerable to religious institutions, and where the very diversity of population is its strength. For Jews, the United States, by and large, continues to be—in the old Yiddish phrase, *der goldineh medina* ("the golden land")—a land of seemingly limitless opportunity, where access to residence, profession, economic success, and life partners are relatively obstacle free.

What such freedom, however, portends for America's Jews remains the question. In twenty-first century America, where Jews are freer not only to accomplish much but less afraid of antisemitism, safer and more secure than anywhere else in the world, including present-day Israel, Jews now confront what it means to be "free Jews," with all the strengths, complexities, and simplicities that that freedom carries with it. How such communities of Jews will, ultimately, work out their personal and collective identities is a chapter in a text yet to be written.

STATE OF ISRAEL

The freedom to "be Jewish" and to "do Jewish" is a hallmark of this nation-state, arising like a phoenix from the ashes of the Holocaust/Shoah at the end of the Second World War, and welcoming Jews who would come to participate in its creation, but one facing two problems radically different from each other and potentially dangerous for its citizenry: first, an entrenched right-wing, politically militant, Jewish religious Orthodoxy, which actively discourages any and all attempts to allow non-Orthodox religious alternatives for its Jewish population, and which, in the process, furthers the secularization of much of Israeli life; second, a perpetually tense, hostile residence in a militarily at-the-ready part of the world that has seen armed conflicts in 1956, 1967, 1973, 1981, and 2006. While political and military scholars do acknowledge that the likelihood of the Israeli state "being wiped off the map" is extremely unlikely—given its highly-developed military system and armaments, including nuclear capabilities—seventy plus years of ongoing tension has resulted in the creation of a kind of "new Jew" (Hebrew, *sabra*, "cactus" or "prickly pear"): fluent in Hebrew, knowledgeable in the Judaic sources of Torah/Hebrew Bible, Talmud, Midrash, and so on, but increasingly estranged from Judaic religious life. Whether such estrangement will result in a new schism of incalculable proportions for future Jewish survival remains an open-ended question.

JEWS WORLDWIDE

For the remaining Jews worldwide, however, these questions and concerns play directly into their own. They are, however, coupled with their own real and evident concerns about their ability to nourish and sustain their own populations, concerns about economic, institutional, and leadership resources, birthrates versus deathrates, intermarriage/ mixed-marriage, and other issues. Examples include the following: the Jewish population of Great Britain is not growing to any appreciable degree; the Jewish population of France remains relatively stable in a country where its increasing Arab population is fast approaching ten percent of the total; the Jewish populations of other European countries remain small (Poland, Romania, Bosnia, the Scandinavian countries—all evidence of Hitler's tragic *success*)—with long-range prognoses for their survival more negative rather than positive.

Ironically, two "bright spots" on the world scene are Germany, where its Jewish (and Israeli) population continues to be the fastest growing on the European continent, and the former Soviet Union, which is experiencing something of a religious revival among its approximately three million Jews and which certainly could never have been predicted during the Communist era, with its opposition to all manner of religious expression, especially that of the Jews.

Thus, for a people who have journeyed so far, concern for its physical survival and its ability to sustain and grow in number remains. However, worldwide, Jews continue to be optimistic; and most of them appear to be working hard to sustain themselves in the present and prepare for the always-unknown future.

ANTISEMITISM: HATRED OLD AND NEW

At the end of the nineteenth century, the "father of modern political Zionism" Theodor Herzl published his tract, *Der Judenstadt*, arguing for the creation of a Jewish state that would, in effect, level the playing field, make the Jewish people a nation-state among equals, and, consequently, lead to a lessening of worldwide antisemitism. Sadly, and tragically, such has not proven to be the case: indeed, as a result of the reality of the modern State of Israel and its ongoing confrontations in the Middle East, antisemitism has not lessened but increased. Whether or not that is true, antisemitism—hatred of the Jews and Judaism and now Jewish Israelis and Zionism/Zionists—remains the oldest hatred and biggest lie, continuing to rear its ugly head, and has experienced something of a resurgence in the last part of the twentieth century and on into this twenty-first century, primarily in Europe, and certainly in the Middle East.

As a minority population in every country in the world except for Israel itself, Jews do remain somewhat at risk where those who oppose them feel free to take matters into their own hands, and/or violate the laws of the nation-state. In the post-Second World War era, Western countries continue to show a remarkable intolerance for those who practice antisemitism, and often fully prosecute its perpetrators. Even the United Nations, with its remarkable record of consistent biases and denigrations of the State of Israel, has condemned antisemitism.

Yet, antisemitism continues, and Jews continue to worry—their own history has taught them the truth of the saying "forewarned is forearmed." Jews, especially in the West, have learned what they perceive as *the* lesson of the Holocaust/Shoah: that such overt hatred of Jews and Judaism cannot be met with silence, indifference, or tolerance, but must be met instead with legal, political, religious, social, educational responses, not only on the part of agencies created specifically for this task (e.g., in the United States, the Anti-Defamation League), but in the workplace, college and university settings, the courtrooms, and in everyday life. While its total eradication may be something of a pipe-dream (given the human reality that there will always be people and groups who do not like each other, for whatever reason, and base their own failings on the supposed "power" of those same others, without the courage to confront their own failings), reducing the power of antisemitism to do evil to Jews and Judaism remains high on the agendas of organized Jewish communities worldwide. Significantly, already in the last century, networks of concern confronting antisemitism exist not only among Jews but now include non-Jews in support of Jews, governmental agencies—e.g., the US State Department regularly publishes its monitoring reports—Christian religious communities, and ordinary citizens. In this arena, too, there is hope as Jews continue to join among themselves and with others to fight what must be understood as a frontal assault on their very right to exist and to continue to be part of the human community.

THE MIDDLE EAST: ISRAEL AND HER NEIGHBORS

Throughout the world, more newspaper column inches and live media coverage continue to be devoted to events in the Middle East than any other topic—long before the events associated with America's 9/11 tragedy, and, perhaps, a reflection of the intimate bond between Jews and Christians in the rise of Western civilization, the intimacy of religious connections between Judaism and Christianity, and the simple fact that the central personage of Christianity—the Christ—was born into the Jewish people in that place. Like every other topic addressed in this text, the ins and outs of this ongoing Middle East conflict between Israel and her neighbors is complex, long-standing, and worthy of the many, many volumes that have already been published, are being published, and will be published, both analyzing the historical story of the conflict, and the temporary solutions and suggestions for its long-term resolution.

Fundamental to any discussion of the Middle East and its conflicts *must* be a discussion as well of the religious and theological understandings that both unite and divide Jews and Muslims, and the place of historical Christianity in the conversation. The "Zionist theology" of the Hebrew Bible/Old Testament is the place to start, as Israelites/Hebrews/Jews continue to understand themselves as stewards of a land given to them by their God. That they have behaved, collectively, marvelously in that place, can historically be documented; that they have behaved towards others less than their best, both in the distant past and the recent present, can likewise be historically documented and verified. However, for Jews—and not only those who live there or who have lived there and those who live outside the land and who fully support the right of Jews to live in their land—it is *their* land, and the decisions that flow from that ownership or stewardship—by divine fiat—must always take that fact into consideration, the present moment notwithstanding.

For the last two thousand years, with the birth and development of the various adumbrations of Christianity (first Roman Catholicism and Eastern Orthodoxy, and later the various Protestantisms), Christians' relationships with Jews and their relationship with the land itself have been uneven and ambivalent. Some have long supported the right of Jews to return and control the land of Israel, out of a theological matrix in which the Jews' return is the first step to their Christ's eventual return. Others, out of their own biases and prejudices against Jews, seem unable to integrate present Jewish hegemony into their own theological worldview, for how can Jewish "success" in returning to the land of their birth be squared with a people who continue to deny the reality of the Christ on whom all success is built and from whom all goodness flows? Still others, out of a far more negative theological interpretation of Jews and Judaism (and perhaps a strong desire to link to the Arabs and Muslims there for religious as well as political agendas) see no legitimacy whatsoever for present-day Jewish control of the land, and still view the last two thousand years of exile as concrete evidence of divine punishment and Jewish perfidy, the present moment only a temporary reprieve before a return to exile.

Six hundred years after the birth of Christianity comes a new voice to the table, that of Mohammed (570–632 CE), experiencing anew God's revelations, coupled with a strong political desire to unite the entire geography under one sovereignty, *Dar al-Islam* (Arabic, "house of submission") versus the world of *Dar al-Harb* (Arabic, "house of war"). That all the lands under this extended banner would be regarded as sacred and holy to Muslims makes sense: a "spot" under the political and religious control of Jews would thus prove and has proven to be an anathema, and thus must be conquered and their leadership and followers subjugated and worse. That they have thus far been unable to do so makes the ongoing crises from Arab and Muslim perspectives, coupled with successive military defeats, that much worse.

Thus, two religious traditions understand the same piece of land as sacred to both, given by God first to one and then to the other, and for whom each represents a threat. That the various forms of Christianity in their own religious-theological assessments overwhelmingly continue to support the Israeli/Jewish side only exacerbates the problem.

Into this heady brew of conflict comes a previous version of *realpolitik* that saw and sees Israel as the one true democracy in the Middle East, and for years the only true window into the affairs of the now former Soviet Union. During the heyday of the Cold War between the two superpowers of the Soviet Union and the United States, Israel (already perhaps perceived by some as a vassal-state rather than an ally of the US) sided consistently with the United States and provided a physical base from which to launch an attack should the need arise. Now, however, in the realignment of the world's nation-states, can such a history of friendship and service sustain a relationship presently and on into the future? Also, given the West's all-consuming need for oil resources, can Israel continue to count on the United States and her allies as it has in the past, or will other, Arab voices and nation-states, including those of the Palestinians, displace Israel in the coming generations? Israelis worry and Jews outside of Israel worry as well.

At the beginning of this twenty-first century, the United States and the West are engaged in what has been labeled a "war against terrorism," which their enemies have seemingly linked directly to the continuing instability of the Middle East and Israel's treatment of its Palestinian population. Whether this is wholly or partially accurate can be seriously questioned and debated. What is true, however, is that, within the current geopolitical boundaries of the sovereign State of Israel exist a people who do not wish to be governed by Israel and Jewish Israelis. Increasingly, many Jews and non-Jews alike both within Israel and throughout the world, have come to the conclusion that a two-state solution is the *only* viable solution to end this crisis of now more than half a century: a Jewish state governed by Jews and those who wish to live under its flag, and a Palestinian state, contiguous to Israel, composed predominantly of Arabs and Muslims and those who wish to live under its flag. Only time and goodwill on both sides, coupled with an overriding commitment to end the blood that has been shed for far too long, will determine whether the Jewish dream of *shalom*/peace and the Muslim dream of *salaam*/ peace can become a reality before it is too late for both sides. Whether this solution in this volatile part of the world will bring about an end to terror remains to be seen.

CONCLUSIONS

I have told the briefest of stories of both Judaism as the religious expression of the Jewish people over the course of their journey of several thousand years and the stories of their lives lived in various places as well. In these chapters, despite their brevity, I have painted (or perhaps sketched) a modern group of people who trace themselves lineally to the ancient biblical period and who understand themselves as inheritors of a rich legacy. They remain committed to this legacy not only in the present generation but for future generations as well, and not only in the largest settings (Israel, the United States, the former Soviet Union), but wherever Jews reside—no matter the size of their communities, their birthrates or the threats to their lives.

For religious Jews, their faith in their future is not augmented by crystal balls or other tools of the magician or soothsayer; for them, the B'rith/Covenant with the God of Israel—the one, true God of all humankind—is an eternal one. And, while at times abused by the disobedient (and punished in response), it is, ultimately, indestructible, shatter-proof, even by those Christians and Muslims who would claim its limitations as a result of their newer readings of past, present, and future. For these Jews, as long as this planet endures, there will be Jews, perhaps in different locations than those where they presently dwell, perhaps in different numbers than those we can presently count; perhaps in different religious configurations than those we presently see, though this remains open to continuous internal debate: the Orthodox convinced that only their approach will guarantee Jewish survival, and the non-Orthodox interpretations arguing that the diversity of approaches is the surest guarantor of that survival.

From an historical perspective, there is truth, indeed, in both these worldviews. The great German-Jewish historian Heinrich Graetz (1817–91) perceived the journey as one of peaks and valleys. That is to say, one could draw a graph of the journey using such a framework: as one Jewish community begins its descendancy, another begins its ascendancy, from the very beginnings, still shrouded in mystery, in the Middle East, through the present moment and on into the future. Though Graetz and others who have followed him have applied the very best scientific methods to their disciplines, they, perhaps, like their Jewish religious counterparts—despite all the evidence at times to the contrary—remain reluctant to recite the Kaddish memorial prayer for the end of the Jewish people and/or the religion of Judaism.

Perhaps, indeed, as a group, Jews are somewhat unique. All attempts at definition have come up short. Mordecai Kaplan, the founder of Reconstructionist religious Judaism, for example, used the term "civilization" to describe both the people and their extended systems of belief, values, culture, and so on, and possessing all the component parts of any civilization; regardless of whether or not they lived in their own land and were governed by those who were like them. Others, including the founders of Reform Judaism, sought to confine Jews and Judaism to religious categories only, divorcing ideas of peoplehood and/or nationhood from their vocabulary, only to be "shocked back" in the aftermath of the Holocaust/Shoah of the Second World War. Even the definition of this author early on in this text is only a point of departure, attempting to address a whole host of the people and the things to which they commit themselves. Perhaps, then, this continuing inability to define either the group or its system of thought and behavior is indicative of its amazing ability to surmount all obstacles and impediments to its ongoing survival.

Based on all the available evidence and given the sweep of Jewish history, the people known as the Jews and the religious traditions known as Judaism should not be here. The story should have come to its end, or been greatly diminished, following the destruction of the northern kingdom of Israel in 721 BCE after the Assyrian invasions. It should have come to its end following the destruction of the Southern Kingdom of Judah in the year 586 BCE. It should have come to its end following the destruction of Palestine in 70 CE after the Roman debacle. It should have come to its end, or been greatly diminished, after the expulsion from Spain in 1492 by King Ferdinand and Queen Isabella. It should have come to its end in the largest community at that time, Poland, in the seventeenth century after the Khmelnytsky massacres. It should have begun an unrecoverable descent after the Holocaust/Shoah of the Second World War. All these "shoulds," however, do not accord with what has taken place: in the aftermath of every destructive tragedy, the Jews have refused to succumb. Though initially reduced in numbers, they have survived, married and remarried, given birth, re-created devastated communities—sometimes in the same locations, sometimes in other locations—and continued to celebrate their religious traditions, both as they have known them in the past and modified them to meet new realities. The threefold mandate of preservation, adaptation, and innovation continues to serve as a cornerstone of their religious and other survivals.

Twenty-first century reality? The American Jewish communities are seemingly slowly growing in number even as they are beset by concerns of intermarriage/mixed marriage in a welcoming environment where antisemitism continues in own downward spiral, despite occasional upturns. The Jewish communities in the former Soviet Union, in the aftermath of the fall of Communism in the late 1990s, are beginning the long, slow road back to vibrancy, both culturally and religiously, even as antisemitism, never fully out of the picture, continues to rear its ugly head. The Jewish communities in a newly reunited Germany (of all places!), surprisingly, reveal a healthy and diverse population, religiously and culturally, slowly growing in numbers, and protected, in large measure, by a government and a population determined to confront their past and less tolerant of neo-Nazism than in that past. The Jewish communities of Great Britain, France, and Australia, while not growing to any appreciable degree, are stable. Their institutions are stable and are committed to addressing problems, including both rising antisemitism and anti-Israelism, and determined not to be overwhelmed by them. The Jewish communities of Israel are growing in number and continuing to build a viable culture and nation-state, despite its internal worrisome agendas of rightist religious Orthodoxy, a rightist government, and the as-yet-unresolved external threat of enemies intent on her destruction, but continually unable to do so. Jewish communities in Latin America, South Africa, and a whole host of other places where Jews live continue to maintain their Jewish lives as Jews have done, continue to do, and will continue to do.

Thus, the story of Judaism and the Jewish people continuously appears to be one of a people who live their lives at the very precipice of their own collective existence, a people who continue to take steps back from that edge only to be met by obstacles and barriers that not only prevent them from doing so, but propel them forward again back to their edge as well. Only time will, ultimately, tell which direction will meet with success. Until then, Jews will leave their fate—and their faith—as they have always done, in the hands of their God. More than that they—and I—cannot say or write.

Bibliography

Ackroyd, Peter R. *Exile and Restoration: A Study of Hebrew Thought of the Sixth Century B.C.* Philadelphia, PA: Westminster Press, 1968.

Aguinis, Marcos. *Against the Inquisition.* Translated by Carolina de Robertis. Amazon Crossing, 2018.

Albertz, Rainer. *Israel in Exile: The History and Literature of the Sixth Century B.C.E.* Translated by David Green. Atlanta, GA: Society of Biblical Literature, 2003.

Alstola, Tero. *Judeans in Babylonia: A Study of Deportees in the Sixth and Fifth Centuries BCE.* Leiden and Boston, MA: Brill, 2020.

Alterman, Eric. *We Are Not One: A History of America's Fight Over Israel.* New York, NY: Basic Books, 2022.

Anderson, Benedict. *Imagined Communities: Reflections on the Origin and Spread of Nationalism.* Revised edition. London and New York, NY: Verso, 2016.

Anderson, Robert T., and Terry Giles. *The Keepers: An Introduction to the History and Culture of the Samaritans.* Peabody, MA: Hendrickson Publishers, 2002.

Anderson, Robert T., and Terry Giles. *The Samaritan Pentateuch: An Introduction to Its Origins, History and Significance for Biblical Studies.* Atlanta, GA: Society of Biblical Literature, 2012.

Appleby, Joyce, Lynn Hunt, and Margaret Jacob. *Telling the Truth About History.* New York, NY, and London: W.W. Norton & Co., 1994.

Avigad, Nahum, Philip J. King, and Lawrence E. Stager, eds. *Life in the Ancient World: Crafts, Society and Daily Practice.* Washington, DC: Biblical Archaeology Society, 2013. E-book.

Baer, Yitzhak. *A History of the Jews in Christian Spain.* Translated by Louis Schoffman. 2 vols. Philadelphia, PA: Jewish Publication Society, 1961.

Bibliography

Bar-Kochva, Bezalel. *The Image of the Jews in Greek Literature: The Hellenistic Period*. Berkeley: University of California Press, 2010.

Barmash, Pamela, and W. David Nelson, eds. *Exodus in the Jewish Experience: Echoes and Reverberations*. Lanham, MD: Lexington Books, 2015.

Baron, Salo W. *History and Jewish Historians: Essays and Addresses*. Philadelphia, PA: Jewish Publication Society of America, 1964.

Barton, George A. *The Religion of Ancient Israel*. New York, NY: A.S. Barnes & Co., 1928.

Barzilay, Tzafrir. *Poisoned Wells: Accusations, Persecution, and Minorities in Medieval Europe, 1321–1422*. Philadelphia: University of Pennsylvania Press, 2022.

Becker, Adam H., and Annette Yoshiko Reed, eds. *The Ways That Never Parted: Jews and Christians in Late Antiquity and the Early Middle Ages*. Minneapolis, MN: Fortress Press, 2007.

Begley, Louis. *Why the Dreyfus Affair Matters*. New Haven, CT: Yale University Press, 2009.

Bell, Dean Philip, ed. *The Routledge Companion to Jewish History and Jewish Historiography*. London and New York, NY: Routledge, 2019.

Bendor, S. *The Social Structure of Ancient Israel: The Institution of the Family (Beit'Ab) from the Settlement to the End of the Monarchy*. Jerusalem: Simor Ltd, 1996.

Benite, Zvi Ben-Dror. *The Ten Lost Tribes: A World History*. New York, NY: Oxford University Press, 2009.

Ben-Itto, Hadassa. *The Lie That Wouldn't Die: The Protocols of the Elders of Zion*. London and Portland, OR: Vallentine Mitchell, 2005.

Berkowitz, Eric. *Dangerous Ideas: A Brief History of Censorship in the West from the Ancients to Fake News*. Boston, MA: Beacon Press, 2021.

Berlin, Isaiah. *Historical Inevitability*. Oxford and New York, NY: Oxford University Press, 1954.

Bernstein, Herman. *The Truth about "The Protocols of Zion."* Reprint. Hoboken, NJ: KTAV Publishing House, 1971.

Bernstein, Michael André. *Foregone Conclusions: Against Apocalyptic History*. Berkeley: University of California Press, 1994.

Biale, David. *Blood and Belief: The Circulation of a Symbol between Jews and Christians*. Berkeley: University of California Press, 2007.

Biale, David. *Not in the Heavens: The Tradition of Jewish Secular Thought*. Princeton, NJ, and Oxford: Princeton University Press, 2011.

Black, Edwin. *The Farhud: Roots of the Arab-Nazi Alliance in the Holocaust*. Washington, DC: Dialog Press, 2010.

Black, Jeremy. *The Holocaust: History and Memory*. Bloomington: Indiana University Press, 2016.

Bloch, Marc. *The Historian's Craft*. Translated by Peter Putnam. Manchester: Manchester University Press, 1954.

Boer, Roland. *The Sacred Economy of Ancient Israel*. Louisville, KY: Westminster John Knox Press, 2015.

Borowski, Oded. *Daily Life in Biblical Israel*. Atlanta, GA: Society of Biblical Literature, 2003.

Bossman, David. "Ezra's Marriage Reform: Israel Redefined." *Biblical Theology Bulletin 9*, no. 1 (1979): 32–8. doi: 10.1177/014610797900900105.

Bottéro, Jean. *The Birth of God: The Bible and the Historian*. Translated by Kees S. Bolle. University Park: Pennsylvania State University Press, 2000.

Boyarin, Daniel. *The Jewish Gospels: The Story of the Jewish Christ*. New York, NY: New Press, 2012.

Braun, Joachim. *Music in Ancient Israel/Palestine: Archaeological, Written, and Comparative Sources*. Translated by Douglas W. Stott. Grand Rapids, MI: William B. Eerdmans, 2002.

Bredin, Jean-Denis. *The Affair: The Case of Alfred Dreyfus*. London: Sidgwick & Jackson, 1986.

Brenner, Michael. *Prophets of the Past: Interpreters of Jewish History*. Translated by Steven Rendall. Princeton, NJ, and Oxford: Princeton University Press, 2006.

Brenner, Reuven. *History: The Human Gamble*. Chicago, IL, and London: University of Chicago Press, 1983.

Brett, Mark G. *Ethnicity and the Bible*. Boston, MA, and Leiden: Brill Academic Publishers, 2002.

Brettler, Marc Zvi. *The Creation of History in Ancient Israel*. London and New York, NY: Routledge, 1995.

Brody, Aaron, and Roy J. King (2013). "Genetics and the Archaeology of Ancient Israel." *Human Biology Open Access Pre-Prints*, Paper 44. http://digitalcommons.wayne.edu/humbiol.preprints/44.

Bronner, Stephen Eric. *A Rumor about the Jews: Reflections on Antisemitism and the Protocols of the Learned Elders of Zion*. New York, NY: St. Martin's Press, 2000.

Brook, Kevin Alan. *The Jews of Khazaria*. Second edition. Lanham, MD: Rowman & Littlefield, 2006.

Brown, William. "Ancient Israelite & Judean Religion." *World History Encyclopedia* (2017). Available online: https://worldhistory.org/article/1097/ancient-israelite-judean-religion (accessed 1 June 2022).

Burrows, Millar. "Ancient Israel." In *The Idea of History in the Ancient Near East*, edited by Robert C. Dentan, 128–9. American Oriental Series Monograph 38. New Haven, CT: American Oriental Society, 1955.

Campbell, Charlie. *Scapegoats: A History of Blaming Other People*. London and New York, NY: Duckworth Overlook, 2011.

Caputo, Nina, and Liz Clarke. *Debating Truth: The Barcelona Disputation of 1263: A Graphic History*. New York, NY: Oxford University Press, 2011.

Carmilly-Weinberger, Moshe. *Censorship and Freedom of Expression in Jewish History: Great Ideological and Literary Conflicts in Judaism from Antiquity to Modern Times*. New York, NY: Sepher-Hermon Press/Yeshiva University Press, 1977.

Carr, Edward Hallett. *What Is History?* New York, NY: Vantage Books/ Random House, 1961.

Cesarani, David. *Final Solution: The Fate of the Jews, 1933–49*. New York, NY: Macmillan, 2016.

Chapman, Guy. *The Dreyfus Trials*. London: Batsford: 1972.

Charlesworth, James H., ed. *The Old Testament Pseudepigrapha*. 2 vols. Peabody, MA: Hendrickson Publishers, 1983.

Chazan, Robert. "The Timebound and the Timeless: Medieval Jewish Narration of Events." *History & Memory* 6, no. 1 (1994): 5–34.

Clark, Douglas R. "Bricks, Sweat, and Tears: The Human Investment in Constructing a 'Four Room' House." *Near Eastern Archaeology* 66, no. 1/2, House and Home in the Southern Levant (2003): 34–43.

Clark, G. Kitson. *The Critical Historian*. London: Heinemann, 1967.

Cohn, Norman. *Warrant for Genocide: The Myth of the Jewish World-Conspiracy and the Protocols of the Elders of Zion*. London: Eyre & Spottiswoode, 1967.

Collingwood, R.G. *The Idea of History*. Revised edition. Oxford and New York, NY: Oxford University Press, 1993.

Collins, John J. *The Apocalyptic Imagination: An Introduction to Jewish Apocalyptic Literature*. Second revised edition. Grand Rapids, MI: William B. Eerdmans, 1998.

Collins, John J. *Between Athens and Jerusalem: Jewish Identity in the Hellenistic Diaspora*. Second edition. Grand Rapids, MI: William B. Eerdmans, 2000.

Coogan, Michael D., ed. *The New Oxford Annotated Bible with Apocrypha*. Fifth edition. Oxford and New York, NY: Oxford University Press, 2018.

Cubitt, Geoffrey. *History and Memory*. Manchester: Manchester University Press, 2007.

Curtiss, John Shelton. *An Appraisal of the Protocols of Zion.* New York, NY: Columbia University Press, 1942.

Davies, Philip R. *In Search of 'Ancient Israel.'* Sheffield: Sheffield Academic Press, 1999.

Davies, Philip R. *On the Origins of Judaism.* London: Routledge, 2011.

Dentan, Robert C., ed. *The Idea of History in the Ancient Near East.* American Oriental Series Monograph 38. New Haven, CT: American Oriental Society, 1955.

DeSilva, David A. *Introducing the Apocrypha: Message, Context, and Significance.* Grand Rapids, MI: Baker Academic, 2018.

Dever, William G. *The Lives of Ordinary People in Ancient Israel: Where Archaeology and the Bible Intersect.* Grand Rapids, MI: William B. Eerdmans, 2012.

Dever, William G. *What Did the Biblical Writers Know & When Did They Know It? What Archaeology Can Tell Us about the Reality of Ancient Israel.* Grand Rapids, MI, and Cambridge: William B. Eerdmans, 2001.

Dever, William G. *Who Were the Early Israelites and Where Did They Come From?* Grand Rapids, MI, and Cambridge: William B. Eerdmans, 2003.

Dorin, Rowan. *No Return: Jews, Christian Usurers, and the Spread of Mass Expulsion in Medieval Europe.* Princeton, NJ: Princeton University Press, 2023.

Douglas, Tom. *Scapegoats: Transferring Blame.* London and New York, NY: Routledge, 1995.

Dubnow, Simon Markovich. *Jewish History: An Essay in the Philosophy of History.* Philadelphia, PA: Jewish Publication Society of America, 1903.

Dunn, James D.G, ed. *Jews and Christians: The Parting of the Ways A.D. 70 to 135.* Grand Rapids, MI, and Cambridge: William B. Eerdmans, 1992.

Dwork, Debórah, and Robert Jan van Pelt. *Holocaust: A History.* New York, NY: W.W. Norton & Co., 2002.

Dworkin, Andrea. *The Jews, Israel, and Women's Liberation.* New York, NY: The Free Press, 2000.

Edelman, Diana Vikander, ed. *The Triumph of Elohim: From Yahwisms to Judaisms.* Grand Rapids, MI: William B. Eerdmans, 1996.

Edwards, Mark U. *Luther's Last Battles: Politics and Polemics, 1531–46.* Ithaca, NY: Cornell University Press, 1983.

Eisenstadt, S.N. *Jewish Civilization: The Jewish Historical Experience in a Comparative Perspective.* New York, NY: SUNY Press 1992.

Eisner, Will. *The Plot: The Secret Story of the Protocols of the Elders of Zion.* New York, NY: W.W. Norton & Co., 2005.

Bibliography

Engel, David. *Historians of the Jews and the Holocaust*. Stanford, CA: Stanford University Press, 2010.

Entine, Jon. *Abraham's Children: Race, Identity, and the DNA of the Chosen People*. New York, NY: Grand Central Publishing, 2007.

Evans, Richard J. *Lying about Hitler: History, Holocaust, and the David Irving Trial*. New York, NY: Basic Books, 2001.

Falk, Avner. *A Psychoanalytic History of the Jews*. Madison, NJ: Fairleigh Dickinson University Press 1996.

Fantalkin, Alexander, and Oren Tal. "The Canonization of the Pentateuch: When and Why? (Part 1)." *Zeitschrift für die Alttestamentliche Wissenschaft* 124, no. 1 (2012): 1–18. http://doi.org/10.1515/zaw-2012-0001.

Faur, José. *In the Shadow of History: Jews and Conversos at the Dawn of Modernity*. Albany: State University of New York Press, 1992.

Faust, Avraham. "How Did Israel Become a People? The Genesis of Israelite Identity." *Biblical Archaeology Review* 35, no. 6 (2009): 62–69, 92–4.

Faust, Avraham. *Israel's Ethnogenesis: Settlement, Interaction, Expansion, and Resistance*. London: Equinox, 2006.

Feinstein, Sara. *Sunshine, Blossoms, and Blood: H.N. Bialik in His Time: A Literary Biography*. Lanham, MD: University Press of America, 2005.

Fernández-Morera, Darío. *The Myth of the Andalusian Paradise: Muslims, Christians, and Jews under Islamic Rule in Medieval Spain*. Wilmington, DE: ISI Books, 2016.

Finkelstein, Israel, and Neil Asher Silberman. *The Bible Unearthed: Archaeology's New Vision of Ancient Israel and the Origin of Its Sacred Texts*. New York, NY: The Free Press, 2001.

Fleming, Daniel E. *The Legacy of Israel in Judah's Bible: History, Politics, and the Reinscribing of Tradition*. Cambridge: Cambridge University Press, 2012.

Frankel, Jonathan, ed. *Reshaping the Jewish Past: Jewish History and the Historians*. Oxford and New York,NY: Oxford University Press, 1994.

Friedenberg, Daniel M. *Tiberius Julius Alexander*. Amherst, MA: Prometheus Books, 2010.

Funkenstein, Amos. "Collective Memory and Historical Consciousness." *History & Memory* 1, no. 1 (1989): 5–26.

Funkenstein, Amos. *Perceptions of Jewish History*. Berkeley: University of California Press, 1993.

Gabirol, Solomon ibn. *A Crown for the King*. Translated by David R. Slavitt. New York, NY, and Oxford: Oxford University Press, 1998.

Gabriel, Richard A. *The Military History of Ancient Israel*. Westport, CT: Praeger, 2003.

Garbini, Giovanni. *History & Ideology in Ancient Israel*. Translated by John Bowden. New York, NY: Crossroad, 1988.

Geisst, Charles R. *Beggar Thy Neighbor: A History of Usury and Debt*. Philadelphia: University of Pennsylvania Press, 2013.

Gellner, Ernest. *Plough, Sword, and Book: The Structure of Human History*: Chicago, IL, and London: University of Chicago Press, 1988.

Gerlach, Christian. *The Extermination of the European Jews*. Cambridge: Cambridge University Press, 2016.

Gidwitz, Adam. *The Inquisitor's Tale, Or, The Three Magical Children and Their Holy Dog*. New York, NY: Dutton Children's Books, 2018.

Gilbert, Martin. *In Ishmael's House: A History of Jews in Muslim Lands*. New Haven, CT, and London: Yale University Press, 2010.

Girard, René. *The Scapegoat*. Translated by Yvonne Freccero. Baltimore, MD: Johns Hopkins University Press, 1986.

Golden, Jonathan. *Ancient Canaan and Israel: An Introduction*. Oxford and New York, NY: Oxford University Press, 2009.

Goldstein, David B. *Jacob's Legacy: A Genetic View of Jewish History*. New Haven, CT, and London: Yale University Press, 2008.

Goldstein, Jonathan. *Peoples of an Almighty God: Competing Religions in the Ancient World*. New York, NY: Doubleday, 2002.

Gordon, Noah. *The Last Jew*. New York, NY: St. Martin's Griffin, 2000.

Gottfried, Ted. *Deniers of the Holocaust: Who They Are, What They Do, Why They Do It*. Brookfield, CT: Twenty First Century Books, 2001.

Gottwald, Norman. *The Politics of Ancient Israel*. Louisville, KY: Westminster John Knox Press, 2001.

Gottwald, Norman. "The Politics of Ancient Israel." *The Bible and Interpretation: News and Interpretations on the Bible and Ancient Near East History* (2001). Available online: https://bibleinterp.arizona.edu/articles/2001/politics.

Gottwald, Norman K. *The Tribes of Yahweh: A Sociology of the Religion of Liberated Israel, 1250–1050 B.C.E.* Maryknoll, NY: Orbis Books, 1979.

Gould, Kenneth M. *They Got the Blame: The Story of Scapegoats in History*. New York, NY: Association Press, 1944.

Grabbe, Lester L. *Ancient Israel: What Do We Know and How Do We Know It?* London and New York, NY: T&T Clark, 2007.

Grabbe, Lester L., ed. *Can a 'History of Israel' Be Written?* Sheffield: Sheffield Academic Press, 1997.

Grabbe, Lester. "The Reality of the Return: The Biblical Picture Versus Historical Reconstruction." In *Exile and Return: The Babylonian Context*, edited by Jonathan Stökl and Caroline Waerzeggers, 292–307. Berlin: de Gruyter, 2015.

Grafton, Anthony. *Bring Out Your Dead: The Past as Revelation*. Cambridge, MA, and London: Harvard University Press 2001.

Gray, Charles. *The Irving Judgment: David Irving V. Penguin Books and Professor Deborah Lipstadt*. New York, NY: Penguin Books, 2000.

Greenberg, Moshe, *The Hab/piru*. New Haven, CT: American Oriental Society, 1955.

Gritsch, Eric W. *Martin Luther's Anti-Semitism: Against His Better Judgment*. Grand Rapids, MI: William B. Eerdmans, 2012.

Gryta, Janek. "Creating a Cosmopolitan Past: Local and Transnational Influences on Memory Work in Schindler's Factory, Kraków." *History & Memory* 32, no. 1 (2020): 34–68.

Gruen, Erich S. *Ethnicity in the Ancient World—Did It Matter?* Berlin: Walter de Gruyter, 2020.

Gurtner, Daniel M. *Introducing the Pseudepigrapha of Second Temple Judaism: Message, Context, and Significance*. Grand Rapids, MI: Baker Academic, 2020.

Guttenplan, D.D. *The Holocaust on Trial: History, Justice and the David Irving Libel Case*. New York, NY: W.W. Norton & Co., 2002.

Gwyer, John. *Portraits of Mean Men: A Short History of the Protocols of the Elders of Zion*. London: Cobden-Sanderson, 1938.

Halter, Marek. *Why the Jews? The Need to Scapegoat*. Translated by Grace McQuillan. New York, NY: Arcade Publishing 2020.

Hardwick, Michael. *Prisoner of the Devil*. New York, NY: Pinnacle Books, 1990.

Harris, Robert. *An Officer and a Spy*. New York, NY: Vantage Books, 2013.

Hartman, Geoffrey H. *Holocaust Remembrance: The Shapes of Memory*. Oxford: Blackwell, 1994.

Harvey, Graham. *The True Israel: Uses of the Names Jew, Hebrew, and Israel in Ancient Jewish and Early Christian Literature*. Boston, MA, and Leiden: Brill Academic, 1996.

Hauser, Alan J. "The 'Minor Judges': A Re-Evaluation." *Journal of Biblical Literature* 94, no. 2 (1975): 190–200.

Hayes, Peter. *Why? Explaining the Holocaust*. New York, NY: W.W. Norton & Co., 2017.

Hendel, Ronald. *Remembering Abraham: Culture, Memory, and History in the Hebrew Bible*. Oxford and New York, NY: Oxford University Press, 2005.

Hertzberg, Arthur, ed. *The Zionist Idea: A Historical Analysis and Reader*. Philadelphia, PA: Jewish Publication Society, 1997.

Herzog, Chaim, and Mordecai Gichon. *Battles of the Bible*. London: Greenhill Books, 1978.

Heschel, Susannah. *Abraham Geiger and the Jewish Jesus*. Chicago, IL: University of Chicago Press, 1998.

Hess, Richard J., and M. Daniel Carroll, eds. *Family in the Bible: Exploring Customs, Culture, and Context*. Grand Rapids, MI: Baker Academic, 2003.

Hitler, Adolf. *Mein Kampf*. New York, NY: Houghton Mifflin, 1939.

Hödl, Klaus (2021). "Major Trends in the Historiography of European Ashkenazic Jews from the 1970s to the Present." *Jewish History* 35 (2021): 153–77.

Hoffmeier, James K. *Israel in Egypt: The Evidence for the Authenticity of the Exodus Tradition*. New York, NY, and Oxford: Oxford University Press, 1996.

Hoffmeier, James K., Allan R. Millard, and Gary A. Rendsburg, eds. *"Did I Not Bring Israel Out of Egypt?" Biblical, Archaeological, and Egyptological Perspectives on the Exodus Narratives*. Bulletin for Biblical Research Supplement 13. Winona Lake, IN: Eisenbrauns, 2016.

Howe, Irving. *World of Our Fathers: The Journey of East European Jews to America and the Life They Found and Made*. Annotated Edition. New York, NY: New York University Press, 2005.

Hsia, R. Po-Chia. *Trent 1475: Stories of a Ritual Murder Trial*. New Haven, CT: Yale University Press 1992.

Hubert, Henri, and Marcel Mauss. *Sacrifice: Its Nature and Function*. Translated by W.D. Halls. Chicago, IL: University of Chicago Press, 1964.

Hughes, Aaron. *Defining Judaism: A Reader*. London and Oakville, CT: Equinox, 2010.

Hughes Aaron. *The Invention of Jewish Identity: Bible, Philosophy, and the Art of Translation*. Bloomington: Indiana University Press, 2010.

Hutchinson, John, and Anthony D. Smith. *Ethnicity*. Oxford: Oxford University Press, 1996.

Jacobs, Janet. *Memorializing the Holocaust: Gender, Genocide, and Collective Memory*. London and New York, NY: I.B. Tauris, 2010.

Jacobs, Steven Leonard. *Antisemitism: Exploring the Issues*. Santa Barbara, CA: ABC-CLIO, 2020.

Jacobs, Steven Leonard. *The Biblical Masorah and the Temple Scroll: An Orthographical Inquiry*. Lanham, MD: University Press of America, 2002.

Jacobs, Steven Leonard (2002), "Blood on Our Heads: A Jewish Response to Saint Matthew." In *A Shadow of Glory: Reading the New Testament After the Holocaust*, edited by Tod A. Linafelt, 57–67. London and New York, NY: Routledge, 2002.

Jacobs, Steven Leonard. "Holy Wars, Judaism, Violence, and Genocide: An Unholy Quadrinity." In *The Routledge Handbook of Religion, Mass Atrocity, and Genocide*, edited by Sara E. Brown and Stephen D. Smith, 37–43. London and New York, NY: Routledge, 2022.

Jacobs, Steven Leonard. *Shirot Bialik: A New and Annotated Translation of Chaim Nachman Bialik's Epic Poems*. Columbus, OH: Alpha Pub. Co., 1987.

Jacobs, Steven Leonard. "The State and Fate of the Jews in the Ottoman Empire and the Early Republic during World War I: A *Necessary* Part of the Conversation." In *Armenians, Assyrians, and the Greeks in the Ottoman Empire*, edited by George Shirinian. New York, NY, and Oxford: Berghahn Books, forthcoming.

Jacobs, Steven Leonard. "Teaching Jesus at the University of Alabama." In *Teaching the Historical Jesus: Issues and Exegesis*, edited by Zev Garber, 48–58. New York, NY, and London: Routledge, 2015.

Jacobs, Steven Leonard. "Two Takes on Christianity: Furthering the Dialogue." *Journal of Ecumenical Studies* 47, no. 4 (2012): 508–24.

Jacobs, Steven Leonard, and Mark Weitzman. *Dismantling the Big Lie: The Protocols of the Elders of Zion*. Jersey City, NJ: KTAV Publishing House, 2003.

Jigoulov, Vadim, Jaco Gericke, and Steven Leonard Jacobs. *The Scriptures of Ancient Israel: A Secular Introduction*. San Diego, CA: Cognella Press, 2020.

Jobes, Karen H., and Moisés Silva. *Invitation to the Septuagint*. Grand Rapids, MI: Baker Academic, 2000.

Joly, Maurice. *The Dialogue in Hell between Machiavelli and Montesquieu: Humanitarian Despotism and the Condition of Modern Tyranny*. Translated by John S. Waggoner. Lanham, MD: Lexington Books, 2003.

Julius, Lyn. *Uprooted: How 3000 Years of Jewish Civilization in the Arab World Vanished Overnight*. Portland, OR: Vallentine Mitchell, 2018.

Kahn, R.A. *Holocaust Denial and the Law: A Comparative Study*. New York, NY: Palgrave Macmillan, 2004.

Kalimi, Isaac. *Writing and Rewriting the Story of Solomon in Ancient Israel*. Cambridge: Cambridge University Press, 2019.

Kapralski, Slawomir. "Battlefields of Memory: Landscape and Identity in Polish-Jewish Relations." *History & Memory* 13, no. 2 (2001): 35–58.

Kaufman, Amy S., and Paul R. Studevant. *The Devil's Historians: How Modern Extremists Abuse the Medieval Past*. Toronto: University of Toronto Press, 2020.

Kaufmann, Thomas. *Luther's Jews: A Journey into Anti-Semitism*. Translated by Leslie Sharpe and Jeremy Noakes. Oxford: Oxford University Press, 2017.

Kierkegaard, Søren. *Fear and Trembling*. Translated by Alastair Hannay. New York, NY: Penguin Press, 1986.

Killebrew Ann E. *Biblical Peoples and Ethnicity: An Archaeological Study of Egyptians, Canaanites, Philistines, and Early Israel, 1300–1100 B.C.E.* Atlanta, GA: Society of Biblical Literature, 2005.

King, Philip J., and Lawrence J. Stager. *Life in Biblical Israel*. Louisville, KY: Westminster John Knox Press, 2011.

Kirsch, Jonathan. *God Against the Gods: The History of the War between Monotheism and Polytheism*. New York, NY: Viking Compass, 2004.

Kitchen, K.A. *On the Reliability of the Old Testament*. Grand Rapids, MI, and Cambridge: William B. Eerdmans, 2003.

Klawans, Jonathan, and Lawrence M. Wills, eds. *The Jewish Annotated Apocrypha*. New York, NY: Oxford University Press, 2020.

Knohl, Israel. *The Messiah before Jesus: The Suffering Servant of the Dead Sea Scrolls*. Translated by David Maisel. Berkeley: University of California Press, 2000.

Knohl, Israel. *The Messiah Confrontation: Pharisees versus Sadducees and the Death of Jesus*. Translated by David Maisel. Philadelphia, PA: Jewish Publication Society, 2022.

Knoppers, Gary S. *Jews and Samaritans: The Origins and History of Their Early Relations*. Oxford and New York, NY: Oxford University Press, 2013.

Koch, Klaus. "Ezra and the Origins of Judaism." *Journal of Semitic Studies* 19, no. 2 (1974): 173–97.

Kratz, Reinhard G. *Historical and Biblical Israel: The History, Tradition, and Archives of Israel and Judah*. Translated by Paul Michael Kurtz. Oxford and New York, NY: Oxford University Press, 2015.

Kurtzer, Yehuda. *Shuva: The Future of the Jewish Past*. Waltham, MA: Brandeis University Press, 2012.

Landes, Richard, and Steven Katz, eds. *The Paranoid Apocalypse: A Hundred-Year Retrospective on "The Protocols of the Elders of Zion."* New York, NY: New York University Press, 2012.

Langer, Jiri. *Nine Gates: The Chassidic Mysteries*. Translated by Stephen Jolly. Cambridge: Lutterworth Press, 2022.

Bibliography

Larsson, Göran. *Fact or Fraud? The Protocols of the Elders of Zion.* Jerusalem: AMI-Jerusalem Center for Biblical Studies and Research, 1994.

Lasker, Daniel J. *Karaism: An Introduction to the Oldest Surviving Alternative Judaism.* London: Littman Library of Jewish Civilization, 2022.

Lemche, Niels Peter. *The Israelites in History and Tradition.* London: SPCK; and Louisville, KY: Westminster John Knox Press, 1988.

Lentin, Ronit, ed. *Re-Presenting the Holocaust for the 21st Century.* New York, NY, and Oxford: Berghahn Books, 2014.

Levenson, Jon D. *The Death and Resurrection of the Beloved Son: The Transformation of Child Sacrifice in Judaism and Christianity.* New Haven, CT, and London: Yale University Press, 1995.

Levenson, Jon D. *Inheriting Abraham: The Legacy of the Patriarch in Judaism, Christianity, and Islam.* Princeton, NJ: Princeton University Press, 2012.

Levine, Lee I. *Judaism and Hellenism in Antiquity: Conflict or Confluence?* Seattle: University of Washington Press, 1998.

Levy, Daniel, and Natan Sznaider. *The Holocaust and Memory in the Global Age.* Translated by Assenka Oksiloff. Philadelphia, PA: Temple University Press, 2006.

Lewis, Bernard. *The Jews of Islam.* Princeton, NJ: Princeton University Press, 1984.

Lewis, Theodore J. *The Origin and Character of God: Ancient Israelite Religion Through the Lens of Divinity.* New York, NY: Oxford University Press, 2020.

Lindemann, Alfred S. *The Jew Accused: Three Anti-Semitic Affairs: Dreyfus, Beilis, Frank, 1894–1915.* Cambridge: Cambridge University Press, 1993.

Lipschits, Oded, and Joseph Blenkinsopp, eds. *Judah and the Judeans in the Neo-Babylonian Period.* Winona Lake, IN: Eisenbrauns, 2003.

Lipschits, Oded, and Manfred Oeming, eds. *Judah and the Judeans in the Persian Period.* Winona Lake, IN: Eisenbrauns, 2006.

Lipschits, Oded, Gary N. Knoppers, and Rainer Albertz, eds. *Judah and the Judeans in the Fourth Century B.C.E.* Winona Lake, IN: Eisenbrauns, 2007.

Lipschits, Oded, Gary N. Knoppers, and Manfred Oeming, eds. *Judah and the Judeans in the Achaemenid Period: Negotiating Identity in an International Context.* Winona Lake, IN: Eisenbrauns, 2011.

Lipstadt, Deborah. *Denying the Holocaust: The Growing Assault on Truth and Memory.* New York: Plume; London: Penguin, 1994.

Lipstadt, Deborah. *History on Trial: My Day in Court with a Holocaust Denier.* New York, NY: Harper Perennial, 2006.

Bibliography

Litvin, Baruch. *Jewish Identity: Modern Responsa and Opinions on the Registration of Children of Mixed Marriages: David Ben Gurion's Query to Leaders of World Jewry: A Documentary Compilation.* Edited by Sidney B. Hoenig. Jerusalem and New York, NY: Feldheim Publishers, 1970.

Longerich, Peter. *Holocaust: The Nazi Persecution and Murder of the Jews.* Oxford: Oxford University Press, 2010.

Maccoby, Hyam. *Judaism on Trial: Jewish-Christian Disputations in the Middle Ages.* Oxford and Portland, OR: Littman Library of Jewish Civilization, 1993.

Macmillan, Margaret. *Dangerous Games: The Uses and Abuses of History.* New York, NY: Modern Library, 2009.

Mansoor, Menahem. *Jewish History and Thought: An Introduction.* Hoboken, NJ: KTAV Publishing House, 1991.

Marcos, Natalio Fernández. *The Septuagint in Context: Introduction to the Greek Version of the Bible.* Translated by Wilfred G.E. Watson. Atlanta, GA: Society of Biblical Literature, 2000.

Marrus, Michael. *Lessons of the Holocaust.* Toronto: University of Toronto Press, 2016.

Matt, Daniel. *Zohar: Annotated and Explained.* Woodstock, VT: SkyLight Paths, 2002.

Matthews, Victor H., and Don C. Benjamin. *Old Testament Parallels: Laws and Stories from the Ancient Near East.* Newly revised and expanded second edition. New York, NY: Paulist Press, 1997.

Mayes, A.D.H. "The Question of the Israelite Amphictyony." *Hermathena* 116 (1973): 53–65.

McKenzie, Steven L., and Stephen R. Haynes, eds. *To Each Its Own Meaning: Biblical Criticisms and Their Application.* Revised and expanded. Louisville, KY: Westminster John Knox Press, 1999.

Mead, Walter Russell. *The Arc of a Covenant: The United States, Israel, and the Fate of the Jewish People.* New York, NY: Alfred A. Knopf, 2022.

Meerson, Michael, and Peter Schäfer, eds. and trans. *Toledot Yeshu: The Life Story of Jesus.* Tübingen: Mohr Siebeck, 2014.

Michael, Robert. *Holy Hatred: Christianity, Antisemitism, and the Holocaust.* New York, NY: Palgrave Macmillan, 2006.

Michelis, Cesare G. de. *The Non-Existent Manuscript: A Study of the Protocols of the Sages of Zion.* Lincoln: University of Nebraska Press, 2004.

Miller, James C. "Ethnicity and the Hebrew Bible: Problems and Prospects." *Currents in Biblical Research* 6, no. 2 (2008): 170–213. https://doi.org/10.1177/1476993x07083627.

Bibliography

Miller, J. Maxwell. "Reading the Bible Historically: The Historian's Approach." In *To Each Its Own Meaning: Biblical Criticisms and Their Application*, edited by Steven L. McKenzie and Stephen R. Haynes, 17–34. Revised and expanded. Louisville, KY: Westminster John Knox Press, 1999.

Miller, Patrick D. *The Religion of Ancient Israel*. Louisville, KY: Westminster John Knox Press; and London: SPCK, 2000.

Mintz, Alan. *Popular Culture and the Shaping of Holocaust Memory in America*. Seattle and London: University of Washington Press, 2001.

Moreh, Shmuel, and Zvi Yehuda, eds. *Al-Farhūd: The 1941 Pogrom in Iraq*. Jerusalem: Hebrew University Magnes Press, 2010.

Mullen, E. Theodore, Jr. *Ethnic Myths and Pentateuchal Foundations: A New Approach to the Formation of the Pentateuch*. Atlanta, GA: Scholars Press, 1997.

Myers, David N. *The Stakes of History: On the Use and Abuse of Jewish History for Life*. New Haven, CT, and London: Yale University Press, 2018.

Myers, David N., and Amos Funkenstein. "Remembering 'Zachor': A Super Commentary [with Responses]." *History & Memory* 4, no. 2 (1992): 129–48.

Myers, David N., and Alexander Kaye, eds. *The Faith of Fallen Jews: Yosef Hayim Yerushalmi and the Writing of Jewish History*. Waltham, MA: Brandeis University Press, 2014.

Myers, David N., and David S. Ruderman, eds. *The Jewish Past Revisited: Reflections on Modern Jewish Historians*. New Haven, CT, and London: Yale University Press, 1998.

Mykytiuk, Lawrence. "Archaeology Confirms 50 Real People in the Bible." *Biblical Archaeology Review* 40, no. 2 (2014): 42–5, 48–50. www.biblicalarchaeology.org.

Mykytiuk, Lawrence. "Archaeology Confirms 3 More Bible People." *Biblical Archaeology Review* 43, no. 3 (2017): 48–52. www.biblicalarchaeology.org.

Nelson, Benjamin N. *The Idea of Usury: From Tribal Brotherhood to Universal Otherhood*. Princeton, NJ: Princeton University Press, 1949.

Nichols, William. *Christian Antisemitism: A History of Hate*. Northvale, NJ: Jason Aronson, 1995.

Niditch, Susan. *Ancient Israelite Religion*. New York, NY: Oxford University Press, 1997.

Niditch, Susan. *War in the Hebrew Bible: A Study in the Ethics of Violence*. Oxford and New York, NY: Oxford University Press, 1995.

Nietzsche, Fredrich. *The Use and Abuse of History for Life*. 1874. Reprinted with translation by Adrian Collins. Mineola, NY: Dover Publications, 2019.

Oberman, Heiko A. *The Roots of Anti-Semitism in the Age of Renaissance and Reformation*. Philadelphia, PA: Fortress Press, 1984.

Oppenheim, Samuel A. *The Historical Evolution of Judaism: With Comparisons to Other Systems of Thought*. Jacksonville, FL: Mazo Publishers, 2012.

Ostrer, Harry. *Legacy: A Genetic History of the Jewish People*. Oxford and New York, NY: Oxford University Press, 2012.

Overberg, Henk. *The Jews' State: A Critical English Translation*. Northvale, NJ: Jason Aronson, 1997.

Pelt, Robert Jan van. *The Case for Auschwitz: Evidence from the Irving Trial*. Bloomington: Indiana University Press, 2016.

Perdue, Leo G., Joseph Blenkinsopp, John J. Collins, and Carol Myers. *Families in Ancient Israel*. Louisville, KY: Westminster John Knox Press, 1997.

Perera, Sylvia Brinton. *The Scapegoat Complex: Toward a Mythology of Shadow and Guilt*. Toronto: Inner City Books, 1986.

Pine, Lisa, ed. *Life and Times in Nazi Germany*. London: Bloomsbury Academic, 2016.

Pitkänen, Pekka. "The Ecological-Evolutionary Theory, Migration, Settler Colonialism, Sociology of Violence and the Origins of Ancient Israel." *Cogent Social Sciences* 2, no. 1 (2016): 1–23.

Pitkänen, Pekka. "Ethnicity, Assimilation, and the Israelite Settlement." *Tyndale Bulletin* 55, no. 2 (2004): 161–82. https://doi.org/10.5375/001c.29171.

Podeh, Elie. "History and Memory in the Israeli Educational System: The Portrayal of the Arab-Israeli Conflict in History Textbooks (1948-2000)." *History & Memory* 12, no. 1 (2000): 65–100.

Powell, Lindsay. *Bar Kokhba: The Jew Who Defied Hadrian and Challenged the Might of Rome*. Barnsley: Pen & Sword, 2021.

Price, Max D. *Evolution of a Taboo: Pigs and People in the Ancient Near East*. Oxford: Oxford University Press, 2021.

Probst, Christopher J. *Demonizing the Jews: Luther and the Protestant Church in Nazi Germany*. Bloomington: Indiana University Press, 2012.

Pummer, Reinhard. *The Samaritans: A Profile*. Grand Rapids, MI, and Cambridge: William B. Eerdmans, 2016.

Rad, Gerhard von. *Holy War in Ancient Israel*. Translated by John H. Yoder and Marva Dawn. Grand Rapids, MI: William B. Eerdmans, 1996.

Rainey, Anson. "Inside, Outside: Where Did the Early Israelites Come From?" *Biblical Archaeology Review* 34, no. 6 (2008): 45–7, 49–50.

Rainey, Anson. "Shasu or Habiru: Who Were the Early Israelites?" *Biblical Archaeology Review* 34, no. 6 (2008): 51–5.

Reed, Annette Yoshiko. *Jewish-Christianity and the History of Judaism.* Minneapolis, MN: Fortress Press, 2022.

Rees, Laurence. *The Holocaust: A New History.* New York, NY: Public Affairs, 2017.

Reston, James, Jr., *Dogs of God: Columbus, the Inquisition, and the Defeat of the Moors.* New York, NY: Doubleday, 2005.

Ringgren, Helmer. *Religions of the Ancient Near East.* Translated by John Sturdy. Philadelphia, PA: Westminster Press, 1973.

Rogers, Guy Maclean. *For the Freedom of Zion: The Great Revolt of Jews against Romans, 66–74 CE.* New Haven, CT, and London: Yale University Press, 2021.

Römer, Thomas. *The Invention of God.* Translated by Raymond Guess. Cambridge, MA, and London: Harvard University Press, 2015.

Rosman, Moshe. *How Jewish Is Jewish History?* Oxford and Portland, OR: The Littman Library of Jewish Civilization, 2007.

Roth, Cecil. *A History of the Marranos.* New York, NY: Sepher-Hermon Press, 1974.

Roth, Michael S., and Charles G. Salas, eds. *Disturbing Remains: Memory, History and the Crisis of the Twentieth Century.* Los Angeles, CA: Getty Research Institute, 2001.

Rovner, Adam. *In the Shadow of Zion: Promised Lands before Israel.* New York, NY: New York University Press, 2014.

Rowley, H.H. *Worship in Ancient Israel: Its Forms and Meaning.* London: SPCK, 1967.

Rule, William Harris. *History of the Karaite Jews.* London: Longman, Green, and Co., 1870; Lexington, MA: Loeb Classical Library, 2016, reprint.

Rumsey, Abby Smith. *When We Are No More: How Digital Memory is Shaping the Future.* New York, NY, and London: Bloomsbury Press, 2019.

Sachar, Howard Morley. *A History of Israel: From the Rise of Zionism to Our Time.* Third revised and updated edition. New York, NY: Alfred A. Knopf, 2007.

Sachar, Howard Morley. *A History of the Jews of America.* Reprint. New York, NY: Vintage Books, 1993.

Sandmel, Samuel. *Alone atop the Mountain.* Garden City, NY: Doubleday, 1973.

Sandmel, Samuel. "Parallelomania." *Journal of Biblical Literature* 81, no. 6 (1962): 1–13.

Sarna, Jonathan. *American Judaism: A History.* New Haven, CT: Yale University Press, 2019.

Schäfer, Peter. *Jesus in the Talmud.* Princeton, NJ: Princeton University Press, 2007.

Schäfer, Peter. *The Jewish Jesus: How Judaism and Christianity Shaped Each Other.* Princeton, NJ: Princeton University Press, 2012.

Schäfer, Peter. *Judeophobia: Attitudes toward the Jews in the Ancient World.* Cambridge, MA: Harvard University Press, 1998.

Schäfer, Peter. *Two Gods in Heaven: Jewish Concepts of God in Antiquity.* Translated by Allison Brown. Princeton, NJ: Princeton University Press, 2020.

Schäfer, Peter, Michael Meerson, and Yaacov Deutsch, eds. *Toledot Yeshu: ("The Life Story of Jesus") Revisited.* Tübingen: Mohr Siebeck, 2011.

Schmidt, Brian B., ed. *The Quest for the Historical Israel: Debating Archaeology and the History of Early Israel.* Atlanta, GA: Society of Biblical Literature, 2007.

Schneer, Jonathan. *The Balfour Declaration: The Origins of the Arab-Israeli Conflict.* New York, NY: Random House, 2012.

Scholem, Gershom. *Major Trends in Jewish Mysticism.* New York, NY: Schocken Books, 1995.

Schorsch, Ismar. *From Text to Context: The Turn to History in Modern Judaism.* Hanover, NH: Brandeis University Press, 1994.

Schwager, Raymund. *Must There Be Scapegoats? Violence and Redemption in the Bible.* Translated by Maria L. Assad. San Francisco, CA: Harper & Row, 1987.

Schwartz, Daniel R. *Judeans and Jews: Four Faces of Dichotomy in Ancient Jewish History.* Toronto: University of Toronto Press, 2014.

Segal, Benjamin W. *A Lie and a Libel: The History of the Protocols of the Elders of Zion.* Translated and edited by Richard S. Levy. Lincoln: University of Nebraska Press. 1996.

Seltzer, Robert M. *Jewish People, Jewish Thought: The Jewish Experience in History.* Upper Saddle River, NJ: Prentice Hall, 1980.

Shandler, Jeffrey. *Holocaust Memory in the Digital Age: Survivors' Stories and New Media Practices.* Stanford, CA: Stanford University Press, 2019.

Smith, Mark L. *The Yiddish Historians and the Struggle for a Jewish History of the Holocaust.* Detroit, MI: Wayne State University Press, 2019.

Smith, Mark S. *The Early History of God: Yahweh and the Other Deities in Ancient Israel.* Second edition. Grand Rapids, MI, and Cambridge: William B. Eerdmans, 2002.

Smith, Mark S. *God in Translation: Deities in Cross-Cultural Discourse in the Biblical World.* Grand Rapids, MI, and Cambridge: William B. Eerdmans, 2010.

Smith, Mark S. *The Origins of Biblical Monotheism: Israel's Polytheistic Background and the Ugaritic Texts.* Oxford and New York, NY: Oxford University Press, 2003.

Sparks, Kenton L. *Ethnicity and Identity in Ancient Israel: Prolegomena to the Study of Ethnic Settlements and Their Expression in the Hebrew Bible.* Winona Lake, IN: Eisenbrauns, 1998.

Spiegel, Shalom. *The Last Trial: On the Legends and Lore of the Command of Abraham to Offer Isaac as a Sacrifice.* Translated by Judah Goldin. Woodstock, VT: Jewish Lights, 1993.

Spronk, Klaas. "Good Death and Bad Death in Ancient Israel According to Biblical Lore." *Social Science & Medicine* 58, no. 5 (2004): 987–95.

Stavrakopoulou, Francesca. *God: An Anatomy.* New York, NY: Alfred A. Knopf, 2022.

Stavrakopoulou, Francesca, and John Barton, eds. *Religious Diversity in Ancient Israel and Judah.* London and New York, NY: T&T Clark, 2010.

Steigmann-Gall, Richard. *The Holy Reich: Nazi Conceptions of Christianity, 1919-1945.* Cambridge: Cambridge University Press, 2003.

Stein, Leonard. *The Balfour Declaration.* New York, NY: American Council of Learned Societies, 2008.

Stern, Kenneth. *Holocaust Denial.* New York, NY: American Jewish Committee, 1993.

Stern, Menahem, ed. *Greek and Latin Authors on Jews and Judaism.* 3 vols. Jerusalem: The Israel Academy of Sciences and Humanities, 1976.

Stier, Oren Baruch. *Committed to Memory: Cultural Meditations of the Holocaust.* Amherst: University of Massachusetts Press, 2003.

Stillman, Norman. *Jews of Arab Lands: A History and Source Book.* Philadelphia, PA: Jewish Publication Society, 1979.

Stillman, Norman. *Jews of Arab Lands in Modern Times.* Philadelphia, PA: Jewish Publication Society, 2003.

Stökl, Jonathan, and Caroline Waerzeggers, eds. *Exile and Return: The Babylonian Context.* Berlin: de Gruyter, 2015.

Talmon, J.L. *The Nature of Jewish History: Its Universal Significance.* London: The Hillel Foundation, 1957.

Thompson, Thomas L. *The Mythic Past: Biblical Archaeology and the Myth of Israel*. New York, NY: Basic Books, 1999.

Tjernagel, Neelak S. *Martin Luther and the Jewish People*. Milwaukee, WI: Northwestern Publishing House, 1985.

Trachtenberg, Joshua. *The Devil and the Jews: The Medieval Conception of the Jew and Its Relation to Modern Anti-Semitism*. Philadelphia, PA: Jewish Publication Society of America, 2002, reprint.

Trouillot, Michel-Rolph. *Silencing the Past: Power and the Production of History*. Boston, MA: Beacon Press, 1995.

Troy, Gil, ed. *The Zionist Idea: Visions for the Jewish Homeland—Then and Now*. Philadelphia, PA: Jewish Publication Society, 2018.

Tumblety, Joan, ed. *Memory and History: Understanding Memory as Source and Subject*. London and New York, NY: Routledge, 2017.

Vaux, Roland de. *Ancient Israel: Its Life and Institutions*. Translated by John McHugh. Grand Rapids, MI: William B. Eerdmans, 1960.

Vermes, Geza. *Jesus in His Jewish Context*. Minneapolis, MN: Fortress Press, 2003.

Vermes, Geza. *Jesus the Jew: A Historian's Reading of the Gospels*. Philadelphia, PA: Fortress Press, 1973.

Vickery, John B., and J'nan M. Sellery, eds. *The Scapegoat in Ritual and Literature*. Boston, MA: Houghton Mifflin, 1972.

Walsh, George. *The Role of Religion in History*. New Brunswick, NJ, and London: Transaction Publishers, 1998.

Walton, John H. *Ancient Israelite Literature in Its Cultural Context*. Grand Rapids, MI: Zondervan Publishing House, 1989.

Watt, James W., ed. *Persia and Torah: The Theory of Imperial Authorization of the Pentateuch*. Atlanta, GA: Society of Biblical Literature, 2001.

Weitzman, Steven. *The Origin of the Jews: The Quest for Roots in a Rootless Age*. Princeton, NJ, and Oxford: Princeton University Press, 2017.

Whitlam, Keith W. *The Invention of Ancient Israel: The Silencing of Palestinian History*. London: Routledge, 1996.

Wiesenthal, Simon. *Sails of Hope: The Secret Mission of Christopher Columbus*. New York, NY: Macmillan, 1973.

Wise, Michael O. *The First Messiah: Investigating the Savior Before Christ*. San Francisco, CA: Harper, 1999.

Wolentarska-Ochman, Ewa. "Collective Remembrance in Jedwabne: Unsettled Memory of World War II in Postcommunist Poland." *History & Memory* 18, no. 1 (2006): 152–78.

Wolf, Lucien. *The Myth of the Jewish Menace in World Affairs: Or, The Truth about the Forged Protocols of the Elders of Zion*. Reprint. Calgary, AB: Theophania Publishing, 2011.

Wolfgram, Mark A. "From the Visual to the Textual: How Nazi Control of the Visual Record of Kristallnacht Shaped the Postwar Narrative." *History & Memory* 33, no. 2 (2021): 107–34.

Wood, Gordon S. *The Purpose of the Past: Reflections on the Uses of History*. New York, NY: Penguin Books, 2008.

Woodward, C. Vann. *The Future of the Past*. New York, NY, and Oxford: Oxford University Press, 1989.

Wright, Robert. *The Evolution of God*. New York, NY: Back Bay Books, 2009.

Wyman, David. *The Abandonment of the Jews: America and the Holocaust, 1941–1945*. Reprint. Lexington, MA: Plunkett Lakes Press, 2018.

Wyman, David. *Paper Walls: America and the Refugee Crisis, 1938–1941*. Reprint. Lexington, MA: Plunkett Lake Press, 2019.

Yaron, Yoseif. *An Introduction to Karaite Judaism: History, Theology, Practice, and Custom*. Troy, NY: al-Qirqisani Center for the Promotion of Karaite Studies, 2003.

Yerushalmi, Yosef Hayim. *Zakhor: Jewish History and Jewish Memory*. Seattle and London: University of Washington Press, 1996.

Yerushalmi, Yosef Hayim, and Sylvie Anne Goldberg. *Transmitting Jewish History: In Conversation with Sylvie Anne Goldberg*. Translated by Benjamin Ivry. Waltham, MA: Brandeis University Press, 2021.

Zimler, Richard. *The Last Kabbalist of Lisbon*. New York, NY: Overlook Press, 2000.

Zimmerman, John C. *Holocaust Denial: Demographics, Testimonies, and Ideologies*. Lanham, MD: University Press of America, 2000.

Index

Abarbanel, Isaac ben Judahk 132
Abraham (*Avram, Avraham, Avraham Avinu*) 24
American Jewish Story 186–90
  B'nai B'rith ("Sons of the Covenant) 188
  Commission for Commemorating 350 Years of American Jewish History 188
  Etting, Reuben 187–8
  Minis, Abigail 188
  Seixas, Gershom Mendes 188
  Sheftall, Mordecai 187
  Solomon, Hayim 187
  Stuyvesant, Peter 186
  United States Holocaust Memorial Museum 188
Augustine 117
Akedat Yitzhak ("binding of Isaac") 46
Aleichem, Sholom (Solomon Naumovich Rabinovich) 165
Alexander the Great 93–4
al-Husseini, Mohammad Amin 120
āl-Yāhaūdu 85, 86
Amarna Letters 9
Antisemitism 200–1
Artaxerxes I 88

Aseret Ha-Dibrot ("Ten Commandments") 70–1, 72
Assembly of Jewish Notables/ Grand Sanhedrin 153–5
Bonaparte, Napoleon 153
Assyrians ("Neo-Assyrians") 21, 83
Assyrian Captivity 48–9
Astruc, Jean 20
Attatürk, Mustafa Kemal 120
Azazel (scapegoat) 47–8

Baal Shem Tov, Isaac Eliezer (Master of the Good Name [of God]) 135, 159, 160
Babylonian captivity 52–3, 85–6
Bar Kokhba, Simon 90, 108
  Bar Kokhba Revolt 108, 115
Baron, Salo Wittmayer 6
Bell, Dean 6
ben Avraham, Yom Tov 132
ben David, Anan 136
ben Gurion, David 2, 168, 190
ben Isaac, Solomon (Rashi) 125
ben Nachman, Moses (Nachmanides) 131
ben Zakkai, Yohanan 33, 115
Berlin, Isaiah 6
Bernstein, Michael André 7

Biale, David 3
Bialik, Chaim Nachman 164–5
Black Death 137
blood libel 128–32, 144
b'nei nevi'im ("sons of the
    prophets"; "prophetic
    guilds")
Bossman, Davidk 88
Bottero, Jean 29
Brenner, Michael 7
Brettler, Marc Zvi 19
B'rith ("Covenant with God") 70,
    88
Brown, William 71, 76
Burrows, Millar 21

Carlyle, Thomas 23
Carmilly-Weinberger, Moshe 7
Chrysologus, Peter 127
Chrysostom, John 117, 127
Clark, George Kitrson 7
Codes 4
Cohanim ("high priests") 23, 46
Collins, John J. 95, 120
Columbus, Christopher 132
Conservative (Positive-Historical)
        Judaism 160, 163, 187
    Eilberg, Amy 163
    Finkelstein, Louis 163
    Frankel, Zacharias 163, 187
    Jewish Theological Seminary
        163, 187
    Kohut, Alexanderk 163
    Mendes, Henry Pereira 163
    Morais, Sabato 163
    Rabbinical Assembly 163
    Schechter, Solomon 163
    Schorsch, Ismar 163
    United Synagogue 163, 187
Constantine, Emperor 116
    Edict of Milan 116
conversos ("converts")
Convivencia ("co-existence")

Council of the Four Lands (*Va'ad
    Arba Artzot*) 141, 144
Crusades 125–6
Cyrus of Persia 87
    Cyrus Cylinder 87
    Edict of Cyrus 87

Da Costa, Uriel 143
Damascus Affair 130–1
David, King of Israel 44
Davidson, Paul 33
Davies, Philip R. 21
de Leon, Mosesl 135
de Torquemada, Tomás (Grand
    Inquisitor) 131
de Torres, Luis 132
deicide 126–8
Dever, William 20, 21, 22
dhimmis ("protected one") 1,
    117
Dönme 150
Dreyfus, Alfred 166–7
    L'Affaire Dreyfus 166–8, 190
    de Barros, Artur Carlos
        167–8
    Drumont, Edouard 167
    Esterhazy, Ferdinand Walsin
        166
    Henry, Hubert-Joseph 166
    Lopes, Isabel Ferreira 168
    Picquart, Georges 166
    Zola, Émile,k 167
Dubnow, Simon Markovich 6

eggel ha-zahav ("golden calf")
Einstein, Albert 3
Emden, Jacob 150
Engle, David 7
Entine, Jon 11
Essenes 102
ethnogenesis 57–9
    ethnicity 58
    ethnoarchaeology 57

ethnocentrism 58
ethnonationalism 58
ethnoreligion 58
Exodus (Y'tziat Mitzrayim, "going
  forth from Egypt") 31
Eybeschütz 150
Ezra 87, 88–9

false messiahs 148–52
Farhud ("violent dispossession")
  120
Fantalkin, Alexander 89
Faust, Avraham 58
Ferdinand II, King of Aragon 131,
  133
Finkelstein, Israel 21
Firkovitch, Abraham 136
Fischer, David Hackett 7
Frank, Jacob 150–1
Freud, Sigmund 3
Funkeinstein, Amos 7

get (rabbinic divorce document)
Glassman, Ronald M. 33
God 5, 20, 28–9, 83, 86, 115
  Yod-heh-vav-heh/Yahweh/
    Jehovah (Tetragammaton)
    28
Goldstein, David G. 11
Goldstein, Jonathan 29
Gottwald, Norman K. 33, 67
Grabbe, Lester L. 22
Graetz, Heinrich 205
Greenberg, Moshe 10

Halevi, Judah 131
halitzah (rejection of Levirate
  marriage) 63
herem ("excommunication")
Hasidism ("Pietism") 159, 160–1,
  174
Schneerson, Menachem Mendel
  161

Vilna Gaon (Elijah ben
  Solomon Zalman)
  161
Haskalah ("Enlightenment") 156,
  159, 163–4
Hasmoneans 97
Heine, Heinrich 3
Hellenism 94–5
Hellenization 94–5
Herod, King of the Jews 98–9
Herzl, Theodor 167, 190
Hirsch, Samson Raphael 156
Hoffmeier, James K. 21
Holocaust/Shoah 8, 174–82
  Barnes, Harry Elmer 183
  Carto, Willis 183
    Institute for Historical
      Review 183
    Journal of Historical Review
      183
  Definitions of 175–82
  Denialism 182–6
    Denialists list of 184–6
  Dolchstoßlegende 176
  Himmler, Heinrich 183
  Hitler, Adolf 175, 188
  Irving, David 184
  Khurban 176
  Lipstadt, Deborah 184
  Marrus, Michael 176
  National Socialist German
    Workers Party (Nazi)
    175
  Porajmos 176
  Rassinier, Paul 183
  Versailles Treaty 175
  Weimar Republic 175
Humanistic Judaism 170
  International Federation for
    Secular Humanistic Jews
    170
  Wine, Sherman 170
Hutchinson, John 58

ibn Aderet Shlomo 132
ibn Ezral Abraham 132
ibn Gabriol, Solomon 123–4
ibn Labrat, Dunash 132
ibn Migash, Joseph 132
ibn Naghrillah, Samuel 123–4
ibn Paquda, Bahya 124
ibn Saruq, Menahem 132
ibn Shaprut, Hasdai 123–4
inheritance 66
    primogeniture 66
Inquisitions 133–4
Isaac (*Yitzhak*) 25
Isabella of Castile 131, 133
Israeli Jewish Story 191–3
    Balfour, Arthur James 191
    Balfour Declaration 191
    el-Sadat, Anwar 192
    Middle East 201–4
    Rabin, Yitzhak 192
    Rothschild, Walter 191
Isserles, Mosesk 144

Jacob (Ya'akov) 25–6
Jesus Christ 99
Jewish People 5
Jews 9, 10, 23
    Ashkenazim 10
    Habiru (Hapiru, 'Apiru) 9, 10,
        30
    Hebrews 9, 10, 23
    Israelites 9, 23
    Jewish Christians 10
    Judeans 9, 10
    Mizrakhim 11
    Sephardim 10
    Shashu (Shutu) 9, 10, 30
    Yehudim 10
jizya ("payment", "tax") 119
Joseph (*Yosef*) 26
Josephus (Flavius Josephus. Yosef
    ben Mattityahu) 103–4
Joshua (*Yehoshua*) 27–8

jubilee year 69
Judaism 5
    Definition of 3
    Jewish Genetics 9
Judges (*Shofetim*) 32

Karaites, Karaism 136
Karo, Yosefk 143–4
kashrut (dietary system) 136, 144
Kaufman, Amy S. 7
kibbutzim 61
Kielce, Poland 130
Kirsch, Jonathan 29
Kitchen, K. A. 21
Kitos War 103, 107–8
Khmelnytsky, Bohdan 141
    Khmelnytsky Massacre 145
Koch, Klaus 89
Kurtzer, Yehuda 7

Lansky, Meyer 4
Lemke, Niels Peter 21
Lessing, Gotthold Ephraim 156
Letter of Aristeas 96
Levi'im ("levitical priests") 23, 46
Levine, Lee I. 95
Lewis, Theodore J. 29
Lowenthal, David 6
Luria, Isaac (Ari, "Lion") 135
Luther, Martin 146–8
    On the Jews and Their Lies
        147–8

MacMillan, Margaret 7
Magreb 117
Maimon, Salomon 3
Maimonides (Moshe ben Maimon)
    100
    Thirteen Principles of the Jewish
        Faith 100
marranos ("forced converts")
Massena, New York 130
Matt, Daniel 135

Mendelssohn, Moses 155–6
Merneptah Stele 9, 59
messianism 99–100
mezzot ("doorposts") 136
Midrash 4
Miller, J. Maxwell 21
Miller, James C. 58
Mishnah ("Second Teaching") 109, 115
mitnagdim ("opponents") 136
Mizrakhim 117–20
Mohammad 117, 119
moriscos (Muslim/Arab converts) 133
Moses (*Moshe, Moshe Rabbeinu*) 26–7
moshavim 61
Myers, David N. 6, 7
mysticism 135
   Kabbalah ("received tradition") 135
   merkavah mysticism ("chariot mysticism) 135
   Zohar ("Book of Splendor") 135

Nehemiah 87, 88–9
Nero, Emperor of Rom 103
Netanyahu, Benzion 134
   Netanyahu, Benjamin (son) 134, 192
   Netanyahu, Yonatan (Yoni, son) 134
Nietzsche, Friedrich 7
Nostre Aetate ("In Our Time") 128

Orthodox Judaism 187
   Rabbi Isaac Elchanan Theological Seminary (RIETS) 187
   Rabbinical Council of America (RCA) 187

Union of Orthodox Jewish Congregations (UOJC) 187
   Yeshiva University (YU) 187
Ottoman/Turkish Empire 119, 149, 168

Pale of Settlement 157, 188
Palestine Liberation Organization (PLO) 134
PaRDeS 135
Parfitt, Tudor 35
Peake, Arthur 33
Pharisees (*Perushim*, "separatists") 46, 101–2, 115
Philip of Macedon 93–4
Philo Judaeus 96
Pitkänen, Pekka 58
Popkin, Jeremy D. 6
Protocols of the Learned Elders of Zion 157–9
   Bonaparte, Louis Napoleon 157
   Goedsche, Hermann 158
   Graves, Philip 158
   Hitler, Adolf 158
   Joly, Maurice 157–8
   Nilus, Sergei 158
Ptolemies 93
Prophets (*Nevi'im*, "bringers of God's/peoples' words") 41–2, 49–52
   Major prophets (Isaiah, Jeremiah, Ezekiel) 49–50
   Minor prophets (Hosea, Joe, Amos, Obadiah, Jonah, Micah, Habakkuk, Nahum, Zephaniah, Haggai, Zechariah, Malachi) 50–2

Qirqisani, Jacob 136

rabbinical academies, Babylonia 116
Rainey, Anson 29, 30
Reconquista ("reconquest") 119, 131
Reconstructionist Judaism 169–70
  Eisenstein, Ira 169
  Federation of Reconstructionist Congregations and Havurot (FRCH) 170
  Kaplan, Mordecai Menahem 169, 205
  Reconstructionist Rabbinical Association (RRA) 170
  Reconstructionist Rabbinical College (RRC) 169
Reform Judaism (Liberal, Progressive) 159, 161–3, 174, 205
  Bennett, Allen 162
  Central Conference of American Rabbis (CCAR) 162, 187
  Columbus Platform 162
  Ellenson, David 162
  Glueck, Nelson 162
  Gottschalk, Alfred 162
  Hebrew Union College 162, 187
  Jacobson, Israel 162
  Jewish Institute of Religion 187
  Magnes, Judah 162
  Meyer, Michael A. 162
  Panken, Aaron 162
  Pittsburg Platform 162
  Priesand, Sally 162
  Rehfield, Andrew 162
  Silver, Abba Hillel 162
  Union for Reform Judaism (URJ) 162, 187
  Union of American Hebrew Congregations (UAHC) 162, 187
  Wise, Isaac Mayer 162, 187
  Wise, Stephen S. 162
  Zimmerman, Sheldon 162
Resolution on Patrilineal Descent (CCSR) 2
Responsa 4
Romaniote 118, 149
Römer, Thomas 29
Rosman, Moshe 6
Roth, Cecil 134
Russian/Communist Revolution 174
  Doctors Plot 174
  Lenin, Vladmir 174
  Stalin, Joseph 174, 188
  Trotsky, Leon (Lev Davidovich Bronstein) 188

Sabbath (*Shabbat*) 5
sabbatical year
Sacrifices 47
Sadducees 101
Samaritans (*Shomrim*) 35, 97–8
Saul, King of Israel 43
Schäfer, Peter 29
Scholem, Gershom 135
Schorch, Ismar 7, 163
sefer kritut ("document of cutting", divorce)
Seleucids 93
Sephardim 117–20
Sevi, Sabbatai 149–50
Smith, Anthony D. 58
Smith, Mark L. 7, 29
Solomon, King of Israel 44–6
Spinoza, Baruch 3, 20, 142–3
Spronk, Klaas 65
State of Israel (*Medinat Yisrael*) 5
Stavrakopoulou, Francesca 29
Streicher, Julius 130
Sturtevant, Paul V. 7
survival 197–200

Tal, Oren 89
Talmon, Judah Leib 6

Talmud 4, 109–10
  Babylonian & Palestinian
    109–10
Tchernchovsky, Saul 165–6
tefflilin (phylacteries) 136
Ten Commandments (*Aseret
  Ha-Dibrot*) 5
Ten Lost Tribes 35, 83
Theophany (at Sinai; "giving of the
  Torah") 31
Thompson, Thomas L. 21
tikkun olam ("repairing the
  world") 85
Titus 103
Tlass, Mustafa 130
Toldot Yeshua ("Generations of
  Jesus") 128
Torah/Hebrew Bible/Old Testament
  4, 19, 20, 23, 47, 49, 61,
  63, 64, 65, 66, 67, 68, 83,
  85, 87, 117. 129, 136,
  190
  Copenhagen School 21
  maximalists 21
  minimalists 21
Torah she-be'al-peh ("Torah from
  the mouth", Oral Law/
  Tradition) 136
Trouillot, Michel-Rolph 7

Twain, Mark (Samuel Langhorne
  Clemens) 164

ummah ("community") 120

Vespasian 103

Weber, Max 32
Wellhausen, Julius 20
White, Hayden 6
Whitlam, Keith 2, 11
Wiesenthal, Simon 132
Wright, Robin 29

Yehud Medinatalk 89
Yehudah Ha-Maccabee (Judah
  Maccabee, "The
  Hammer") 97
Yehudah ha-Nasi ("Judah the
  Prince/Exilarch") 33,
  109
Yerushalmi, Yosef 6, 8
yibbum ("Levirate marriage") 63
Yohanan be Zakkai 104–5

Zealots (*Kana'im/Sicarii*) 102
Zionism 159, 168–9
  Balfour, Arthur James 168
  Rothschild, Lionel Walter 168